Heroes, Villains, Dames & Disasters

150 Years of Front-Page Stories
from the
Rocky Mountain News

MICHAEL MADIGAN

MADIDEAS
LLC

DENVER

For information go to
www.michaelmadiganauthor.com

Madigan, Michael, 1949-
  Heroes, villains, dames & disasters : 150 years of
front-page stories from the Rocky Mountain news /
Michael Madigan.
  p. cm.
  Includes index.
  LCCN 2009903942
  ISBN-13: 978-0-9823775-0-5
  ISBN-10: 0-9823775-0-9

  1. Rocky Mountain news. 2. Denver (Colo.)--History.
I. Title.

PN4899.D45R598 2009   071'.8883
                 QBI09-200047

Production Management by
Paros Press
1551 Larimer Street, Suite 1301   Denver, CO 80202
303-893-3332   www.parospress.com

Book Design by Scott Johnson

Printed in the United States of America
3   5   7   9   10   8   6   4   2

To Julie,
my bedside editor...

To Patricia,
who first read to me ...

And, to the thousands
of employees – past and recent –
who loved the 'Rocky'

M.M.

Contents

Dedications and Disasters

Heroes, Villains and War

New Beginnings

Challenge

Foreword

Washington Post publisher Philip Graham called newspapers "the first rough draft of history." Graham's observation begins to suggest what an immense loss befell future historians of Denver and Colorado when the *Rocky Mountain News* published its final issue on February 27, 2009. Newspapers come and go – always have and, so long as people are hungry for information, always will. But very few communities have been fortunate enough to have a single newspaper chronicle its entire existence. Denver was one such community. Until now.

William J. Convery

The book you hold in your hands, *Heroes, Villains, Dames & Disasters: 150 Years of Front-Page Stories from the Rocky Mountain News,* chronicles the incredible 150-year history of Colorado's pioneer newspaper, from its beginnings in a leaky saloon attic on the banks of Cherry Creek to its all-too-abrupt ending in early 2009. The sudden finale of the *Rocky Mountain News* raised questions about whether or not Denver was big enough to support two major newspapers. Observers asked the same question on April 23, 1859, when the first issue of the News hit the streets just twenty minutes ahead of its competitor, *The Cherry Creek Pioneer*. The *Pioneer* closed up shop after a single issue. At least forty-five other daily newspapers met a similar fate between 1859 and 2009. The *Rocky* endured.

Denver, of course, continues to support more than two newspapers, including the estimable *Denver Post*, whose rivalry with the *Rocky* over the years improved the city's standard of journalism. Yet the loss of the *Rocky* represents a dis-

tancing from our roots. In pioneer settlements such as Denver, newspapers not only shaped and disseminated public opinion, they literally, and occasionally literarily, puffed communities into existence.

And from the outset, Denver was extraordinarily fortunate to have a dedicated community booster in the *Rocky Mountain News*. In 1860, when Denver City was still little more than a village, William Byers, the paper's founder and first editor, proclaimed: "Denver will stand a shining mark to all the world—a great city built up in three short years on a barren plain... A city that will stand second to no other in its modern improvements, arts, and customs." For better or for worse, Denver's pioneer newspaper never backed down from its vision of Denver as a great city.

More so than even blogs and online news sources have thus far been able to capture, newspapers represent a daily accretion, a daily reinvention of a community's identity. Readers looked forward to a new edition of the *Rocky* every day for more than 54,000 issues. This book highlights some of the best, and some of the most controversial, headlines that the *Rocky* published in its storied 150-year career. It is a reminder of how one newspaper reflected and in turn shaped our hopes, fears and aspirations, our triumphs and tragedies. It is the story of ourselves—in the rough. □

William J. Convery
State Historian
Colorado Historical Society

Acknowledgments

The challenge I face is to thank so many, for so much, in so few words.

The first must be John Temple, editor, president and publisher of the *Rocky Mountain News* until its end. John accepted my initial proposal for the series, *The Rocky @ 150 Years,* and when it became apparent the newspaper would not survive to finish the series, he immediately supported my idea for this book. He did this at a time when I know he felt deeply about far more urgent issues – the wake for a Colorado institution, more than two hundred suddenly jobless employees, his family, and his own future. He responded to all of it in his usual style – with grace and compassion – and still found time for a friend.

Another former colleague and steady friend, Denny Dressman, handled every curveball I threw him in the planning and execution of the book. I can't imagine a better bench coach over my career. It was Denny's idea to break the book into "eras," which I believe lends some structure to the history. He's a pro who always has another idea.

Several other former *Rocky* colleagues played key roles. John Moore edited the series and wrote the headlines for the first one hundred chapters until the paper closed. If so much as a comma is out of place, it is my fault and not his. Andy Piper set the design tone under the calm, considered direction of Kathy Bogan, who even after the paper closed helped herd pieces of the book together. Randall Roberts patiently answered my requests until the day he turned the lights out.

The series and the book simply could not have been possible without the resources and assistance of the Colorado Historical Society. The Historical Society possesses the hardware to produce scanned files of original *Rocky* front pages from microfilm archives. Many members of its staff helped in this process. They are not named here at their own request.

However, Ed Nichols, president and CEO, committed the Historical Society's support at the first meeting with the *Rocky*. And I can't thank enough Bill Convery, the state historian, for his willingness to write the Foreword.

The Western History Collection of the central Denver Public Library is one of Colorado's true treasures. It is where I conducted most of my research, and found pages that didn't exist in either the *Rocky* or Historical Society archives. J. Wendel Cox, Ph.D. and senior special collection librarian, embraced the project from the first day I outlined it for him. Librarian Bruce Hanson always produced new nooks in which to find things. Coi Drummond-Gehrig fulfilled every request for historical photos and errant front pages.

Chris Brown, government document librarian at the University of Denver's Penrose Library, helped me plot research strategy and gave me my first microfilm scanning lesson.

When I decided to publish the book, I knew that I needed a partner who had experience dealing with the heroes, villains, dames and disasters that legends say fill the netherworld of independent publishing. Judy Joseph of Paros Press is one of the heroes.

Scott Johnson, chief designer at Sputnik Design Works, knitted a dizzying array of elements into the elegant, worthy book that I wanted. Scott also unearthed the old Underwood typewriter – that's a typewriter, kids! – and I thank Dave Ball for the photograph.

I wish to especially thank my family, which loves nothing more than to watch each other meet a challenge, and cheer them along the way. Julie has probably read every word I've written for the last 40 years – usually with a smile of encouragement, but occasionally with a look that says "you've got to be kidding." Petra St. George unfailingly plays her part as literary sounding board and my writing conscience; her thinking elevated *Heroes, Villains, Dames & Disasters* from the subhead into the main title. Tim Madigan is a trusted critic, constant inspiration and the best son I could ever have.

Finally, the idea for the 150 series and book is drawn from years of experiences at the *Rocky,* a perverse pleasure in tackling big projects and seeing them through, and trust that generations of colleagues would approve. ☐

M.M.

Introduction

Rocky Mountain News
1859-2009
R.I.P.
(Rest In Print)

The Rocky @ 150 Years project, as it was conceived, was to be an anniversary reprise.

Now, it is an obituary.

What was to have been a series of 150 stories commemorating historic front pages that led up to the paper's 150th anniversary on April 23, 2009, instead abruptly ended at No. 103. It was on Feb. 27, 2009, which not coincidentally was the day the *Rocky* also came to an end.

The Rocky @ 150 Years connected with many readers, at least judging from the emails and letters and condolences that I received. For many, it seemed to open a window to the past.

For if Page 1 of a daily newspaper is a sneak peek at daily events, then a trip through 150 years of front pages is truly pressing your nose up against the cool panes of history.

Despite its abbreviated sesquicentennial year, the *Rocky* reached a peak in Colorado terms of performance. Since William Newton Byers' first edition in 1859 – counting weekly editions, dailies and Extras!, and deducting only a few missed editions due to weather and more for the loss of a Sunday edition – the paper published about 54,320 front pages. After the 1864 Denver flood, the *Rocky* missed only one other day of publication, that I could find, although a couple editions couldn't be delivered due to blizzards.

The historic front pages represent an amazing record of communication and an immensely entertaining transformation of the written word. Think about it: we've progressed from advertising dentures on Page 1 to promoting "Twitter" on an electronic front page that exists we know not where exactly.

Page 1 has always been history's billboard.

My objective in writing both the series and presenting it in this book is to study 150 years of history – Colorado, U.S. and even world history – through the eyes and words of one of America's great newspapers.

I want readers to *feel* what it was like to read the actual battle dispatches exchanged between Grant and Lee. To read the first report at the foot of the Rockies of Lincoln's assassination. To read how women in Colorado got the vote, but not necessarily equal rights. To understand the dread at the start of World War I, and the exhilaration at its end. To share the excitement of such man-over-mountain achievements as building the Moffat and Eisenhower tunnels, landing on the moon, and photographing the stars in back of heaven. To read the overnight review of the Beatles in Denver, and the over-the-top coverage when the Broncos finally won the Super Bowl. To not forget how we felt after Columbine and 9/11.

Heroes, Villains, Dames & Disasters live on every front page.

I tried to choose front pages that I think matter to readers. In some cases – the early days of frontier journalism – The Big Story didn't appear on Page 1, but sometimes on Page 2, or even deeper inside the paper. Usually, this simply reflected the newspaper's format back in the day.

Occasionally, The Big Story was treated like The Little Story – a matter of news judgment. As a former news editor responsible for editing Page 1, I can think of many nights when I would have cut off a finger to have had the *complete* "Chronicle of the 20th Century" on my desk to consult regarding the historic portent of a breaking story. I point out such editorial decisions only as historic oddities, not fatal blunders.

News judgment on a breaking story has always been an unforgiving told-you-so. Oftentimes, it isn't until a story unfolds for two or three days that it becomes The Big Story. One can track a path of major events leading up to World War I, so singling out one representative front page is a tricky business. Trinity Church was a congregation in 1859, but it became one of Denver's enduring landmarks in 1888, which is why I chose a front page from that year.

Such perspective is also the reason why I selected some pages to represent an important historical trend or ongoing Big Story. The emerging skiing industry in Colorado, and Denver's infamous "brown cloud" are examples.

I also didn't attempt to pick one story for each of the 150 years. There's that scary news judgment again. I felt it was more important to honor history than a calendar. If someone questions the choices of FDR's death, the demise of Hitler, VE Day and the bombing of Hiroshima – all world-shifting events in 1945 – well, then, we need to have a talk.

The choices are all mine.

This applies as well to my arbitrary fashioning of five eras in the *Rocky's* publishing history, and the years that fell into them. The eras may seem subjective and uneven, and they are, but this is how I think of them.

The fact that I worked at the *Rocky* from 1973 to 2007 (with a four-year adventure as general manager of the *Daily Camera* in Boulder wedged in) did not influence my designation of much of that period as an era of New Beginnings. After all, it was between 1978 and 2000 that the newspaper achieved its highest daily circulation (446,465) and regained the critically important Sunday lead (552,085) from the rival *Denver Post*.

The secondary vignettes and notes that I included in most chapters were chosen either for their news value, the flavor of the moment that they capture, their bizarre nature, or the writing.

Since the beginning of journalism, it has been the mission of writers and editors to eliminate typos and misspellings. In all cases of original reporting, I intentionally left them in. Including some truly bizarre hyphenations in headlines. I did so in the interest of accurate reporting and, to me, they add grit to the writing of the time, rather than detract from it.

The most enjoyable experience of this project for me was to witness how the writing evolved.

On the frontier, Indian skirmishes were frequent and the accounts, often days old, were written in breathless detail. Damon Runyon's ode to William Jennings Bryan, after his third nomination for president, surprised me with its boosterism. Read the excerpts from Molly Mayfield's column,

and her cheeky good sense leaves no doubt why she became the model of advice for Dear Abby and Ann Landers. Ernie Pyle's reports from the battlefronts of World War II are written with mesmerizing humanity. Heroes, villains and damsels in distress tumble off the front pages, brought to life by events and reporters' words.

War and tragedy cannot be ignored in any honest accounting of history. Such times immortalize front pages. Readers squirrel them away so that decades later they can be extracted, yellowed and frayed, and offered as their piece of The Big Story.

Such important stories written by skilled men and women who elevate their craft to match these moments is impressive. Al Nakkula attacked such stories as the slaying of Adolph Coors III, and tornadoes that swooped down on Denver, like one of his native Finnish bears after a snack. Columnist Greg Lopez had a knack for befriending complete strangers, like the wildfire hero who told him what he dreamed the night after escaping Storm King Mountain. Mike Anton wove together non-stop reports from dozens of colleagues at the scene to tell the first story from Columbine.

In the end, I realized that I lived through history in my career, as well. I witnessed – a little closer than most readers – wars, blizzards, celebrations and more. Maybe the next best thing to making history is to be able to write about it. I say this with humble apologies to David McCullough and McKay Jenkins and William Convery and all real historians.

I'm just a writer.

My boldest wish is that *Heroes, Villains, Dames & Disasters* proves a worthy vault for the *Rocky's* rich history to rest in print.

Michael Madigan
Arvada, Colorado
April 23, 2009

Frontier Journalism

ROCKY MOUNTAIN NEWS.

THE MINES AND MINERS OF KANSAS AND NEBRASKA.

The Cherry Creek flood of May 1864 swept away the first home of the *Rocky,* **a second-floor attic office above a saloon. A competitor,** *The Daily Commonwealth,* **published in the white building at left.** *(Western History Collection/Denver Public Library)*

"One of the most astonishing feats performed by the flood
was that of carrying a Printing Press, belonging to the News office,
which weighs upwards of three thousand pounds,
over half a mile from its original position ..."

❧

The Daily Commonwealth

May 23, 1864

ROCKY MOUNTAIN NEWS.

THE MINES AND MINERS OF KANSAS AND NEBRASKA.

VOL. 1. CHERRY CREEK, K. T., SATURDAY, APRIL 23, 1859. NO. 1.

Rocky Mountain News.

WM. N. BYERS & CO.,
Editors, Publishers and Proprietors,
CHERRY CREEK, K. T.

TERMS.—Five Dollars per annum in advance. Single Copies for Mail, 25 cents.

THE OPENING OF JAPAN.

The present age is signalized by the rapid succession of striking events in the history of divine providence. Nations and continents which had maintained a rigid exclusiveness, or had been enveloped in unbroken obscurity, are now brought into friendly communication with the rest of the world, and doors are opening for the introduction of the gospel where heretofore it has not been allowed a foothold.

Scarcely had the news of the opening of China to the commerce and Christianity of the Western world reached us, when tidings came that a treaty with the United States, granting the fullest privileges, had been ratified by the Emperor of *Japan*.—This empire is composed of several islands the largest of which is about eight hundred miles in length, some of the others being larger than Great Britian, and has a population of about forty millions. In consequence of the commercial rapacity and fraud of the Portugese, whose enterprise opened a trade with Japan in the sixteenth century, and of the intrigues of the Jesuits who followed in their train, a fierce persecution arose against the Christians, that did not cease till every thing bearing the name was extirpated. For over two centuries the empire has been closed against the nations of Christendom with the exception of the Dutch, who have been allowed a few privileges.

A little over four years ago, Commodore Perry of the United States navy was sent to Japan, and succeeded in negotiating a treaty. In consequence of that treaty, the first that had been made with any western country, Mr. Townsend Harris, a gentleman who had spent many years in the East, was appointed Consul-general of the United States. Though at first regarded with no favor by the Japanese authorities, he soon gained their good will, and at length obtained permission to visit Jeddo, the capital city, and had an audience with the Emperor, the first obtained by any foreign minister. While at the capital, he received the kindest attentions from all classes. During his residence of about two years in the country, Mr. Harris has exhibited the principles of Christianity as far as he was able, statedly observing the Sabbath, refusing to make or receive vists, or to transact business on that day.

In the meantime he was able to arrange the articles of a treaty with the emperor, conferring far grater privileges than the former. In July last, being visited by the United States fleet, he thought that a favorable time for having it ratified.—Two Imperial Commissioners were sent by the emperor to conclude and sign the treaty, which was done on board the frigate Powhatan, with appropriate ceremonies.

The treaty provides for the opening of additional ports to Ameriban commerce, for the residence of an American minister at Jeddo, and of a Japanese minister at Washington, for the liberty of maintaining Christian worship, and erecting Christian chrches in ano part of the empire, for the abolition of the annuol custom of trampling on the cross that has existed since 1620, and for the extension of religious freedom to all Japan. These great and unexpected privileges were gained without resort to force or bribery, by the energy and wisdom of one unaided man, to whom not only his country but the world is indebted for thus opening this empire, which till lately, had been the most exclusive land on the globe. Lord Elgin, the English plenipotentiary who had negotiated the treaty with China and, the Russian ambassador, soon followed, and secured for Great Britian and Russia, treaties similar to that made with the United States.—*American Messenger.*

BOOTS AND SHOES.—It is estimated that not far from 75,000,000 pairs of boots and shoes are required for the consumption of the United States, whose whole value is not far from $180,000,000. Of these, 12,000,000 are made in Massachusetts, at a value of 40,000,000, employing 45,000 men, and 32,825 women. One half of these are made at Lynn, which is the largest shoe shop in the country; the next is Philadelphia. Every eighth man in Massachusetts is a shoemaker. Boston has 218 shoe houses, doing a business of $62,000,000 annually. New York has 65 houses in the trade, doing a business of $16,000,000.

CAPE HORN TO BE AVOIDED.—A company has been formed at New York to establish a line of powerful tug steamers to tow vessels through the Straits of Magellan, from ocean to ocean, thus obviating the delays, dangers and difficulties of the stormy passage around Cape Horn. It is calculated that fully twenty days would be saved to vessels passing through the straits, compared with doubling the Cape.

ALPHABETICAL CONUNDRUMS.

Why is the letter A, like a meridian? Because it is the middle of day.

Why is the letter B, like a hot fire? Because it makes oil boil.

Why is the letter C, like the ocean? Because it makes the "sea."

Why is the letter D, like a fallen angel? Because by associating with "evil" it becomes Devil.

Why is the letter E, like the end of time? Because it is the beginning of eternity.

Why is the letter F, like death? Because it makes "all," fall.

Why is the letter G, like wisdom? Because it is the beginning of greatness and goodness.

Why is the letter H, like the dying words of John Quincy Adams? This is the end of earth.

Why is the letter I, like the American Revolution? Because it is the beginning of independence.

Why is the letter J, like the end of spring? Because it is the beginning of June.

Why is the letter K, like a pig's tail? Because it is the end of pork.

Why is the letter L, like a young lady giving away her lover to another? Because it makes over a lover.

Why is the letter M, like the first glass of rum? Because it is the beginning of misery.

Why is the letter N, like a newly-married woman? Because it is the end of maiden.

Why is the letter O, like a courageous woman in disguise? Because it makes her a hero.

Why is the letter P, like two winds meeting? Because it makes air pair.

Why is the letter Q, like a king? Because it is attached to the Queen.

Why is the letter R, like a treaty ratified? Because it is the end of war.

Why is the letter S, like the end of hogs? Because it is the beginning of sausages.

Why is the letter T, like a victory? Because it is the end of conquest.

Why is the letter U, like fragrance? Because it is the centre of the "bud."

Why is the letter V, like two extremes? Because it is the beginning of vice and virtue.

Why is the letter W, like a dying christian? Because it is the end of sorrow.

Why is the letter X, like a scolding wife? Because it is "cross."

Why is the letter Y, like sight? Because it is in the centre of the "eye."

Why is the letter Z, like S? Because it "is" (is.)

METHODIST EPISCOPAL CHURCH.—The minutes of the Annual Conference for the last ecclesiastical year show that the present number of members and probationists is 956,555; an increase of 136,000 within the year. They have 9,063 churches, 6,502 travelling preachers, and 7,530 local preachers; 11,500 Sunday-schools. 125,000 officers and teachers, and 650,000 scholars, with over two million volumes in the libraries. The appropriations by the General Missionary Committee for 1859 are $261,549, of which $131,490 are for domestic missions, and $84,059 for foreign missions. At a recent meeting they determined to send six additional missionaries to India, to increase the work in China, and to form a mission at Salt Lake. The Methodist Church South has a membership of 655,000; 2,434 travelling, and 4,907 local preachers.

CRIME IN NEW YORK CITY AND VICINITY.—The first annual report of the Metropolitan Police states that the total number of arrests has been 60,865, of which 49,410 were for offences against the person, and 11,455 were for offenses against property. Included in these were 15,001 for intoxication without disorderly conduct, 2,918 for vagrancy, 2,170 for violating corporation ordinances, and others to the amount of 18,718, which should be deducted from the number of arrests for absolute crime, reducing the total to 42,147. Of these arrested, 30,065 were natives of Ireland, 10,208 of the United States, 5,932 of Germany, 2,588 of England, 886 of Scotland. The amount of property reported as having been stolen is $137,477 78, of which $83,342 47 was recovered.

OUR VOCABULARY.—Hon. George P. Marsh in a recent lecture stated that there are nearly 100,000 English words found in use by good writers, but that no single writer employed more than a very small proportion of the whole. Few scholars use as many as 10,000 English words, and ordinary people not more than 3,000. In all Shakespeare there are not more than 15,000 words, and in all Milton but 8,000. There were but 800 of the Egyptian hieroglyphics.

THE WORLD WITHOUT A SABBATH.

What would it be? Labor without rest; care without solace; probation without preparation; a night without day.

To the *laboring man*, the loss of the Sabbath would bring unceasing toil without increased compensation, and a consequent wasting of physical strength which would soon wear out the machinery of life. It would rob him of the allotted period for mental and spiritual improvement, and for home duties and enjoyments.—Brutalized in mind, body, and association, he would sink to the level of the *serf*, be the sport of capital, and end his days in heathenism.

To the *family*, the Sabbath lost would entail the loss of the *home day*—the day of domestic re-union, instruction, worship, and charity. Family government would lose its tone; family joys would die out; domestic purity would be imperiled—for the two oldest institutions in the world are interlinked—and family piety would become extinct.

To the *church*, a lost Sabbath would involve the loss of its solemn assemblies, its godly ministry, its day for edification and action, its season for domestic and associated instruction of the young, and its antetype of the "rest that remaineth for the people of God." An Arctic winter—without light, or heat, or food—is but an emblem of the state of the Christian world without the Sabbath and its ordinances.

A *state* without a Sabbath must be without liberty. To a free state the Sabbath brings the support of some of the most powerful elements of self-government. It inspires respect for law, divine and human. It fosters the sense of omnipresent Deity, and of man's dependence and accountability. It engenders a lively conscience, *more* potent to restrain from crime, than all legislative or judicial guards. Its educational force, through the pulpit, the Sabbath school and the fireside, quickens the intellect and moulds the heart of a nation. It gives the weekly occasion for illustrating the equality of man before God, and of inculcating the great lesson of human brotherhood. It is the foe of despotism, and the ally of freedom. The nation that has the Sabbath may dispense with armies and tax-gatherers for their support; no nation on the globe without the Sabbath, or with only a profane holiday in its stead, has free institutions, or dare disband its standing armies.

The *soul* without the sabbath would grope its way through a rayless night to the "blackness of darkness forever."—For while man might give heed to eternal concerns on any or all days, universal observation proves that contemners of the Sabbath despise and wonder and perish. No man who defies the authority of God, and willfully profanes the Lord's day, can have the temper of a child of God on other days. Think of a world of souls without a Sabbath, and the image of hell rises upon the vision. Think of a world waking each seventh day to the consciousness of the presence and power of a creating, redeeming God and Saviour; the families of earth bowing in worship before their several altars, going up to his temples to render their homage and hear his truth, and bearing forth the principles and spirit of the gospel in all the relations of life; and you have antedated that millenial Sabbath which promise, prophecy, and providence are hastening on, and which the day, the word, and the Spirit of God conspire to usher in.

He is the enemy of the laborer, of the family, of the church, of the state, and of the soul, who profanes or degrades the Sabbath, and who would rob either of its priceless blessings. R. S. C.

—*American Messenger.*

"THEY SAY" PUNISHABLE BY LAW.—A woman in Massachusetts, who was recently sued for slander, was defended on the ground that she only repeated what was currently reported. The Supreme Court justly decided that it was no defence, but that a tale-bearer who repeated a false and slanderous story, no matter how widely it had been circulated, did so at his peril. The origin of a slander cannot always be traced, and its power of mischief comes from its repetition.

WHAT OUR FOREFATHERS THOUGHT OF TOBACCO.—The following is extracted from the proceedings and debates in the House of Commons:

"Wednesday, April 18, 1621. Sir William Strand moved that he 'would have tobacco wholly banished out of the kingdom, and that it may not be brought in from any part nor used among us;' and Sir Grey Palmes said that 'if tobacco be not banished, it will overthrow one hundred thousand men in Egland; for now it is so common that he hath seen ploughmen take it at the plough.'"

COMMUNICATIONS RECEIVED BY THE NEBRASKA IMMIGRATION SOCIETY.

MONROE, N. T. Nov. 30, 1858.

DEAR SIR: The Circular of the Nebraska Immigration Society of which you are Secretary has been received, and I will cheerfully give any information that I can, at any and all times. In regard to his country:

First. Labor is worth from $1 to 2$ per day.

Second. The soil is simular to the prairies of Illinois; perhaps a little more sandy.

Seventh. Wood is plenty; in fact this is one, if not *the* best timbered counties in the Territory. The timber consists of Black Walnut, Ash, Elm, Cedar, and Cottonwood; the latter predominates.—Water is also abundant. The following streams run east and west through the county:

Platte River, Loup Fork, Looking-Glass Beaver, Shell, and Maple Creeks. (Lime stone has been found.)

Tenth. Elk, Deer, Antelope, Ducks, Geese, Quails, and Turkeys are found in abundance.

Owing to the newly settled character of this country, the remainder of the questions are not applicable to this country, but I will make a few remarks on the settlement of the country, and chances for Immigrants. This country was first settled in May, 1857, by a company of persons from Oneida county N. Y. They started this town—MONROE. In June, a company of Mormons settled in the western part of the county and started the town of Genoa. In July, a few persons from Florence, started the town of Cleaveland, in the eastern part of the county. In Aug., of 1857, the county seat was located here, and the county organized. Since when, the emigration has been gradually, settling up the country; but still there are good chances for emigrants to get good claims on the direct route to the new gold region, plenty of good claims can be had in this immediate vicinity for the mere taking. The land is principally prairie, as level as the city of Omaha; yet perfectly free from swamps, the streams are all clear and pure. We have had very little ague for a new country. There is an excellent ford across the Loup Fork, at this place and a good ferry at Genoa.

Respect. Yours,
L. GERARD.

FARMING VS. GOLD DIGGING

From present appearances, our citizens are likely to all be taken off with the Cherry Creek Yellow Fever, inasmuch that the farming interest of our Territory is likely to suffer materially, and the miners will also have to suffer for want of supplies.

This is all wrong; and our opinion is that farmers who stay at home, and spend as much money to improve and cultivate their farms, will realize more clear profit by so doing, than they will to go to the mines.

There will be enough to go to dig all the gold all the Union will need, and those who raise stock and produce for the miners will get their equal share of the gold in exchange for their produce. Everything must be high, and will bring cash next fall; and those who live at home will be perhaps the best off. Many mechanics will leave for the mines, and those who remain, will be much the best off in two years from now, as on the frontier along the Missouri, the emigration is going to settle up the country very fast, and wages will be very high.

Those who wish to get real estate will never be able to purchase it as cheap, nor on as good terms again, as the gold mines has turned the heads of all those who have bought property in the Territory, and all they think of is to dig gold and wash gold.

It is our candid opinion that those who have a few dollars to spare, will make more by buying property in eastern Nebraska at present, while the excitement is so high, than they will to go to the mines.

THE INDIANS.—According to the annual report of the Commissioner of Indian Affairs, presented to Congress, there are within the limits of the United States about 350,000 Indians, comprised in 175 tribes, with 44 of which we have treaties. There have been 393 treaties ratified with them since the adoption of the Constitution, by which 581,163,188 acres of land are acquired, and the entire cost of fulfilling them will be about $49,816,344. From the lands that have been sold, the government has received a surplus of at least $100,000,000 above the expense incurred for their acquisition, survey and sale. The whole amount of trust funds held on Indian account is $10,570,619.

YANKEE VISIT TO CARLYLE.

The Rev. Theodore Clapp, of New Orleans, in an autobiography, gives the following account of his introduction to the "Great Censor of the Age," Thomas Carlyle. Having received letters from Mr. Bancroft, the American Ambassador at the English Court, he called at the door of his residence. A lady, with a very intelligent appearance, received the visitor. "I have called this morning, he said, "to see Mr. Carlyle; is he at home?" She replied, "Mr. Carlyle has just entered his study, and no *gentleman* can see him this morning. If the Queen of England should now call and request an interview, it would not be granted." The Doctor asked if she could oblige him by taking a written message to his study. An affirmative answer was given, when he wrote with a pencil the following words:

"Dear Sir: No *gentleman*, but a man is at your door—a Unitarian, a Yankee, a Democrat, and a radical, all the way from the banks of the Mississippi; a careful reader, and a great admirer of Mr. Carlyle, and begs the favor of a short interview, which must be granted now, or never this side of the grave."

The letter of introduction was sent with this unique note. Directly the invitation came, "walk up sir; I shall be happy to see you."

We copy Dr. Clapp's account of this interview:

"I was received in the most kind and unceremonious manner. The topics on which we conversed were so numerous that I have not room even to mention them. The colloquial style is plain, easy and unaffected, and bears no resemblance to that of his later writings; has none of those qualities commonly called transcendental. Our conversation was protracted till afternoon. Though I rose several times to depart, he insisted on my staying longer so earnestly that I acceded to his wishes. Much of the time was spent in answering his inquiries concerning the statistics of the United States, the peculiarities of our government, laws, manners, schools, churches, literature, &c. He professed to be much gratified with the information which I gave him in regard to these subjects."

CAUTION TO SORGHO GROWERS.—The Independence (Iowa) *Guardian* gives an account of the destruction of seven head of cattle, belonging to I. G. Freeman, from eating the refuse of Chinese Sugar Cane, after it had been compressed in the mill. The outer coating of the stalks are of a very viterous character; when thus broken up and taken into the stomach, it operates like broken glass, cutting, and in some cases penetrating through the coats of that organ, producing violent inflamation. A post-mortem examination in this case revealed this as the cause of death. This important fact should be known to every farmer, as it may be the means of preventing a serious destruction of their stock. Besides this danger, there is nothing to be gained by feeding the bagasse. Even that of the tropical cane is considered quite worthless for everything but fuel. —*New York Tribune.*

Every body remember M'Donald Clark, who was so well known in New York a few years, as the "Mad Poet." During the last years of his life Clarke was made free of the Astor House table, and oftentimes this errant man of genius could be seen accepting its hospitalities when other doors were closed on his fallen fortunes. Every one knew Clarke by sight; and one day while quietly taking his dinner, two Southerners, seating themselves, commenced a conversation intended for the ears of Clarke. One said:

"Well! I have now been in New York two months, and have seen all I wish to see with one exception."

"Ah!" said the other, "what is that?"

"M'Donald Clarke, the great poet," responded No. 1, with strong emphasis.

Clarke raised his eyes slowly from his plate, and seeing the attention of the table was on him, stood up, placing his hand on his heart, and bowing with great gravity to the Southerners, said:

"I am M'Donald Clarke, the great poet."

The Southerner started in mock surprise, gazed at him in silence for a few moments, and then, amidst an audible titter of the company, drew from his pocket, a quarter-dollar, and laying it before Clarke, still looking at him without a smile. Clarke raised the quarter in silence and dignity, bestowed it in his pocket, drew thence a shilling, which he deposited before the Southerner with these words:

"Children half price."

The titter changed to a roar, and the Southerners were missing instanter.

What key is that that opens the gate of misery? Whis-key.

Rolling out a rich history

A cheer went up along Cherry Creek late the night of April 22, 1859. William Newton Byers, 28, and a crew of three men – not all experienced printers, as you will learn – cranked out the first edition of the *Rocky Mountain News,* beating its very first competitor, *The Cherry Creek Pioneer,* to the streets of Denver by 20 minutes. Colorado had its first newspaper.

Byers had arrived from Omaha only one night earlier, setting up shop on the second floor of a log building operated by Uncle Dick Wooton as a general store and saloon. Immediately, he found himself in a race against the *Pioneer,* as he explained on page 3 in the first edition:

William N. Byers, founder of the *Rocky Mountain News*

QUICK WORK. – On the 21st, at 7 p.m., the wagons carrying our press were driven to the door and we began unloading. We set up our press, arranged our matter, and the next day at 10 p.m. began printing the outside of our first issue.

One man working with Byers, Ike "Buckskin" Chamberlain, may have had some printing experience. But Byers apparently wasn't so sure that he could out-race the *Pioneer* that he would turn down help from an unlikely volunteer. The following account appeared in the paper's anniversary edition 38 years later:

O.P. Wiggins, the well-known policeman ... was in the city on the day and had never seen a press. Hearing that one was about to be operated he went to The News office and requested to be allowed to assist in the printing. Mr. Byers gave him a chance to run the roller which distributed the ink over the type. He accepted the offer and worked faithfully for an hour ... Chamberlain was killed about a year later on the trail between Pueblo and Taos. Mr. Wiggins subscribed for The News at that time and has been a continuous subscriber ever since. Amos Steck divides the honor with Mr. Wiggins, having taken the paper as regularly.

History-maker

Byers went on to become one of the most influential leaders in the state's history. He was instrumental in gaining statehood for Colorado; helped bring in telegraph lines and the railroad; served on the committee that founded the Colorado Seminary, later the University of Denver; trekked with the first party known to climb Longs Peak, and helped found the Colorado Historical Society, the Natural History Society and Denver's first library.

The *Rocky* first published as an evening weekly. It went on to become one of the leading newspapers in the country and an integral part of Coloradans' lives. In 1926, it became part of the Scripps newspaper chain and media family. It has been a rich and colorful 150 years, as you will see.

From Byers' first editorial

Fondly looking forward to a long and pleasant acquaintance with our readers, hoping well to act our part, we send forth to the world the first number of the ***Rocky Mountain News.***

(In the early days of newspapering, "number" meant edition.)

Paper's first home

The original site was the second-floor attic of a saloon near the Market St. bridge in Auraria, one of three towns that made up what was to soon become Denver. The other two towns were Montana City and St. Charles. Denver City eventually won out over St. Charles as the city's name because, in one prospector's opinion: "There ain't no saints in St. Charles." ☐

A painting by artist Richard Brogan was commissioned by the *Rocky* to depict its original setting – a second-floor office above a saloon approximately where the Market Street bridge crosses Cherry Creek today. The large painting filled a wall in the paper's lobby on the day it closed, Feb. 27, 2009.

Gold fever pans out to be first 'Extra'

It took the *Rocky* only six editions to establish a proud tradition of responding to big news in a big way by publishing its first "EXTRA." On Saturday, June 11, 1859, it printed a one-page edition. Beneath the fledgling paper's name, it added a special headline:

EXTRA. – GREELEY's REPORT.

"Gold fever" had swept across the Kansas Territory, as Colorado was first designated. Reports of rich strikes of gold in the foothills of the Rockies reached editor William Byers and citizens along Cherry Creek almost daily. But as frequent as the claims, were the revelations of barren mines and exaggerated stories. The gold rush that brought easterners and commerce to the towns was in danger of petering out.

Horace Greeley already had built a reputation as a reporter for the *New York Tribune*. With two other reporters from eastern newspapers, he visited the gold fields, and their report was printed by Byers under the headline:

THE KANSAS GOLD MINES.

We herewith submit a report, written at the "Gregory Diggings," of such facts as we witnessed there, and obtained from the lips of miners. We endeavored to make it definite and specific as possible, and to give an unbiased statement of the PRESENT condition and progress of the first important gold discoveries in the eastern slopes of the Rocky Mountains.

Respectfully,

HORACE GREELEY

A.D. RICHARDSON

HENRY VILLARD

Greeley and his colleagues went on to fill the entire four columns of the single sheet with details of what they found.

At Gregory Diggings near Clear Creek:

... Witnessed the operation of digging, transporting, and washing the veinstone, (a partially decomposed, or rotten quartz, running in regular vein, from southwest to north-east, between shattered walls of an impure granite,) have seen the gold plainly visible in the riffles of nearly every sluice, and in nearly every pan of the rotten quartz washed in our presence.

Sopris, Henderson & Co. (from Farmington, Indiana,) have run their sluice six days in all with four men – one to dig, one to carry, and two to wash: four days last week produced $607; Monday of this week $280; no further reported.

But, the report went on to warn,

Great disappointments, great suffering are inevitable ... for the latter who arrive at Denver City after September without ample means to support them in a very dear country ... through a long winter.

"Gregory Diggins" along Clear Creek between Black Hawk and Central City in 1859. *(Library of Congress Prints Division)*

In *Colorado: A History of the Centennial State,* the authors state that 100,000 gold seekers may have started for the fields in 1859. They believe only 40,000 reached Denver, and only 10,000 remained at the end of the year. ☐

Fighting words

Secession.

This was the single-word headline that greeted *Rocky* readers at the top of the far-left column in the first edition of the new year. The type size was small – smaller than printed above – for such momentous news.

> At last South Carolina has made good her threats, by a formal withdrawal from the Union … She goes out with dignity and equanimity, and proposes to treat with the Government of the United States, for the Federal property within her limits.
>
> Never before in the history of the nation, has such a crisis presented itself; never since the trying days of '76 has the independence of the 'American Colonies' been in such danger.

This was one of the first reports of the prelude to Civil War to reach the Rocky Mountains. Newspaper style of the time was to use smallish headlines. But often they screamed with editorial fervor, and even assumed to know whose side God was on.

Mystery poet

The report of South Carolina's secession was accompanied in the second column by a complete poem with this tantalizing introduction:

> The following lines were written recently … by one of the brightest literary stars our country can boast … The name of their author will be readily guessed from the initials … Hardly had these lines greeted us here in our Pike's Peak home, when there came in a lightning's flash the words which must startle every true American: "South Carolina has Seceded!"

Lydia Howard Sigourney

The patriotic poem's title printed by the paper was *STARS OF MY COUNTRY'S SKY,* at the end of which were the initials L.H.S. No further identification was provided. In fact, the exact title of the work was *Stars In My Country's Sky* by prolific poet Lydia Howard Sigourney.

By telegraph

One of the *Rocky's* early practices was to reprint whole columns of news dispatches, on this date received from Missouri and Western Union Telegraph. One of the last on this front page:

> ST. LOUIS, Dec. 20 – A duel was fought this A.M., between Brigadier Gen. D.M. Frost, and a civil engineer named Sayers. Twelve paces with pistols. No harm done.

Weekly and daily

While it started printing as a weekly, by 1860 editor William Byers added a *Daily Evening News.* □

Printing was a battle, as war erupts

As events of major importance to the country unfolded hundreds of miles away, Colorado and its first newspaper must have felt like they were on the fringes of history. The *Rocky* endeavored to give its readers the latest news. But it could be confusing — starting with the incorrect spelling of the battle site.

Beneath the headline

MOST EXCITING NEWS!

on page 2 of the April 18 edition, the main news story provided a detailed account of the Confederate States' bombardment and siege of the Union's Fort Sumter in Charleston harbor. As most feared, it was the start of the Civil War.

A dispatch from Charleston, dated Apl. 12th, says the batteries of Sullivan's Island, Morris Island and other points were opened on Fort Sumpter at 4 o'clock this morning. Fort Sumpter has returned the fire, and a brisk cannonading has been kept up. No information has been received from the seaboard yet.

But in the news column immediately beside the report, comes later word:

Rumored Surrender of Fort Sumpter.

From Hon. B.D. Williams, who arrived in this morning's (April 18) coach, we learn that at the moment the coach left Fort Kearney, a despatch was coming

through, reporting the surrender of Fort Sumpter. There is nothing of the kind in our despatches, but such an event is not unlikely to have occurred. Our next despatches will settle this matter.

Uncertain times

Days before the newspaper's second anniversary, it was clear that just the act of printing each day on the frontier remained a challenge. The notice at the top of page 2, above the Sumter headlines:

Our Paper – In consequence of the non-arrival of a supply of paper which left St. Joseph more than a month ago, we are compelled to use a smaller sized sheet today. We may be compelled to continue this size for several days, but we hope to receive our regular sized paper in a day or two. The provoking necessity which compels us to reduce the size of our paper will not long exist. Meantime we give our usual amount of reading matter.

Friendly reminder

From its first edition, local merchants and purveyors of services filled the *Rocky's* pages with advertisements. The paper wasn't shy in pursuing business.

This same day, under "Special Notices":

Remember that to succeed in business you must advertise. ☐

Territory, paper join fight

It wasn't long after the first shots of the Civil War that troops from Colorado Territory joined the action, and the *Rocky* reported it like it was Fort Sumter.

Latest from New Mexico
Particulars of the Battle.
Noble Deeds of the Colorado Boys.
Captain Cook Not Dead.

On March 28, outside Santa Fe at Glorieta Pass, the Union's first Colorado Volunteer Regiment surprised a slightly larger Confederate force of Texans, according to the report by Major A.H. Mayer, which the *Rocky* printed:

The enemy had about 2,000 men and one six pounder (cannon). We had 1,800 men and one each, six and twelve pounder, and four howitzers. The enemy lost their entire train (64 wagons and provisions,) and 230 mules, – about 150 killed, 200 wounded and 93 taken prisoners.

It's to be assumed Mayer's casualty count were Texans, not mules.

Mayer didn't mention that the Coloradans rapelled down the canyon walls in the attack.

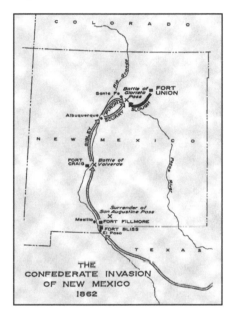

The Union troops had to overcome some other challenges, Mayer went on:

Capt. Cook, was wounded, but is doing well. His heaviest injury was sustained by his horse falling down and bruising his ancle. Lieut. Marshall, of Cook's Co., shot himself while trying to break one of the Texan guns lying in the field after the battle …

Our command falling back in the morning of the 30th, having done, as all say, wonders. Even the Texan officers and privates acknowledge this.

Name to be heard again

The commanding officer of the Colorado Volunteers was Major John M. Chivington, who was hailed as the hero of Glorieta Pass. More than two years later, he would be the central figure in a military action reported in the *Rocky* with far more historical significance. Chivington would rise through the Army to become Colonel Commanding the Colorado Expedition Against Indians on the Plains. He would lead the attack on the Sand Creek Indian reservation. □

Reserved proclamation

It is an understatement to observe that the headlines of the early *Rocky* were understated. But was this simply the newspaper style of the day or, in 21st century hindsight, a gross case of underplaying a story?

Whatever the answer, no better example exists than the reporting of Lincoln's Emancipation Proclamation.

It was enacted on Jan. 1, 1863, and the *Rocky* reported it on Jan. 8 near the bottom of the fifth news column under the headlines:

WEDNESDAY'S DISPATCHES.
The President's Proclamation.

"That on the 1st day of January 1863, all persons held as slaves within any State or district, or part of a State, the people whereof shall be in rebellion against the United States, shall be henceforth and forever free, and the Executive Government of the United States, including military and naval authority thereof, will recognize and maintain the freedom of such persons …

"In witness whereof, I have hereunto set my hand, and caused the seal of the United States to be affixed. Signed, **ABRAHAM LINCOLN.**"

The significance of the document, read on the page as the citizens of the Colorado Territory must have read it, seem all the more staggering today.

Support for Abe

Regular readers of the *Rocky* weren't surprised by the proclamation. Nine months earlier, on April 8, 1862, the newspaper printed the president's announcement of his intention to seek adoption of the proclamation by Congress. The paper made its position clear on the matter in an accompanying note:

The last mail … brought scores of Eastern and Western papers with similar recommendations. The voice of the press is almost unanimous in its approval. That is a pretty correct index of popular opinion, and we may therefore set down that almost the entire loyal States endorse the action of the President. It must be expected that the ultra Abolitionists will kick against it, as too conservative for their radical views. Let them squirm! 'Honest Abe' has shown that he will be no tool of theirs.

Growing circulation

At different times in its history, the *Rocky* followed the practice of printing its circulation in daily editions. On April 8, 1862, the day it first published Lincoln's proclamation, it was 550. □

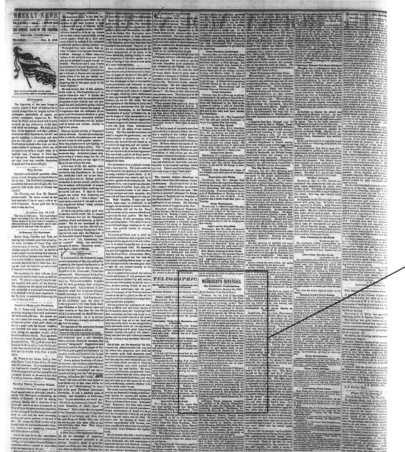

Gettysburg dispatches

Even on the *Rocky's* page 2, the size and mix of headline fonts, replete with editorial vigor and even holy invocation, trumpeted the epic battle of the Civil War.

**THE GREAT BATTLE
OF THE WAR
SPLENDID TRIUMPH!
TERRIBLE SLAUGHTER!
Rebel Loss 50,000 Men!
LEE RETREATING!
Entire Rebel Army Broken Up**
GLORY TO GOD

It is fascinating today, in a time when communication is instantaneous, to think that news from such a major military engagement in America's history took days to reach across the country.

Below the headlines follows a string of dispatches, not all in chronological order, from various cities reporting news about Gettysburg. Some are eyewitness accounts, even from generals fresh off the battlefield. The most authoritative report is datelined from Hanover, Pennsylvania., July 5, yet it refers to still another account:

A semi official dispatch, dated Headquarters of the Army of the Potomac, July 3d, says a great and decisive battle was fought to day. This was repulsed with terrific loss … An entire rebel brigade belonging to Longstreet's corps marched to our lines last night and gave themselves up. The bearer of dispatches from Jeff Davis to Lee orders him to return immediately to Richmond.

Victory at Gettysburg turns the tide for the Union. *(Harpers Weekly, 1861)*

Even though days after the battle, the detail contained in the continuing report conveys the awful toll.

The house used by (Union) Gen. Meade for headquarters was perforated with several shells, and many of his staff killed. General Butterfield was struck by a a piece of shell and badly injured … Too much credit cannot be given to our batteries which for hours served under a burning sun surrounded by missiles of death.

Rebel and Union troops sparred in the first days of July around Gettysburg. The first word that *Rocky* readers received of the impending battle were printed in the July 6 edition. The report appeared under a smaller headline:

**HIGHLY INTERESTING
AND IMPORTANT.**

Paper plows way through flood

The *Rocky's* early location along Cherry Creek was picturesque and quaint. It was good for business as well, positioned smack in the middle of the bustling young city where news and commerce converged.

But five years after it printed its first newspaper, citizens less familiar with editor William Byers' fierce sense of survival may have wondered whether the paper had printed its last edition.

The waters of Cherry Creek began to rise the afternoon of May 19, 1864, and that night they engulfed Byers' entire newspaper operation. It would be just one of the city's great floods.

For more than a month the *Rocky* was printed by one of Byers' competitors, *The Daily Commonwealth*. When Byers resumed publishing, the first thing he did was buy out the *Commonwealth*.

The *Rocky's* June 29 edition led with a farewell from *The Commonwealth's* publisher, Simeon Whiteley:

> **This afternoon I have sold to Messrs. Byers & Dailey, the Commonwealth Printing Establishment, and with it the good will of the same. The circumstances which led to this change, are mainly connected with the late Flood, which spoiled so many dreams of the future for so many of our fellow citizens.**

Immediately below Whiteley's letter, Byers also addressed his readers and explained his plight under the headline:

> **PLAIN TALK**
>
> **It is a little more than a month since our old office was swept away. In the building itself, and its contents, for carrying on the business, we had invested over twelve thousands dollars in cash.**

Byers went on to implore the business community to increase its advertising and subscriptions while at the same time informing them he would be raising rates. He wrote that this was necessary because before the flood, the paper's printing rates were "not in proportion with others" and that his margin of profit for the first quarter of the year was $142.63.

The flood

The Commonwealth provided some of the first details of the flood for readers in its May 23 edition. It accounted by name for 11 deaths, including a 4-year-old boy and at least four other children.

> **In this number we have not included any mere rumors of lives lost, deeming actual facts sufficiently heart-rending.**
>
> **From the head of Cherry Creek to this City, and down the Platte no correct estimate can be made, but one million dollars will not cover it.**

The paper's reporting of the catastrophe was excellent, even down to this detail:

> **One of the most astonishing feats performed by the flood was that of carrying a Printing Press, belonging to the *News* office, which weighs upwards of *three thousand pounds,* over half a mile from its original position, which was a stone floor, so that it had nothing to float on, but was actually forced on by the power of the awful torrent.** □

WEEKLY NEWS.

DENVER, COLORADO.

WEDNESDAY, - - - JUNE 29, 1864.

From the Daily Commonwealth, 28th inst.

TO THE READERS OF THE COMMONWEALTH:

This afternoon, I have sold to Messrs. Byers & Dailey, the Commonwealth Printing Establishment, and with it the good will of the same. The circumstances which led to this change, are mainly connected with the late Flood, which spoiled so many dreams of the future for so many of our fellow-citizens. I need not here repeat them. My successors have a far wider reputation throughout Colorado than I have, consequently it would be a work of supererogation in me to introduce them to the readers of the Commonwealth.

As publishers of the *Rocky Mountain News* they gave to the country a paper thoroughly devoted to the best interests of Colorado, and of the United States; this is the best assurance that they will continue to do so; and I hope that every reader will continue to give them a warm support; for in no way can they contribute more to the general welfare, than in sustaining generously their efforts to magnify the country at home and abroad.

I leave the paper not without some regrets. My relation to the public at large has been very pleasant; I may have made enemies, but they are mostly the enemies of good order, of social advancement, of fair dealing between man and man, and of the government under which we live. I have found friends whom I shall ever cherish; and in my short experience in journalism in Colorado, new proofs of the old maxim—"It always pays to do right."

To the readers of the Commonwealth, and to its cotemporaries, I bid a kind farewell.

SIMEON WHITELEY.

PLAIN TALK.

In resuming the publication of the Rocky Mountain News, it will doubtless be excusable for us to indulge in a little plain talk to its friends, patrons, and the public generally.

It is a little more than a month since our old office was swept away. In the building itself, and its contents, for carrying on the business, we had invested over twelve thousand dollars in cash, all of which was a total loss. With it we lost all our files, and many of our books—in the latter of which were unpaid accounts amounting to many more thousands of dollars—together with notes, due-bills, county warrants, packages of letters, legal papers, and many other articles, the monetary loss of which we cannot estimate. Many of these things we valued far more than money, and their loss is irreparable. In addition to these absolute losses, we had devoted more than five years to building up a business, which thus far had given but little satisfaction, and allowed but little enjoyment in its pursuit. Of this, we expect yet to reap some return, since we have again resumed it; otherwise, that labor, too, would have been a dead loss, and it may even prove so yet, though we have a strong hope to the contrary. At any rate, we believe Colorado has

the way of subscriptions. We must forward immediate orders to the type founders, and they must be accompanied with money; therefore, we want it now, and [illegible]. The current expenses of our office will not fall below seventy dollars per day, therefore our prices must be advanced; but the increase will be made as slight as possible, whilst some things will not be affected at all. The new schedule will be announced on the first proximo, and when published, it will be strictly adhered to.

SUBSCRIBERS.

Persons who were subscribers to the News, for themselves or friends, who have not received the Commonwealth since our suspension, will please notify us of the fact at once, with the address of the paper, and the time paid for. We desire to supply every subscriber for the full time ordered, but our subscription books were lost, and we have no means of making them up, except by information from the subscribers themselves. Despite the great advance in printer's stock, the price of the Weekly News will remain the same—five dollars per year—and we hope old subscribers will promptly renew, and induce their friends and neighbors to subscribe in order to help us out of a tight place.

ADVERTISERS.

On the first of July our advertising columns will be revised. Advertisers are requested to notify us prior to that date, of all changes desired. If advertisements are to be discontinued, we also wish to know it by that time; otherwise they will be kept in and *payment collected therefor.* We are determined to establish our business upon a *paying* basis and "fight it out on that line," or "bust." Do Not Neglect This Matter.

TO NEWS AGENTS.

Under the new postal law prohibiting the transmission of newspapers through the mails on *the Overland line,* we are unable to supply agents with their usual quantity of papers. We have laid the matter before the Department for a decision, and hope, with a good deal of confidence, that we will in a short time be allowed to transmit packages of newspapers and other printed matter under the old regulations; at least to agents in New Mexico and Colorado, if not to Utah, Nevada, Idaho and Montana Territories. The last four named may be ruled out because the mails for them pass a portion of the way over the Overland line, yet the Rocky Mountain News does not leave either "from the western boundary of Kansas, or the eastern boundary of California." Upon all other routes, except the Overland, we feel quite sure the prohibition does not apply, yet it is so construed at the Denver Post Office at present.

P. S. Since writing the above, the acting Postmaster in this city has given it as his opinion that the new postal regulation does not affect any mail routes but the Overland. In consequence we forward the usual supply of papers to our agents in New Mexico and Colorado. As eastern papers cannot be received, we hope they will find it advantageous to increase their orders for the News. Utah, Idaho and Montana are still cut off from the munificent benefits of Uncle Sam's postal facilities, even as re-

The jailor's fault was in trusting in the slightest degree [illegible] and [illegible]. But the [illegible] of law-abiding citizens who have all [illegible] themselves to [illegible] in the [illegible], seems to have arisen from want of a conception of the obligations they owe to their government and the laws of the land. For the present we refrain from more definite reflections, preferring to wait for awhile the course of events.

NEW DISCOVERY.

We saw last evening, in the hands of a gentleman of this city, some very rich appearing specimens of iron pyrites that were found in or near Cherry creek. Exactly where it came from is yet a secret known only to the discoverer, but the place will doubtless be made known in due time, when assays have been made and the value of the ore is established.

It has long been the belief, among those who had the best means for arriving at such a conclusion, that rich gold bearing veins would yet be found in the low hills along Cherry creek. It is certain that the very considerable deposits of gold in and near this stream, and for some miles up the Platte, have come down the creek and the now dry arroyas that reach down from the divide parallel with it. No such gold is found along the Platte, except for the distance of a *few* miles above Denver. In the recent floods, good prospects were found in the floating sands brought down, whenever and wherever tried. A prospect hole sunk in the bed of the creek within the city limits, gave from two to three cents to the pan, at the depth of three or four feet. A few months ago a boulder was picked up in the bed of the creek, by an employee of the News office, which was composed of white quartz and pyrites. The recent floods have of course laid bare many new indications of leads, so that no better time than now, for prospecting, will ever be found. The dry ravines and gullies are all cut out anew, and if leads exist they will doubtless show themselves in such localities. We have every confidence that some valuable discoveries will soon be made, and if so, they will prove of incalculable advantage to Denver.

NEW MEXICO ITEMS.

From the Santa Fe *Gazette,* the Albuquerque *Press,* and last and best, the Arizona *Miner,* we glean some items afloat in the two southern Territories. We might have had more, had the Santa Fe *New Mexican* arrived, but that delectable sheet has "soured" on us for a few weeks past.

Capt. Anderson has completed a new and correct map of New Mexico, which is something that will prove desirable to citizens here and there.——Mrs. Dr. McNulty gave a brilliant party at Santa Fe, on the evening of the 16th.——Major McFerran, Quartermaster of New Mexico, went to the States, on a business trip, by last week's coach.——Gov. Goodwin, of Arizona, has re-located the capital at Prescott, on Granite Creek, and has appointed the 18th of July as the day for holding an election for a Delegate to Congress, and for Members of the first Territorial Legislature.——Schultz & Bro., merchants of Franklin, Texas, across the Rio Grande from El Paso, old Mexico, have lately been in Santa Fe, purchasing their large sum-

MASONIC.

Oration delivered before the Fra[illegible] on St. John's Day, 24th [illegible] 1864, by [illegible] GEORGE C. BETTS.

[*At the request of those that heard this most excellent address, as delivered by its gifted author, we present it to our readers, knowing it cannot fail to prove of interest and instruction.—Ed.*]

—Ladies and Gentlemen, Most [illegible] [illegible] Masons, [illegible], Brethren, [illegible] Sir Knights:—

We are met together this evening [to] celebrate a day peculiar to all "Ancient Free and Accepted Masons," wherever gathered or dispersed upon the face [of] the globe;—a day whose dawning [illegible] to every true brother's remembrance the hour when first Masonic light burst [upon] his anxious eyes, and whose setting should bear with its last rays into eternity, promises of fidelity and renewed vows;—the day of all other days which more nearly restores him to the scenes of the past, and presents to him again the thoughts and feelings that with the ever increasing delight flooded his [being], when through right angles, horizontals and perpendiculars—through darkness and danger, but without doubt or dread, he won his way to the Sanctum Sanctorum:

It is very meet on such occasion, when the veil that hides Masons and Masonry from the outer world is partly lifted, [and] the uninitiated is permitted to snatch [a] glimpse of its inner beauties as the beam from the Orient, where the column of Wisdom maintains its position, [is] reflected from the *West* and *South,* where *Strength* and *Beauty* emulate each other in the glorious strife of *Benevolence* [and] *Holy Charity,* all united in one solemn league and covenant, to be good [and] true; that the hand that parts the curtain should be sustained by the knowledge that a *Mason's* trust being only [in] God, he may pursue his journey, fearing no danger.

With this assurance, my Brothers, [let] us step within the charmed circle [of] memory, and go back in the history [of] our lives to a time ere we heard the sound of the Gavel, or were presented with the twenty-four inch gauge. [We] were not Freemasons, however much we might have coveted the honor [and] the sacredness of the Masonic home, [we] found ourselves outside a well tyled door and gates, whose warden's were vigilant. "Knowledge is power," says one; [but] knowledge obtained without a struggle is scarcely worth the having. Yet who so bold as to approach the Sacred Temple without due preparation? If [we] turned to those who had already passed the portals, and asked for light, they told us *that they had not so received.* If we *plead* with the exalted of earth, [the] wealthy and the intelligent, they, [in] common with the poor and the ignorant, confessed their inability to dispel the gathering mists. We might have tried the power of *bribery, that* almost omnipotent instrument of bad men; but here was a faithfulness incorruptible; an integrity as far removed from price as "the heavens are above the earth." [We] might have descended to intimidation and threats, the resort of the coward [and] the autocrat; but here was courage [and] resolute determination, that met us with a moral force *invincible,* and never, [till] the Gavel of Truth had broken from [our] minds the rough corners of [illegible]

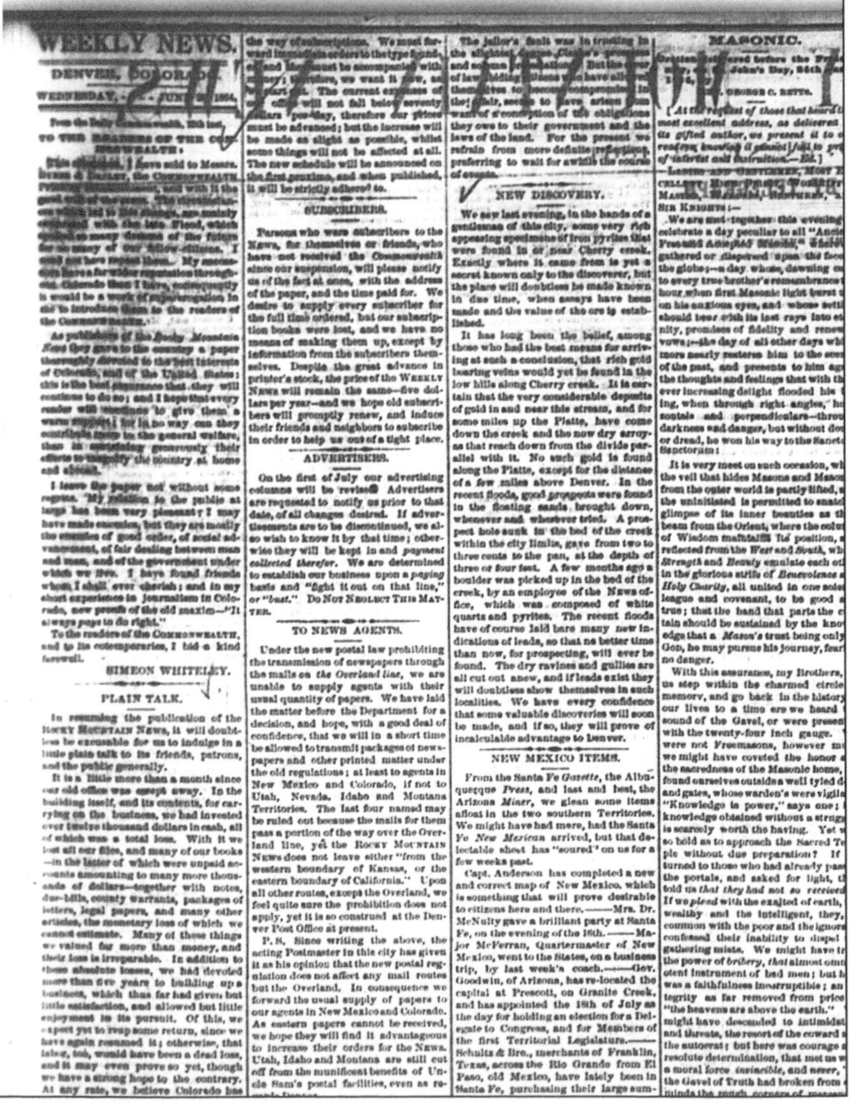

Sand Creek Massacre

History has been a harsh judge of what has come to be known as the Sand Creek Massacre and the man who led the raid, Colonel John M. Chivington. The *Rocky's* first report of the attack, which took place Nov. 29, 1864, was based solely on military dispatches from the battlefield. It came shortly after a period when Indian raids wreaked bloody havoc on the Plains.

The front page of *The Weekly Rocky Mountain News* on Dec. 14:

Great Battle with Indians!
The Savages Dispersed!
500 INDIANS KILLED
Our Loss 9 Killed, 38 Wounded.
Full Particulars.

The report begins with a brief editor's note of the following dispatch received at Army headquarters:

To Major General S.R. Curtis, Fort Leavenworth:
General: – In the last ten days my command has marched three hundred miles – one hundred of which the snow was two feet deep. After a march of forty miles last night, I, at daylight this morning, attacked a Cheyenne village of one hundred and thirty lodges, from nine hundred to one thousand warriors strong. We killed Chiefs Black Kettle, White Antelope and Little Robe, and between four and five hundred other Indians; captured between four and five hundred ponies and mules. Our loss is nine killed and thirty eight wounded. All did nobly. I think I will catch some more of them about eighty miles on Smoky Hill. We found a white man's scalp, not more than three days old, in a lodge.
J.M. Chivington
Col. Com'g District of Colorado, and First Indian Expedition.
I am, gentleman, very respectfully, your obedient servant.

Chivington was at first widely praised for his role in the "battle" of Sand Creek. Shortly after, he was honored with a parade through the streets of Denver. Soon, though, rumors began to circulate that soldiers butchered unarmed women and children. No criminal charges were ever filed against him. But an Army judge later stated that Sand Creek was "a cowardly and cold-blooded slaughter." Chivington was forced to withdraw from the militia in disgrace.

Black Kettle, in fact, was not killed. He died four years later when Gen. George Armstrong Custer attacked his camp in Oklahoma.

Frontier journalism

In the same edition it reported the Sand Creek attack, the *Rocky* also printed excerpts from a Teton chief's speech at a recent peace parley. The editors may have thought it would present the Indians' slant on the tension with the whites. But looking back, the paper's bias appears obvious. And the chief's message all the more tragic.

At the top of page 2, the headline over a short story read:

WHAT INDIANS THINK OF US.

Below we publish a portion of a speech ... by a chief who sports the sobriquet of "Bear Rib" ... It shows what the "red skins" think of us – after they got whipped.

"Man is but moral. He has but once to live and but once to die. A brave man is not solicitous whether his time comes sooner or later; but cares more to live in comfort and dignity as long as he is obliged to remain on Earth, and to leave the prospect of the same prosperity to his children when he dies.

"The traders and other whites (agents) got us into this war in the first place, then we thought we could secure the blessings just spoken of by making war on the whites. We have tried it, and know we are fools; and our hearts are heavy and sad." □

Fallout from Sand Creek

In the *Rocky's* early years, hardly an edition was published that didn't include news about Indian sightings, or movement, or raids by or against them, or the latest peace prospects. Less than a month after Sand Creek, the newspaper reported several more attacks. In future days they would be viewed as the Indians' retaliation for the massacre.

On Jan. 9, 1865, at the top of page 2, under a small headline:

FROM DOWN THE PLATTE

A dispatch was received on Saturday evening from Clark's and Keith & Cook's trains, bound eastward, stating that four of the teamsters had been killed by the Indians. Also, a dispatch was received from the Julesburg office on Saturday evening, saying that the Indians had cleaned out the town, smashed all the windows, doors and furniture in all the houses, robbed everything from the Express coach coming this way, except one package of greenbacks, which the messenger chanced to save, and escaped with to the fort adjoining town, which the few citizens and soldiers occupied.

Also, that five dead bodies were lying on the townsite.

… Men went down the road to-day to look after the men that were killed by the Indians yesterday. We found men killed and scalped, and the horses and wagons burned.

… My scout just in reports … Indians attacked Dennison's ranch … They killed and wounded 7 white men. The force on the Republican (River) is not less than 4,000 warriors.

In days, details of the military's response were printed under the headline:

THE BATTLE AT JULESBURG

A squad, returning with artillery, drove the enemy to the bluffs. The highest bravery and coolness was displayed by every officer and soldier of the command, several times cutting their way through overwhelming numbers and emptying double their numbers of saddles. Col. Sumner of the Seventh Iowa, killed the commanding Chief with his own hands … Bodies of thirteen soldiers and five citizens were brought in, presenting every form of ghastly mutilation. Fifty-five Indians were slain, and the battle-field strewed with Indian relics.

Plea for help

Life at the edge of the Plains was still a precarious existence with a tenuous economy. The Indians were seen as a threat.

S.H. Elbert

On the same day the *Rocky* printed the first report from Julesburg, it also ran this urgent message under the headline:

PREPARING FOR WAR

Immediately upon his arrival from Golden City … Acting Governor Elbert sent the following dispatch to Governor Evans, at Washington:

"Governor Evans: The Indians are again murdering travelers and burning trains on the plains. Get authority to raise a regiment of cavalry for one year's service. We must have five thousand troops to clean out these savages or the people of this Territory will be compelled to leave it. Everything is already at starvation prices. The General Government must help us or give up the Territory to the Indians.

"S.H. Elbert, Acting Governor"

Sorting out surrender

By now the front page of *The Daily Rocky Mountain News* was usually filled almost entirely with small ads taken by an array of businesses – Hallett & Sayre, Attorneys at Law; Dr. N.N. Greene, Surgeon of the Missouri Country; Frank W. Cram, Flour Inspector; Hodges' Boot and Shoe Store, and the Tremont Hotel.

Even news of the end of the Civil War took its place on page 2:

The Latest!
Lee Has Surrendered

Just before going to press we received the following important special:

"WAR DEPARTMENT, WASHINGTON, April 7 – To Maj. Gen. Dix: Sheridan has whipped and routed Lee, capturing Generals Ewell, Corse, Bennett, Kershaw, and many other general officers; also several thousand prisoners and many guns, and we hope soon to capture or annihilate what remains of Lee's army. We will send particulars soon, though the telegraph lines are working badly.

"E.M. Stanton, Secretary of War."

The next day's *Rocky* proved just how fickle communication still could be:

NO DISPATCHES.

About six o'clock last evening the wires got down east of Valley Station, and have kept dumb as beetles ever since, so that we reluctantly must go to press without a line additional from Grant or Lee, Ed Stanton or from "any other man."

Finally, in the April 10 edition, came official word – even if delivered in somewhat bewildering fashion:

CONFIRMED.

The glorious news of Lee's surrender is fully confirmed, with all the correspondence and particulars, in to-day's dispatches; but it was not consummated until yesterday. The report published by us on Friday last (April 7) was doubtless founded on the first correspondence between Generals Grant and Lee, aided by the vivid imagination of some reporter.

The editors seemed to have forgotten the report was signed by the Secretary of War.

Grant, Lee negotiate

Two days later, the *Rocky* published an amazing exchange of tense dispatches between Grant and Lee:

"April 7 – To Lee: The results of the last week's operations must convince you of the hopelessness of further resistance by the army of Northern Virginia in this struggle. I … regard it as my duty to shift from myself responsibility any further offusion of blood, by asking of you the surrender of that portion of the Confederate States Army.

"Grant."

And then this:

"April 7 – To Grant: I have received your note of this date, and though not entirely of the opinion you express of the hopelessness of further resistance on the part of the army of North Virginia, I respect your desire to avoid the useless offusion of blood; therefore before considering your proposition, we ask the terms which you will offer as the conditions of surrender.

"Lee."

The war was all but over. ☐

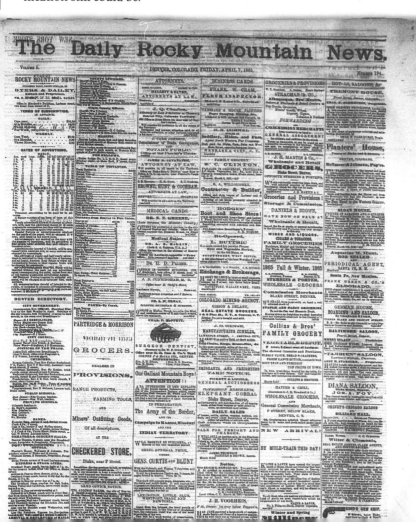

DAILY NEWS

DENVER, COLORADO

SATURDAY, ... APRIL 15, 18..

THE NATION MOURNS.

Never did lightning flash such sad news as is borne upon the wire to-day. PRESIDENT LINCOLN IS DEAD! Hung to the heavens is black, for the man upon whom the world looked is no more! The bright sunshine seems a mockery; Life to have lost its charm! A whole nation is plunged from the acme of hope, to the lowest depth of despondency and woe. The guiding spirit, whose hands have held its destiny for more than four years past, have passed away.

[body text largely illegible]

ONE EASTERN MAN'S OPINION OF "FRIENDLY INDIANS."

[body text largely illegible]

LATEST STATES NEWS.

[body text largely illegible]

Latest by Telegraph

ASSASSINATION

OF

PRESIDENT LINCOLN

AND

SECRETARY SEWARD,

A NATION

IN

Mourning.

WASHINGTON, April 15, 1:30 a. m.,—Last evening, about 9:30 p. m., at Ford's Theatre, the President, while sitting in his private box with Mrs. Lincoln, Mrs. Harris and Major Rathbone, was shot by an assassin, who suddenly entered the box and approached behind the President. The assassin then leaped upon the stage, brandishing a large dagger, and made his escape in the rear of the theatre.

[body text largely illegible]

WASHINGTON, April 14.—President Lincoln and wife, with other friends, this evening visited Ford's Theatre for the purpose of witnessing the performance of "Our American Cousin." ...

[body text largely illegible]

WAR DEPARTMENT, WASHINGTON, April 15.—To Dix: Abraham Lincoln died this morning, at twenty-two minutes after seven o'clock.

[Signed] E. M. STANTON, Secretary of War.

[third and fourth columns largely illegible]

RICHMOND HAS FALLEN

AND

DOWN COMES THE PRICES!

A. B. REA, MERCHANT-TAILOR,

Up stairs in Blake & Williams' Block, Blake street, Denver,

J. H. HENSON,

MANUFACTURING JEWELER,

LAWRENCE STREET, — CENTRAL CITY.

Geo. W. Brown,

MONEY AND EXCHANGE BROKER

DENVER, ... COLORADO

Warren Hussey & Co.,

Bankers,

Denver and Central City,

Colorado.

GOLD DUST, COIN AND BULLION

BANK OF CALIFORNIA,

AGENCY,

VIRGINIA, — NEVADA.

FAMILY GROCERY.

S. C. CLINTON,

MARKET

[price table and body text illegible]

A. S. PARKER & CO.,

ATCHISON, KANSAS,

Storage & Commission

MERCHANTS,

AND

General Forwarding

Agents.

REFER TO

VOUCHER LOST.

A GOVERNMENT VOUCHER...

April 11, 18..   S. C. GALLUP.

Winter and Spring

Millinery

WINTER STYLES

Notice.

NEW YORK STORE.

30 DAYS

IMMENSE

NEW STOCK

OF

DRY GOODS,

GENTS' CLOTHING

& FURNISHING GOODS

For Gents and Ladies,

WILL BE SOLD

BY

Wholesale and Retail

AT

Reduced Prices.

LARGE SPRING SUPPLIES

Now is Your Time to Buy

~ 14 ~

Death of a president

To any reader, the front page of *The Daily Rocky Mountain News* on April 15, 1865, looked like any other edition. At the top of the page there were the usual subscription rates ($24 for a year). The rest of page 1 was taken up with text ads for attorneys, business cards, hotels and saloons. Even the single graphic element on the page – a set of dentures fashioned by Dr. Eugene C. Gehrung – was familiar.

But it took only a glance at page 2 to know there was terrible news. The entire page was bordered in black and the gutters between columns of text were black as well.

**Latest by Telegraph
ASSASSINATION
OF
PRESIDENT LINCOLN
AND
SECRETARY SEWARD.
A NATION
IN
*Mourning.***

WASHINGTON, April 15, 1:30 a.m. – Last evening, about 9:30 p.m., at Ford's Theatre, the President, while sitting in his private box with Mrs. Lincoln, Mrs. Harris and Major Rathborne, was shot by an assassin, who suddenly entered the box and approached behind the President. The assassin then leaped upon the stage, brandishing a large dagger, and made his escape in the rear of the theatre.

The pistol ball entered into the back of the President's head, penetrating nearly through the head. The wound is mortal, and the President has been insensible ever since it was inflicted, and is now about dying.

About the same hour an assassin, whether the same or not, entered Mr. Seward's apartment, and under pretence of having a prescription ... inflicted two or three stabs in the throat and two in the face.

Another story followed with more details:

The screams of Mrs. Lincoln first disclosed the fact to the audience that the President had been shot, when all present rose to their feet, rushing towards the stage, many exclaiming "hang him."

A later bulletin followed, written by Edwin M. Stanton, Secretary of War:

WASHINGTON, 4:10 a.m., April 15. – The President continues insensible, and is sinking.
... It is now ascertained with reasonable certainty that two assassins were engaged in the horrible crime

– (John) Wilkes Booth being the one that shot the President.

Lincoln's last breath

Considered too critically wounded to be moved to the White House, Lincoln was carried from Ford's Theatre to a nearby boarding house. From there, a stream of reports regarding his condition, written two or three hours behind events, were dispatched across the city and the nation. The reports, as they finally appeared in the *Rocky:*

WASHINGTON, April 15, 11 a.m. – The Star says the President breathed his last at 7:30 this morning, closing his eyes as if falling asleep; his countenance assuming an expression of perfect repose, giving no indications of pain. Rev. Dr. Gurley, of the New York Avenue Presbyterian Church, immediately on it being known that he was extinct, knelt at the bedside and offered an impressive prayer, which was responded to by all present.

History claims it was at this moment when Secretary Stanton declared: "Now he belongs to the ages."

WASHINGTON, April 15, 12 p.m. – The President's remains were removed from the private residence opposite Ford's Theatre to the Executive mansion at half past nine, in a hearse, wrapped in the American flag and escorted by a small guard of cavalry, with General Auger and other military officers on foot. A dense crowd accompanied the remains to the White House, when a military guard excluded all but persons of the household and personal friends of the deceased. The body is being embalmed with a view to its removal to Illinois.

Denver in mourning

The *Rocky* continued coverage of the President's assassination the next three days. It reprinted much of it in *The Weekly Rocky Mountain News* on April 19, the day of Lincoln's funeral procession through the capital, on more black-bordered pages. That day on page 3 it also carried a poem entitled FAREWELL TO ABRAHAM LINCOLN, signed Minnie Auk, Denver:

" ... We'll weep, for our sorrow is due to his memory
"Who labored and suffered to vanquish our foe.
"Farewell Abraham Lincoln! thy memory shall flourish."

Making tracks for the future

The announcement on page 1 of the *Rocky Mountain News* on June 29, 1870, marked the most significant step in Colorado's development to date, despite the typically understated, small-headline, second-column style of the day.

The Denver Pacific Finished.

Even though the headline wasn't much larger than the words you are reading here, it was a huge deal. Denver had a railroad.

The Denver Pacific line traveled 106 miles north to Cheyenne to connect with the Union Pacific and the transcontinental railway. The "Denver Crowd," as the railroad's backers were called, beat out the rival "Golden Crowd," who at the same time were attempting to build the Colorado Central railroad from Golden City to connect in Cheyenne. The story began:

> Denver and Colorado rejoice in the completion of the Denver Pacific railroad. We are now brought into close connection with the valley of the Mississippi and the Atlantic and Pacific sections, and a new era of

progress and prosperity opens before us ... And, without forgetting the high deserts of others of our prominent citizens, we may say that to Governor John Evans belongs pre-eminently and conspicuously the credit of giving to Denver and Colorado their first railroad.

Ex-governor Evans was Colorado's second territorial governor and one of the leaders of the "Denver Crowd." In order to complete the Denver Pacific, he had to negotiate a deal with the Kansas Pacific line from Kansas City for support.

The *Rocky's* story, barely eight inches long, concluded:

> Cheers for the Denver Pacific and its builders! Cheers for the Kansas Pacific! Cheers for the Colorado Central! And three times three and a tiger for the live men who have conquered every difficulty and given to us the key of success and prosperity!

Worthy of the front page

At the bottom of the page on the same day, a short story of a different sort appeared. It ran beneath the headline:

Breaking Bad News.

It seems Judge Bagley had tripped, fell down the courthouse stairs, and died of a broken neck, and "a simple creature" named Higgins who hauled rock was recruited to deliver the news – and the body – to Mrs. Bagley. He was instructed, though, to be gentle in how he told her what had happened. So the story goes:

When Higgins got there with his sad freight, he shouted till Mrs. Bagley came to the door. Then he said:

"Does the widder Bagley live here?"

"The widow Bagley? No sir!"

"I'll bet she does. But have it your way. Well, does Judge Bagley live here?"

"Yes, Judge Bagley lives here."

"I'll bet he don't. But never mind – it ain't for me to contradict. Is the Judge in?"

"Not at present."

"I just expected as much. Because, you know – take hold o' suthin, mum, for I am a-going to make a little communication, and I reckon maybe it'll jar you some. There's been an accident, mum. I've got the old Judge curled up out here in the wagon – and when you see him you'll acknowledge, yourself, that an inquest is about the only thing that could be a comfort to him!"

A city Springs into existence

One of the earliest mentions in the *Rocky* of a new "city" to the south of Denver occurred on Aug. 9, 1871. Under a simple headline at the top of page 1 ran a lengthy recitation of the ground-breaking ceremonies, which actually occurred more than a week earlier:

COLORADO SPRINGS
The first stake in the new town – The interesting ceremonies – Speech by General Cameron – Beauties of the new resort – Its superior inducements.

COLORADO SPRINGS, July 31, 1871.

The ceremony of driving the first stake in the new town of Colorado Springs was witnessed, this morning, by a large concourse of ladies and gentlemen. The morning was bright and beautiful, and everything conspired to make the occasion a success.

At 8 o'clock a.m., under the superintendence of General (Robert) Cameron and Engineer Nettleton, the first stake touched the ground.

William Jackson Palmer, the city's founder, was never mentioned in the report. Cameron was hired by Palmer to be the city planner. He also took on the job of "orator of the hour," according to the reporter, who mostly quoted his speech.

"Immediately before us looms up Pike's Peak," Cameron said, "whose glorious dome realizes the poet's dream of beauty; which is to be as it has been for hundreds of unappreciated years – a joy forever …

A narrow-gauge Denver & Rio Grande train crosses Marshall Pass in southern Colorado.

"Then we are not to forget, and could not if we so desired, the famous soda springs in our immediate vicinity – springs well known to the aborigines of the older days, and famous already to the new civilization skirting the borders of the Rocky mountains."

And so readers learned of the birth of Colorado Springs.

Shiny new railroad

At the time, Palmer was president of the Denver and Rio Grande Railway, which would have tremendous impact and influence in the region. So it was somewhat fitting, if slightly overplayed, that in the *Rocky* column next to the Springs story on page 1, there appeared an account of the arrival in Denver of two new narrow gauge passenger cars.

They must have been marvels.

Armed and equipped with pencil and note book, one of our reporters accompanied (a railway official) to the depot, to inspect the new arrivals, and view the latest achievements in the way of railway architecture. They are, indeed, a novelty, and as the first ever constructed, cannot but be pronounced a perfect and complete success.

Each car was capable of carrying 34 passengers. The exterior was painted a brownish-cinnamon with gilt trim. The interior was finished in walnut and ash with scarlet plush velvet seats, silver mounted hooks and French glass windows.

The railway was apparently ahead of its time in one other respect: It had two smoking cars. ☐

Custer's Last Stand

By 1876, the newspaper had dropped "The" from its *Daily Rocky Mountain News* name. It had also changed its format to print the most important stories on the front page instead of page 2. That's where the bad news about Gen. George Armstrong Custer and the Seventh Cavalry appeared.

Gen. Custer's Command Cut to Pieces.
"Not a Man Returned to Tell the Tale."

Oddly, the story carried a Chicago dateline, and contained about eight inches of details about how Custer's command separated to fight the Sioux in the Dakota Territory before finally reporting in the last six lines that the general had been killed.

General Custer left the mouth of Rosebud with two companies to follow the Indian trail of a large band of hostile Sioux ... General Terry, with Gibbons' command of five companies of infantry and four of cavalry, started east of the Big Horn to attack the enemy in the rear.

On the morning of June 25, the story reported, Terry's force saw smoke from an Indian village they believed Custer had attacked.

The next morning the head of the column entered a plain bordering on the banks of the Little Big Horn, where had recently stood an immense Indian village, three miles in length. The ground was strewn with slaughtered horses, cavalry equipment and the dead bodies of nine Indian chiefs.

... Custer's command had apparently made an attack on the Indians and were compelled to retreat, but were cut off from the main body. They were forced into a narrow recess, where the horses and men lay slaughtered promiscuously. Here were found the bodies of Custer, his two brothers and nephew, Mr. Reed, Colonel Yates and Cook, and Captain Smith, all lying in a circle of a few yards, and here one after another of Custer's brave command fell. Not a man returned to tell the tale.

Near the bottom of the front page, appeared a related item under the headline:

Michigan Mourning for Custer

TOLEDO, July 6 – A special to the Blade from Monroe, Michigan, the home of General Custer, says that the startling news of the massacre of the general and his party by Indians created the most intense feeling of sorrow among all classes. General Custer passed several years of his youth in Monroe. □

Gen. George Armstrong Custer

Statehood for Colorado

Colorado's statehood was a proud moment in its history. Whether because of the challenges of time or means of communication, the *Daily Rocky Mountain News* reported the event with only one paragraph on Aug. 2, 1876, reprinting Ulysses S. Grant's wordy proclamation under the headlines:

The President's Proclamation Declaring Colorado a State.

WASHINGTON, August 1, – The President, in accordance with the provisions of an act of congress, approved March 3, 1875, has issued his proclamation declaring and proclaiming the fact that the fundamental conditions imposed by congress on the state of Colorado to entitle that state to admission to the Union have been ratified and accepted, and the admission of said state into the Union is now complete.

Can't-miss advertising

Paid advertising still commanded a hefty portion of the daily front page, both display and classified "For sale" and "Wanted" ads. On the same day that statehood was reported, a Denver grocer made sure readers would see his ad on page 2, printing at the top just two words in thick type one inch tall:

President Ulysses S. Grant

MY WIFE

says that the only place in Denver where she can buy her Groceries and have them always turn out satisfactory is at WINFIELD & HODGEs'.

SHE BUYS

Granulated sugar, 8 lbs. for $1.00
Coffee A. Sugar, 8 lbs. for 1.00
6-lb box Silver Gloss Starch, .50
Best Green Rio Coffee, 4 1-2 lbs. 1.00
Fairbank's Lard, 10-lb. cans, 1.50
White Russian Soap, 16 pieces, 1.00
California Salmon, large cans, .35
Star Raspberries, 2 lbs, .25
3 lbs. Peaches, Extra Quality, .25

'Personals'

Denver was becoming a thriving city. But in many ways it was still a small, intimate town. The comings and goings of citizens and visitors were of business and personal interest. The *Rocky* published a log daily. A few from this same edition:

G.H. Baxter, western passenger agent of the Missouri Pacific railroad, is in Denver.

J.D. Henry, a prominent citizen of Pueblo, arrived here yesterday from the centennial, which he says is a pretty good show.

Messrs. Beck, of Bouldor, and C.P. Elder, of Arapahoe, are spoken of in connection with the position of chairman of the republican state central committee.

And the newspaper simply couldn't claim to be the city's authority on all things local without this report:

Mr. Chapin, of the Grand Central (hotel), has a pet tobacco worm. It's a perfect beauty. □

'Red letter' day in Boulder

The *Rocky* reported in some detail on the "Dedicatory Exercises" of the University of Colorado in Boulder. But the story was published one day late, perhaps because of a transportation mix-up. And the story never referred to the college by its proper name.

THE STATE UNIVERSITY

BOULDER, September 5, – This has been a "red letter" day in the annals of Boulder. The great event, so long delayed and so anxiously awaited, has at last been consummated, and the citizens of this thriving town are now in the possession of a full-fledged university. To-day's proceedings are the realization of their fondest hopes and proudest aspirations, – evinced not less by the efforts and sacrifices they have made in the past to obtain it

… The morning train from Denver brought up the reporters, Gilman's full band, members of the board of regents, and a number of invited guests. Owing to the idiotic blunder of somebody – each one demonstrating that somebody else is to

Old Main, the first building on the University of Colorado campus.

blame – the crowd of visitors from Denver was small, there being no arrangements for a return train in the evening over either of the roads, and compelling everyone to remain over night. The forenoon was spent in examining the university building. It is situated on the plateau on the south side of the creek opposite the town. It is an imposing structure of brick, with stone trimmings, 81x112 feet, 65 feet to the roof, and 110 feet from the ground to the summit of the tower.

There was more that the reporter wasn't happy with, though.

The entire cost of the building has been about $30,000. Much of the work in the upper stories is of a cheap character – the size and necessary appointments of the building being too great for the amount of money available.

Denver or Boulder?

One of the earliest printed mentions of the university was in the *Rocky's* legislative report on Nov. 6, 1861. The newspaper printed the daily legalities on the front page in exhaustive detail – every bill, every vote, every roll call. At this time, there was still debate over exactly where the university should be built.

There was a roll call to vote on the city. Those receiving votes included Golden City, Denver, Georgia Gulch, Silver City, Mill City, Bradford, Platte City, McNulty, Pueblo, Conejos and Boulder.

Finally, after three roll calls, Boulder won out and the site was added to the bill.

Worth every nickel

The *Rocky* now printed the price for a daily paper on the front page – 5 cents. □

Higher ed, taller tales

Colorado's early newspapers did the best they could with limited resources and uncertain communications to give readers news from the surrounding region. Even Fort Collins seemed far away.

One of the *Rocky's* first reports on the state's new Colorado Agricultural College, today known as Colorado State University, appeared on Sept. 2, 1879:

LARIMER COUNTY
Rich Agricultural Region – Cheering Reports from the North

FORT COLLINS, September 1. – The News representative takes especial pleasure in noting the rapid and marked progress of this pretty town ... When the Colorado Central railroad extension was projected through Larimer county Fort Collins was an ill shaped and save its natural location unprepossessing town. But order has been brought out of chaos.

... I had a pleasant ride to the agricultural college, public school building and the new fairgrounds. Each of these places add much to the new prosperity of Fort Collins. The college is an imposing brick edifice immediately in the line of the railroad and in the suburbs of the town ... The state may well feel proud of its agricultural college.

College president's pay

The *Rocky* reported the previous May that E.E. Edwards, Ph.D., had been named the college's first president at an annual salary of $1,800.

That's entertainment

Twenty years after its first edition, the *Rocky* was now usually printing an eight-page daily paper, and on Sundays at least 12 pages. The advertisements continued to show the most dramatic change in the appearance of the paper.

An eight-column ad on Sunday, Aug. 31, 1879, left no doubt one of the first circuses was coming to town. It included drawings of horned horses, giants and flying horse riders. Huge type proclaimed:

You Have Seen the Pigmies!
Now
BEHOLD THE GOLIATH!
for the
Canvas Colossus of the Continent is Coming!

EARTH'S ONLY GREAT EUROPEAN
7 ELEPHANT RAILROAD
MENAGERIE AND CIRCUS

It was too grand. But two days later in the same edition as its report on the ag college, the newspaper upheld the advertising claims in an eyewitness "review" on page 8:

The show is certainly an excellent one and deserves the liberal patronage of our citizens. It is the first visit to Colorado of Sills Brothers, and when they may elect to again visit the "Queen City of the Plains" they are assured of a generous welcome.

In headlines and the story, the names of the circus owners were spelled three different ways – Selles, Sells and Sills. ☐

The Daily News

THURSDAY, OCTOBER 2, 1879.

The ROCKY MOUNTAIN NEWS Printing Company will not be responsible for any bill or other indebtedness contracted by any employé of THE NEWS office, except upon the written order of the Manager, previously obtained; nor will any such sum be allowed upon any indebtedness due this company.

J. M. BARRET, Manager.

Democratic State Ticket.

For Associate Justice of the Supreme Court:
GEORGE Q. RICHMOND, of Pueblo.

FOR DISTRICT ATTORNEYS:
First Judicial District.
FRANCIS M. BROWN, of Boulder.
Second Judicial District.
J. W. NORVELL, of Larimer.
Third Judicial District.
ROBERT A. QUILLIAN, of Huerfano.
Fourth Judicial District.
ALLEN T. GUNNELL, of Lake.

Democratic County Ticket.

Clerk and Recorder—A. MANTY.
Sheriff—S. W. KEENE.
Assessor—J. M. HAMRICK.
Coroner—C. K. McHATTEN.
Justice of the Peace—J. H. LESTER.
Constable—PETER J. MAQUIRE.
Superintendent of Schools—REV. W. J. PHILLIPS.
Chairman County Committee—W. N. BABCOCK.

Democratic City Ticket.

Mayor—HON. GEORGE W. MILLER.
ALDERMEN.
1st Ward—ISAAC N. CAMPBELL.
2nd Ward—PATRICK RILEY.
3rd Ward—E. L. GALLATIN.
4th Ward—E. J. BURKE.
5th Ward—GERHARDT HAGUS.
6th Ward—ROBERT BANDHAUER.

AS a receiver, Ellsworth is a success.

THE court house clique is a self-perpetuating ring.

THE greatest obstacle to silver mining is Radicalism.

JAY GOULD is the pivot on which Denver's future turns.

MINING investments are as safe as railroad investments.

THE bottom of a true fissure vein never has been found yet.

EVERY vote for Sopris will be a vote against practical sewerage.

THE organs are as dumb as dead men on the anti-silver attitude of their party.

THE Angel "Mike" is spreading his wings for the political bummer's spirit land.

THE republican organs represent everything that is hostile to the laboring men.

WHAT has become of our four per cent. of taxes that the republican party has collected?

THE golden autumn leaves are falling. Old age is upon the year. It is in the yellow leaf.

Is Grant not hostile to silver? Yet he has been indorsed and applauded by Colorado republicans.

THE new mines discovered this year vouchsafe two hundred thousand additional permanent residents.

THE republicans are seriously alarmed at the numerous splits and defections from their party in this city.

HUNDREDS who were republicans before that party arrayed itself against silver are republicans no longer.

SHALL Colorado proclaim to the world that she intends to continue to act with the party that defeated the silver bill.

THE democrats of Colorado are the only true friends of silver. They act with the party that supports the silver bill.

RAILROADS are to be pushed in every direction from this city, which is the blazing central star of a vast undeveloped inland region.

THE farmers all detest Spangler because they know he has pocketed the large percentage they have lost every time they have served on a jury.

THE binding part of the republican platform pledges the party here to the national party and to Grant both of whom are solid against silver.

EVERY German who does not intend to swallow Grant, who hates and ostracises their nationality, may as well pull up stakes and get out of the republican party.

EVERY republican is expected to go to the polls next Tuesday.—*Tribune.*

And by electing a gamblers' tool for mayor to deal a death blow at morality.

WHAT has become of the hundred thousand dollars in revenue which the city collected from the taxpayers last year? Can Mayor Sopris give an account of it?

NOBODY dares to deny that Sopris is sworn to execute the laws and that he notoriously refuses to close up the prostitution and gambling houses. To this point there is no answer.

AT last Colorado has an Indian war with real blood in it. The surprise, defeat and death of Major Thornburgh will attract the attention of the whole country to the Ute question, and their speedy extinction will follow. The death of Thornburgh will rank next to that of Custer and is one more proof that fighting Indians must not be treated by our army officers as mere child's play. The Utes know that their day is well nigh over, and have doubtless resolved to imitate the followers of Sitting Bull and extort what terms they can from a bloody war. They know perfectly what they are about and the tragic assault at Milk river is only the commencement of a general war which they have deliberately determined to make. It would be well for prospectors in the vicinity of their grounds to beat a retreat until sufficient troops come up.

General Hamill and the Utes.

In case of the use of state troops against the Utes General Hamill will doubtless be called upon to take command. He has already, at going to press, acquired full details of the number of men available in Clear Creek and Grand counties, and has two Georgetown companies in complete equipment, ready for marching orders. The quickness with which his mind grasps the details of successful organization, and at once seizes every strategic point has been noticed before in business and politics, and may now have a new field in Indian fighting. As adjutant in the army of the Potomac he saw several years' service. Ever since the first telegram he has been in active correspondence with the governor, and if there is to be a campaign, the militia may congratulate themselves on his leadership.

Municipal Economy.

Last year there was collected nearly a hundred thousand dollars for municipal purposes. What has become of it? There have been no public improvements. No attention has been given to the streets—no sewerage—no highways graded, no public buildings erected. But the money has been spent and we have nothing to show for it. Will Mayor Sopris explain what has been done with this enormous sum of money, or will he countenance the inference that it has been frittered away in useless expenditures. One fact is potent to the public, we have had no benefit from the enormous revenues that have been drawn from the tax-payers of this city. The money must have gone somewhere—but where? As rich as Denver is it cannot afford to throw its revenues away. There will come a time when every dollar will be needed to carry forward some needed and indispensible reform, and when that time arrives it will be found that the money needed for it has been thrown away by reckless and incompetent executives. Such a condition of affairs ought not to exist. A clear and accurate account should be kept of all municipal expenditures, and every dollar spent should be applied to some useful purpose.

"Republicans Don't Believe In It.'

Our charge that the republican silver resolution is a sham, a fraud and a swindle is being confirmed by republicans everywhere. Outside of the state it is denounced as being totally antagonistic to the views of the party, but is apologized for as "a necessary concession" to trap the silver men. Within the state the frank and manly sentiment of the party is not hypocritical enough to sanction the deception even for the sake of success. The Colorado Springs Gazette says:

No intelligent republican in the state really believes in the resolution, and we therefore said that our leaders were cowardly in assenting to this resolution against their convictions. We say too if our senators saw it and did not protest they were cowardly because it condemns them for their votes. The Tribune, Times and Republican, also accepted the snub of the convention very quietly when it endorsed the position of THE NEWS in the controversy which the metropolitan papers have had.

The Register-Call, whose editor wrote the platform, says in his paper that Hill and Teller both saw and assented to the resolution. Of course the Gazette is right in denominating their action as cowardly. We ask the city organs to digest the following additional remarks from their brothers at Colorado Springs:

Now, THE DENVER NEWS continued its assaults and, backed by the influence of bonanza owners like Tabor, compelled the republican convention to adopt a resolution embodying the views of THE DENVER NEWS, and giving up the only issue which was between THE NEWS and the republican press.

So far as Tabor backing THE NEWS is concerned, he simply came to its position, as all the rest will do in time. He would have been unworthy the mining interest he represents had he done otherwise. One more sentence from the Gazette, and we will let the snubbed and excoriated organs rest. It goes on to say: "The resolution was a decided reflection on the action of our senators last spring. They then voted against the free coinage of silver which was as good a policy in February, 1879, as it is now. Mr. Frank Hall, of the Times, introduced a resolution which correctly represented the position of our senators and the party, but it was ruthlessly set aside."

An Inconsistent Plank.

If a "silver and gold" plank in their state platform makes the New York democracy in favor of silver, will THE NEWS tell us how a straight-out silver plank in the Colorado platform makes all Republicans standing thereon gold bugs?—*Republican.*

Nothing is easier. A state platform to be rational must be consistent with the attitude and tendency of its party at large. Especially is this so upon a question that requires national legislation. The New York republican platform declared for gold alone. This was perfectly consistent with the course of its party in congress in opposition to the silver bill. It was an utterance that represents the well known sentiment and tendency of the republican party everywhere except in this locality. To make such a declaration here would be open suicide. Therefore, the difficulty was straddled. A silver plank, wholly incongruous, was thrown in as a tub to the silver whale to elude a sharp pursuit. But it was wholly neutralized by two declarations that fly in its face. One was that of unswerving fidelity to the republican party, and the other was the resolve to support Grant. Thus the silver plank is destroyed, and the devotion to the party and to Grant avowed makes the platform really and substantially a gold standard pledge, in spite of the silver plank.

Anybody who will reflect a moment will see that this is so. To vote for the ticket nominated on that platform is to help elect another republican president and congress next year. Nobody will deny this. Everybody knows that they will prevent the passage of any complete silver bill. The mosquito delegation from Colorado will not weigh a feather in shaping the course of the party at Washington. There is no hope for silver except with the vote of the south. There is not a remote possibility of passing the bill except through the agency of the democratic party. For Colorado to vote with the republicans under these circumstances is to throw away her vital interest, and for our local republicans to put a silver plank in their platform is to perpetrate an unblushing swindle upon their own voters.

The Milk Creek Massacre.

The White River Utes On the War Path.

Major Thornburgh's Command Ambushed and Put to Retreat.

The Gallant Commander Killed While Leading a Charge.

A Graphic Description of the Battle from a Scout.

Full Details of the Battle--The List of Killed and Wounded.

Agent Meeker and Family Murdered and the Agency Buildings Burned.

Troops Concentrating at Rawlins--Governor Pitkin's Action Yesterday --A Bloody War Predicted Notes from the Battle Field.

Description of the Battle--A Government Scout's Graphic Account of Thornburgh's Gallant Fight.

Special to THE NEWS.

RAWLINS, WYOMING, October 1.—On the twenty-sixth instant Grafton Lowry, one of the scouts, was sent by Major Thornburgh to the White River agency to ascertain the condition of affairs there and to communicate with Agent Meeker. Upon his arrival at the agency he found things in the utmost confusion. The Indians had sent all the old men, squaws and pappooses south, toward Blue river.

THE WARRIORS WERE PAINTED

in the most hideous manner and everything indicated that they had really taken the war path. They were about to murder Meeker and burn the agency buildings, but Mr. Lowry being well known and respected by the Indians succeeded in persuading them to abandon their hellish scheme, at least for the time being.

Meeker instructed Lowry to inform Major Thornburgh that

THE INDIANS WERE READY FOR WAR

and that they would open fire whenever the troops advanced toward the agency. Meeker informed Lowry that he would have abanboned the agency with his family and employés but was prevented by the Indians.

Lowry now attempted to return to the command, but was stopped by the Indians who informed him that he could not go. They were loud in

THEIR COMMANDS AND THREATS,

but the good feeling existing between him and the Indians again came to his assistance, and he was allowed to depart. He was accompanied, however, by about thirty warriors, who rode with him for a while, but finally left him. He arrived at the command on the evening of the twenty-eighth and gave Thornburgh the above information.

The next morning, Semtember 29th,

THE COMMAND ADVANCED

under the guidance of Joe Rankin, who is well acquainted with the country. About 9 o'clock a. m. Rankin discovered fresh Indian signs, and so informed Thornburgh.

At about 10 o'clock the command reached a cañon, through which the road passed.

Rankin informed the Major that

THERE WAS A TRAIL

leading up over the hill, and advised that they follow it, as the road through the cañon gave the Indians an excellent opportunity of ambushing the command.

THORNBURGH ORDERED HIM TO FOLLOW

the trail, and by this keen foresight of Rankin, the entire command owe their lives, for on reaching the top of the hill Rankin discovered the Indians on either side of the road leading through the deep, dark cañon. He sent Lowry back to inform Thornburgh of the situation. The major then drew

HIS COMMAND UP IN LINE

on top of the hill and the Indians mounted their horses, apparently being greatly astonished at the appearance of the troops, and disappointed at the failure of their scheme to lead them into the trap. Rankin was now with the command, and after the line was formed rode up to Thornburgh and asked him why he did not open fire?

The major replied:

"CAN'T DO IT, JOE,"

and then rode along the line ordering his officers to allow no firing. Rankin told him if he did not open on them that they would soon have the drop.

Thornburgh quietly remarked:

"MY HANDS ARE TIED."

The wagons were some distance in the rear and the Indians were now discovered to be between the command and the wagons.

Rankin again approached the major and begged him for God's sake to open on them, saying:

"If you don't we will all be murdered. We must fight now or never."

DEATH SOONER THAN DISOBEDIENCE.

Thornburgh turned in his saddle and said: "Joe, under my instructions I dare not fire a shot. My orders are positive, and must be obeyed at all hazards. Should I open this ball I would not only be court-martialed and cashiered, but would be disgraced with the army and the world. No sir, they must open the ball, and then

WE WILL DO OUR BEST."

Just at this time two Indians came out of the brush, and rode up to within a hundred yards of the command. One of them dismounted, took deliberate aim at Payne's company and fired.

This was the signal agreed upon for the attack, for instantly the war-whoop was given by all the Indians, which disclosed their position, showing that the major, with his little squad of doomed men, were surrounded. Thornburgh immediately ordered the troops to fire, and in a few moments he ordered the "charge," which he himself gallantly lead, attempting to cut his way toward where his wagons were.

THE TROOPS HEMMED IN

This movement, it seems, had been anticipated by the Indians, as they were encountered in great force in this direction, but after a desperate battle they succeeded in cutting their way out. The battle now grew more furious, as the Indians concentrated and kept up a galling and deadly fire.

When the command had reached a point within about five hundred yards of the wagons Major Thornburgh received two shots through the head, which

KILLED HIM INSTANTLY,

and he fell to the ground a corpse.

Captain Payne now assumed command and directed the movement of the command, which soon reached the wagons, where a severe fight was kept up till eight o'clock p. m., when the Indians drew off a short distance and went into camp.

A SCOUT KILLED.

Grafton Lowry was shot through the head about the time the wagons were reached, and died in a few minutes. His last and only words were directed to a soldier who stopped to look at him: "Never mind me. I am gone."

LIST OF THE KILLED.

During the engagement Major Thornburgh, Grafton Lowry, Wagonmaster McKinstry and twelve enlisted men were killed outright.

LIST OF THE WOUNDED.

The following persons were wounded:
Captain Payne, right arm and side.
Captain Lawson, foot.
Dr. Grimes, left shoulder.
Lieutenant Woolt, slightly, left leg.
Lieutenant Paddock, right thigh.

In addition to these thirty-five men were wounded and one hundred and fifty horses and mules killed.

A wagon train owned by George Gordon and loaded with supplies for the fort for the Indians were burned. Gordon is missing.

THE TROOPS FORTIFYING.

Nothwithstanding Captain Payne's doubtful wound, he retained command and proceeded to fortify his position. He has rations enough to last four or five days, and has plenty of wood and water. He hoped to be able to hold his position until reinforcements could reach him, but it is generally conceded that should the Indians renew the attack on the following morning, the little band of men must

SURELY BE SLAUGHTERED.

Agent Meeker reported that the sale by outside parties of arms and cartridges had been exceedingly brisk within the last few days.

It was Lowry's opinion as well as the opinion of all parties that Agent Meeker, his family and employés

HAD ALL BEEN MURDERED,

and the agency buildings burned, yet this is not positively known. Rankin left the command at about 8:15 p. m. September 29, with dispatches, and arrived here in thirty-six hours—a distance of one hundred and sixty miles.

NOTIFYING THE SETTLERS.

He notified the settlers along his route of what had happened, and they are now flocking in here for safety. A messenger from Lieutenant Price, who is seventy-five miles this side of the battle field of the date of twenty-ninth, says that reinforcements must come quick or they will be too late. Troops are concentrating here and General Merritt will leave here early to-morrow for the scene of action.

A general war is anticipated and great excitement prevails.

THORNBURGH'S BODY NOT RECOVERED.

Thornburgh's body had not been recovered when Rankin left. The above information was obtained from Rankin himself, who was an eye-witness and is reliable.

J. B. ADAMS.

THE BATTLE IN BAD CANON.

Special to The News.

LARAMIE CITY, October 1.—Thornburgh's command was met and repulsed by the Indians at Bad cañon at noon on the twenty-ninth, one mile from Milk river. Thornburgh retreated to his wagon train.

KILLED IN RETREATING.

On the retreat Major Thornburgh was killed, Captain Payne wounded slightly in two places, Lieutenant Paddock and Dr. Grimes wounded, though not dangerously. Ten soldiers and Wagon Master McKinsley were killed and twenty-five men and teamsters wounded.

Later reports are that the troops were retreating and the Indians in pursuit.

A PROMINENT PARTY IN DANGER.

Anxiety is felt for the safety of the miners and others in North park. Also for First Assistant Postmaster General Tyner, Governor Hoyt, General Burnside and Dr. Hayford, who are out on a hunting trip towards the Ute country.

MOVEMENTS OF TROOPS.

Troops from Fort Russell will make forced marches from Rawlins to-morrow morning with 300 men and three companies of cavalry.

Major Thornburgh's staff consists of Captains Lawson, Volkman and Payne, and Lieutenants Price and Cherry.

General Merritt will take command on his arrival at the scene of action.

A SHORT ACCOUNT.

Special to the News.

LARAMIE CITY, October 1.—The Utes attacked Thornburg's command at Milk river, thirty miles from the White River agency, and they killed Major Thornburg and sixteen of his men and wounded thirty men. The belief among the troops, so Rankin the scout says, who brought into Rawlins the dispatches, was that the Indians had left the agency and were not within a hundred miles of it.

Every available soldier within reach is ordered immediately to the field.

MEEKER REPORTED KILLED.

Special to The News.

GEORGETOWN, October 1.—Considerable excitement prevails here over the telegram of Governor Pitkin to General Hamill on the Indian question. There are quite a number of Georgetown people in the park, and their friends are growing uneasy. Public opinion here favors a war to the knife with the Utes this time, with no quarter.

It is rumored here to-night that Agent Meeker was killed at the agency Sunday night. No particulars. Parties who have cattle in the park are making up a company to go out and protect them.

CALLING OUT THE FORT RUSSELL TROOPS.

Special to The News.

CHEYENNE, October 1.—Fort Russell is all confusion and bustle to-night. Supply wagons are being loaded, and almost the entire force at the fort are under marching orders from General Sheridan. It is estimated that nearly 750 men can be mustered from this division. Reports of Major Thornburgh's brush with the Utes are very conflicting, but tend to the opinion that he was ambushed. He was well known here and much esteemed.

BIOGRAPHY OF MAJOR THORNBURG.

Special to the News.

RAWLINS, October 1.—Major Thornburg, the first victim of the Milk River tragedy, was transferred from the pay department to to the cavalry arm of the service at his own request, to satisfy his inclination for service in the field. He commanded an unsuccessful pursuit of the hostile Cheyennes last winter, but has never been noted as an Indian fighter. His action in the Milk river battle shows that he was a man not lacking in courage, but a stickler for obedience, to which virtue he can attribute his death. He was much esteemed here both as a gallant officer and a gentleman.

The Situation Locally Considered.

The threatening attitude assumed by the Ute Indians during the past few weeks has at last culminated in an encounter between a band from the White River agency and a detachment of United States troops, in which the latter were worsted.

The first particulars of the difficulty were received at the executive department yesterday afternoon, and were afterwards verified by press telegrams from the scene of the battle.

FATHER MEEKER'S FEARS.

Ever since the attack on Father Meeker at the agency some weeks ago, trouble has been brewing, and the fears expressed by Mr. Meeker seems to have been well founded. Governor Pitkin was apprised of the encounter between the Utes and the soldiers by the following telegram received yesterday:

AN APPEAL FOR HELP.

LARAMIE CITY, October 1, 1879.—*To Governor Pitkin, Denver:* The White River Utes have met Colonel Thornburgh's command, sent to quell disturbances at the agency, killing Thornburgh himself, and killing and wounding many of his officers, men and horses, whereby the safety of the whole command is imperilled. I shall warn our people in the North park, and trust that you will take such prompt action as will protect your people and result in giving the war department control of the savages, in order to protect the settlers from massacres provoked by the present temporizing policy of the government with reference to Indian affairs in all time to come. STEPHEN W. DOWNEY.

THORNBURGH'S DEATH REPORTED.

RAWLINS, October 1.—*To the Governor of Colorado*—Messengers from Thornburgh's command arrived during the night. Utes attacked the command at Milk creek, twenty-five miles this side of the agency. Major Thornburgh killed and all of his officers but one wounded. Stock nearly all killed. Settlers in great danger. About one-third of command wounded. Settlers should have immediate protection. J. B. ADAMS.

These are the only messages that were received by the executive department during the afternoon.

INFORMING THE WAR DEPARTMENT.

Immediately upon the receipt of the first, Governor Pitkin proceeded to take effective measures for protecting the settlers from any further encroachments, and to inaugurate plans for a brush with the Indians should the war department see fit to take cognizance of the fact that the lives of soldiers and settlers were imperilled. To this end the following telegram was sent to the secretary of war:

DENVER, October 1.—*George W. McCrary, secretary of war, Washington, D. C.*—Dispatches just received from Laramie city and Rawlins inform me that White River Utes attacked Colonel Thornburgh's command twenty-five miles from agency. Colonel Thornburgh was killed, and all his officers but one killed or wounded, besides many of his men and most of his horses. Dispatches state that the whole command is imperilled. The state of Colorado will furnish you, immediately, all the men you desire to settle permanently this Indian trouble.

I have sent couriers to warn settlers.

FREDERICK W. PITKIN,
Governor of Colorado.

THE GOVERNOR ORDERS OUT COURIERS.

Governor Pitkin followed the dispatch up with telegrams to the military staff of the state militia.

A telegram was wired to General W. A. Hamill, at Georgetown, apprising him of the encounter with the Utes and ordering a courier dispatched into Middle park to warn the settlers of their danger.

Another telegram was sent to General Joseph Wilson, at Leadville, directing a courier to proceed up the Gunnison country and work his way on over to Summit, where there are a number of miners working on the edge of the Indian reservation. General Wilson was also informed that in case a call for troops was made that he would be expected to take the field with his Leadville companies.

A third telegram was sent to Captain George J. Richards, at Lake City, ordering a courier dispatched to the settlers in that section, and requesting Captain Richards to gather the Lake City and Ouray guards together for an emergency.

These messages were all wired before 3 o'clock, and the governor before proceeding further waited for additional information from the seat of the encounter. In the meantime the associated press brought a few meagre accounts of the battle.

A DESCRIPTION OF THE BATTLE GROUND.

After the receipt of the telegrams announcing the battle, a NEWS reporter visited Hon. Wm. N. Byers, the postmaster, to gather some facts in relation to the locality in which the encounter took place, as well as to ascertain the opinion of Mr. Byers regarding the feeling that induced the Indians to make the attack.

Mr. Byers was found in the postoffice looking over the associated press telegrams regarding the battle.

"I know that country well," said he, "and was over it only a few months ago, when I visited Middle Park. It is an excellent place for an Indian ambush, and I judge that is the way Thornburgh and his command met with much disaster."

WHERE THE TROOPS WERE AMBUSHED.

"This Milk creek is about twenty-five miles from the White River agency. There is a wagon road leading by it to the agency and an Indian trail on the crest of the hogback or mountain that rises there. The wagon road runs along the foot of a gulch, and after crossing Milk creek and leaving it about half a mile, enters a brushy cañon covered with oak brush. My opinion is that the troops were ambushed, and after leaving the road and going into the cañon were attacked by the Indians."

WHO LEADS THE INDIANS.

"Who do you suppose led the attack?"

"That I have no means of knowing positively, though I suspect that it might be Douglas. Colorow is with the band, no doubt."

"You saw a great deal of the delegation when they were here some weeks ago, did you not?"

"Yes, I presented them to the governor."

"Who was in the party?"

"There was Captain Jack, Sahwitz, Unkum Good and Musceeco."

"What seemed to be their grievance at that time?"

"A fear that they were to be driven off the reservation, and a dislike for Meeker."

"What occasioned the feeling against Meeker?"

"I think they said he threatened to bring soldiers into the agency, and they threatened to attack them if they came."

"Do you anticipate that there will be serious trouble?"

"That is hard to tell. The Indians are well fitted out with arms and horses and could give the soldiers a great deal of trouble."

COLORED TROOPS IN THE PARK.

Mr. Byers, continuing, said that it was not generally known that there was a company of soldiers now in the park. They were sent there on General Pope's order at the time of the recent difficulty at Meeker's house. They are colored troops from Pagosa springs.

Mr. Byers stated that he had just received a letter from G. M. Rand, an old settler on the western border of the park, stating that the troops had left their station there and proceeded nearer to the agency. Rand, in his letter, charged that the troops had been threatened by the Indians and were afraid to remain where they had first camped.

THE FORCE AT THE AGENCY.

It was feared that the silence of Father Meeker was ominous. Nothing was heard from him at the executive department, and there were rumors that the Indians had attacked the agency and massacred all its inmates. The force at the agency comprises six men besides Father Meeker, the agent. There is also in addition Mrs. Meeker, her daughter and a Mrs. O'Neil, wife of the blacksmith at the post. Mrs. O'Neil also had charge of the boarding house where the men were lodged. An opinion regarding Meeker's silence is that the marauding party, hearing of the approach of the troops sent out from Fort Steele, first raided the agency and then proceeding to Milk creek, prepared an ambush for Major Thornburgh's command. How well it succeeded the reports of Major Thornburgh's death only tell too plainly.

WHO ARE THE WARRIORS?

It was the opinion of Mr. Byers, whose long residence in the park and his familiarity with the Utes enables him to speak intelligently, that the warriors are composed largely of the White River Utes. There are four tribes of Utes in Colorado—the White River or Middle Park Utes, the Uncompahgre Utes, the Uintah Utes and the Los Pinos tribe. The Uintah tribe is a small one and is located about 125 miles west of Meeker's agency. They are peaceably disposed in ordinary times, but are closely allied to the White River tribe by reason of intermarriages. Ouray's band, considered the most peaceable in the state, comprises the Los Pinos and Uncompahgre Utes. They contain a number of outlaws who would not hesitate a moment to join in any insurrection like that THE NEWS is now chronicling.

A Talk With Governor Pitkin.

Probably there are few in Denver or in the state who have a correct idea as to how the present trouble with the Utes began. It had its origin some months ago and has grown from bad to worse, culminating in a series of terrible tragedies.

A NEWS reporter had an interview with Governor Pitkin last evening concerning the present outbreak, and gives his version of the difficulty as the most correct one.

It will be remembered that early in June the Indians began to burn the forests all along the reservation—over 300 miles in length. The motive in starting these fires was inspired by malice and a desire to destroy valuable property. Complaint having been made to the authorities at Washington, a company from the Pagosa springs station was ordered on the strength of an official telegram sent by Governor Pitkin to the war department. This company, composed of colored troops, got into the Middle park on their way to the White river agency for orders, and detected two Indians in the act of burning Major Thompson's house and barn. Complaint was made against them at Georgetown, and a warrant issued for their arrest. The officer entrusted with the warrants pursued the men to the White river agency, but could not find them.

DOUGLASS GROWS DEFIANT.

Douglass, the chief of the band, was called upon to surrender the men but refused, claiming that the whites had no right to arrest an Indian on the reservation. This was reported to Governor Pitkin who immediately telegraphed General Pope, at Leavenworth, Kansas, and called on him to furnish troops to assist the sheriff in arresting the Indians who burned Thompson's place. General Pope then ordered the colored company from the Ninth cavalry at Pagosa, which had already started out, to proceed on to the White river agency and make the arrest.

THE ATTACK ON THE AGENCY.

This was all that was heard until the twentieth, when agent Meeker's letter arrived, stating that his plowman had been shot at in the field and he himself thrown out of his houses by a lot of Douglass' band. In this letter Mr. Meeker desired Governor Pitkin to call on Pope for troops to protect the agency, but urged that the fact that he made the request should not get out either to the Indians or the newspapers. So when Mr. Meeker's letter was published in THE NEWS some weeks ago the portion referring to his appeal for aid was suppressed. On this appeal for protection General Pope ordered three additional companies from Fort Steele. In the meantime, while Meeker was being threatened, the colored company from Pa-

The Meeker Massacre

When the *Rocky Mountain News* reported the Milk Creek Massacre (or Meeker Massacre), it wasn't simply about another flareup with the Indians. It was the beginning of the end for a proud tribe, the Utes, in Colorado.

The headlines on page 4 on Oct. 2, 1879:

**The Milk Creek Massacre.
The White River Utes On the
War Path.
Agent Meeker and Family Murdered
And the Agency Build-
ings Burned.**

Nathan Meeker was the government agent at the White River Ute Agency near the present-day town that bears his name. The Utes already felt oppressed and stripped of their native lands. Chief Ouray tried to hold the Ute nation in check. But, according to one historical account, when Meeker plowed the Indians' race track, where they staged wild pony races and gambled, it ignited the incident.

The *Rocky's* coverage consisted of reports from scouts, witnesses' letters and official reaction. The reports were printed one after another in the journalistic style of the day, so events sometimes read out of order. Accounts were interrupted by capitalized subheads. They filled nearly two pages.

**Nathan Meeker, agent at the
White River Ute Agency**

Grafton Lowry was a scout who first witnessed the attack at the agency and was later killed.

It was Lowry's opinion as well as the opinion of all parties that Agent Meeker, his family and employees **HAD ALL BEEN MURDERED,** and the agency buildings burned, yet this is not positively known.

Meeker and 11 other men at the agency were killed. Two women and three children were taken by the Utes. Fourteen U.S. soldiers, led by Major Thomas Thornburgh, were ambushed and died when they attempted to save Meeker.

The *Rocky's* founder, William Byers, now held the office of postmaster. He had traveled extensively in Middle and North parks, and he was quoted for his knowledge of the Utes and the tensions in the area.

"I know that country well," Byers said. "It is an excellent place for an Indian ambush, and I judge that is the way Thornburgh and his command met much disaster."

Eventually, a treaty was signed in Washington with Chief Ouray. It led to most of the Utes leaving Colorado and being relocated in Utah. □

A sketch of the Meeker massacre site, drawn by Lt. C.A.H. McCauley, 3rd U.S. Cavalry, and printed in *Frank Leslie's Illustrated Newspaper*. *(Western History Collection/Denver Public Library)*

A violent end for Billy the Kid

By the start of the *Rocky's* third decade in business, news content had pushed all advertisement off the front page.

The lead headline the morning of July 19, 1881:

GOING TO LEAVE.
Orders Issued to Re-
move the Utes

But a secondary headline and story would prove to be the source for legends and books and movies for more than a century to come:

Sheriff Garrett Disposes of Billy
the Kid.

The report started with a simple lead-in:

The End of the Kid.

LAS VEGAS, July 18. – The Gazette received positive information this morning from Fort Sumner of the death of "Billy the Kid." This noted desperado was killed at Fort Sumner, on the Pecos, 120 miles distant from this city, on the 14th instant, by Patrick Garrett, sheriff of Lincoln County ... Late in the night he went to the house of Pete Maxwell and went in ... Billy just then stepped into the room in his stocking feet. He had a six-shooter in one hand and a bowie knife in the other. He saw Garrett standing at the foot of the bed and asked in Spanish: "Who is that?" Billy again asked, "Who is that?" and as he did so Garrett fired, shooting the kid through the heart, who fell back dead.

... Billy has been roaming about the country in the neighborhood of Fort Stanton since he killed Deputy Sheriffs Bell and Olinger in Lincoln and escaped early in May, a few days before he was sentenced to hang for the murder of Deputy Sheriff William H. Brady of Lincoln county, during the war of the stockmen.

Great joy is shown among the cattle men over his death.

The *Rocky* had printed its first photograph one month earlier, but there were no images of Billy.

Four days later, the paper followed with a footnote about "the kid," who was using the name of William Bonney and was believed to be about 23 when he died:

Billy the Kid

Antecedents of Billy, the Kid.

NEW YORK, July 22. – There is a general belief in the Fourth ward that Billy, the kid, was brought up in that ward ... (and) his real name was McCarthy ... "There is one way to make sure of it," said a Fourth warder. "McCarthy, when ten years old, was badly burned with acid and was treated at the Chambers street hospital, but I think he must have a scar on the upper part of one of his legs and body."

Business and sports

The *Rocky* wasn't all about desperadoes and Indians. It now included a daily Commerce & Finance section, and weekly it printed columns on society, music and stage, fashion and church news. Regular reports were published about horse racing, even on races in Europe, and interest in boxing matches also foretold of the city's early hunger for sports. □

New hopes – bitter end

Inventions were changing life at the foot of the Rocky Mountains with almost as much frequency, it seemed, as its leading newspaper changed its name. In 1881 it was simply *Rocky Mountain News*. With the period.

Edison had invented electricity, and Bell had perfected the telephone. It was news when someone was in line for phone service. On Aug. 23, it was Boulder and beyond.

> **The Colorado Telephone company has at last made arrangements for the erection of a telephone line from Denver to Boulder, with branch lines from here to Gold Hill, Nederland, Caribou and Longmont ... This enterprise when carried through (and there is now no doubt but what it will be) will be a great convenience for communication not only between Boulder and Denver and Boulder and Longmont where there are already telegraph lines, but more especially between Boulder and the mining camps of Caribou, Gold Hill, Nederland and other points where there is no quicker communication at present than by overland. Merchants, mining men and people doing business in or outside of Boulder will have cause to rejoice when this, the latest improvement is completed.**

Garfield's ordeal

On the same day, the *Rocky* continued its nearly daily report on the condition of President James Garfield, who survived an assassination attempt nearly two months before but would suffer with a bullet lost inside him for 11 weeks before finally dying. The newspaper reported his condition in exhausting detail with stories from Washington, New York and Chicago.

Today the front-page headlines were not encouraging:

GOING TO PIECES
Less Chance Than Ever for The President.
His Loss of Strength Affecting His Mind.

The president had awoken the previous night and acted disoriented and confused, a symptom that had

> **not occurred at any other time and is perhaps due to extreme weakness.**
>
> **The swelling of the parotid gland remains about stationary.**
>
> **The feeling at the executive mansion this morning is one of anxiety, but the general impression seems to be that there is no greater excuse for alarm now than there has been for two or three days.**

Garfield died Sept. 19, 1881.

A more lively look

The first examples of artwork had begun to appear in the *Rocky*, breaking up the gray pages of dense type. Most of the art appeared in health-related advertisements, to illustrate:

Dr. Price's Cream Baking Powder
The Howard Galvanic Shield
Tropic Fruit Laxative
Safe Kidney-Liver Cure
And, Dr. Sanford's Liver Invigorator □

ROCKY MOUNTAIN NE

VOL. XXII. DENVER, COLORADO, TUESDAY, AUGUST 23, 1881.

GOING TO PIECES.

Less Chance Than Ever for the President.

His Loss of Strength Affecting His Mind.

The Utes Will March for Utah on Thursday.

Lively Times in Chicago's Grain Market.

A Freight Train Tumbles Near Antonito.

Serious Accident Between Pueblo and Canon,

In Which the Engineer and Fireman Are Badly Hurt.

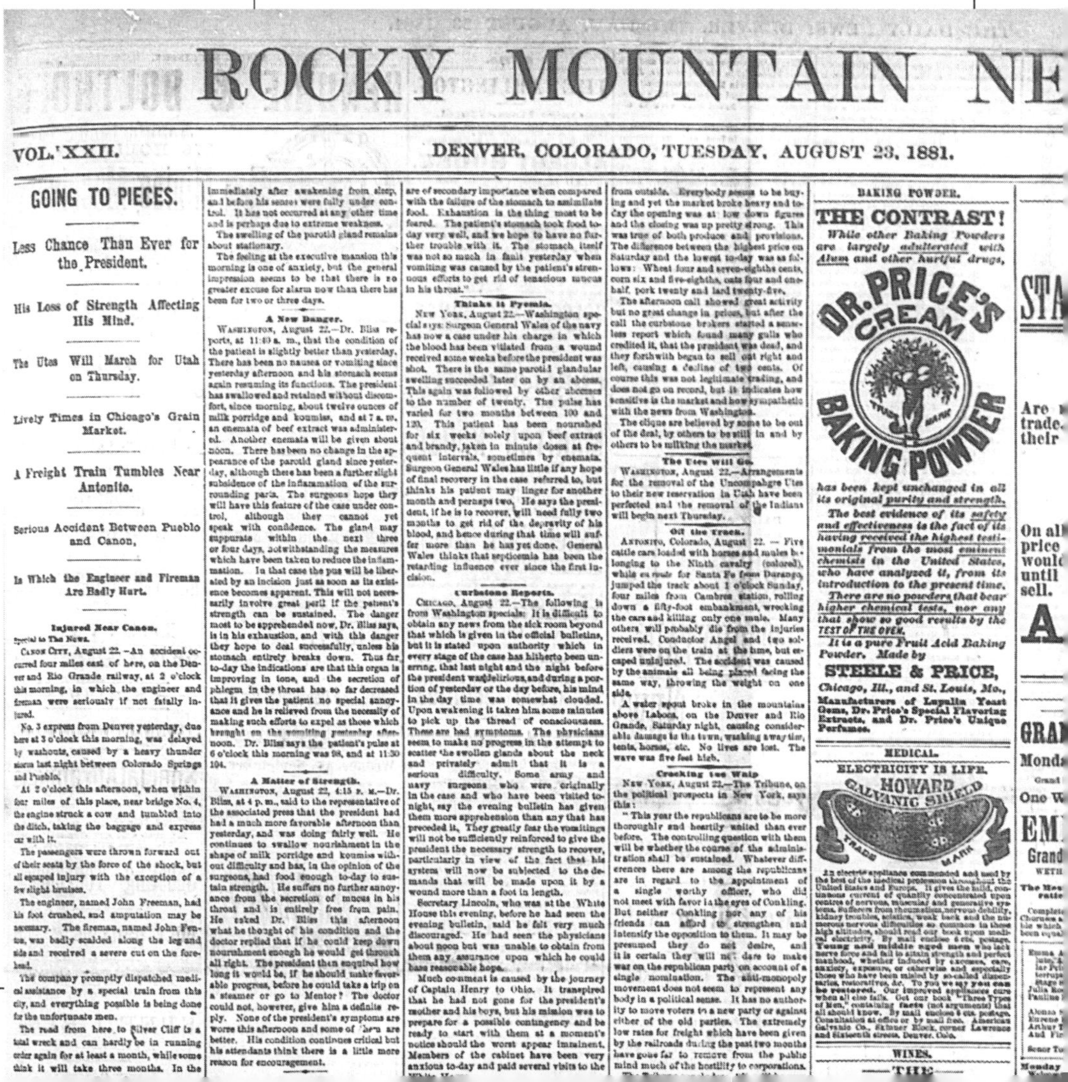

Colorado's cannibal

The first report in the *Rocky* of one of Colorado's most infamous incidents and history's most despised villains appeared on July 11, 1874, on page 4 under the inconspicuous, but memorable headline:

Man Eaters in Colorado.

Alfred Packer – aka A.G. Parker and Alfred Packard – didn't dine alone. He just dined last.

The horrible stories current some time since about man eaters in the San Juan country are apparently confirmed by advices from Salt Lake. One Driver writes from the Adams district, San Juan, that a party of six, respectively denominated S. Swan, J. Humphreys, Frank Miller, George Noon, J.S. Bell and A.G. Packer, sometime in May, set out on a four hundred mile tramp, between stations, and, not long after starting, became hard up for want of food. So great was their destitution that, when they were ten days on their way, Swan died from exhaustion, and to preserve themselves from starvation, strong as their natural repulsion was, the remaining five cooked and ate their defunct comrades. Almost a week later, Humphreys, whose digestive organs don't seem to have relished human flesh, also gave out, and soon his bones were picked as clean as those of the unfortunate he had assisted in picking.

One might criticize or chuckle today at the word choice and syntax if the story wasn't so authentic and mesmerizing. It was based on the sworn statement of Packer after he was finally captured. It went on for about six column inches in one single paragraph.

Miller was next on the menu. Then Bell shot Noon, and when Bell attacked Packer with the butt of his gun,

Parker was smart enough to get out of the way, and Bell struck a tree instead, and completely demoralized his weapon in so doing. Parker, indignant at this attempt on his life, killed and ate Bell.

It took 13 years – Packer later set the act in 1873 – before he was tried and convicted in Gunnison. That headline and story, on Aug. 6, 1886, offered still more drama.

FOR FORTY YEARS.
Packer, The Man Eater, After Thirteen Years, Receives a Punishment In-adequate To His Crime.

The reporter recorded the final courtroom moment:

Packer's face, very pale up to this time, flushed at the sentence. It was evident that although he had been expecting it all along, this long term of imprisonment rather shook him up.

"Forty years," said he, in a low tone and bowed his head.

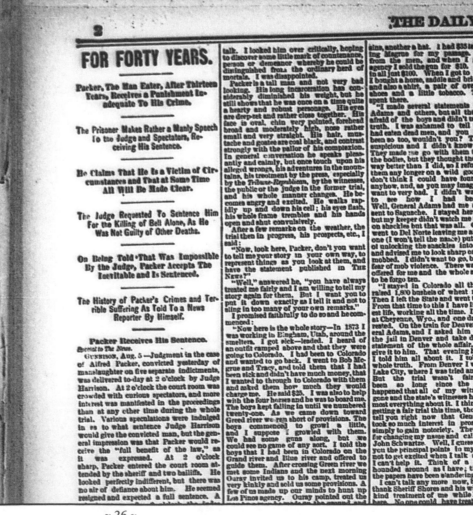

Spreading the word

In addition to the City of Denver and the *Rocky Mountain News,* one other enduring endeavor celebrated its 150th anniversary in 2008-2009 – Trinity United Methodist Church, the pinkish-gray stone spire and landmark at 18th and Broadway.

On Aug. 2, 1859, minister William H. Goode and yet-to-be-ordained Jacob Adriance established the Auraria and Denver City Methodist Episcopal Mission, known today as Trinity Church.

Research doesn't show that the *Rocky* attended the first service. The congregation opened its first church at 14th and Lawrence in 1865. One of the earliest references in the newspaper, although there had to be earlier still, appears to be Dec. 9, 1888. What by then was known as Trinity Methodist Episcopal was preparing to christen its impressive Broadway church and its New York-made organ, worthy of a full two-column ad in the *Rocky* inviting the city to the first concert for $1.50 per seat.

On Dec. 21 the paper reviewed the occasion on page 3:

FESTIVAL OPENING.
THE GREAT ORGAN IN TRINITY
METHODIST CHURCH.

The first audience in the main auditorium of the Trinity Methodist Episcopal church assembled last evening and was composed of 1,500 of the representative citizens of Denver and surrounding towns. The occasion, it is hardly necessary to state, was the first opportunity to see the great organ and to listen to the most eminent musicians in the country.

The story went on about the organ – "46 feet across the front of the church, 19 feet deep and 35 feet high" – but with little mention of the new church in which it played.

The organ was indeed a showpiece. It still is. While only 108 of its 4,202 pipes are visible today, the remainder hidden behind an enclosure, it still thunders with heavenly sound. Its original cost was $30,000; after several restorations, the cost to replace it today is estimated at $2 million.

The church was designed by Robert Roeschlaub, Colorado's first licensed architect. The exterior and 184-foot tall corner steeple are entirely fashioned of rhyolite quarried in Castle Rock. In 1888, it was one of the tallest stone towers in the U.S.

100 years later

The *Rocky* gave Trinity United Methodist considerably more attention in 1988, when it celebrated its 100th anniversary. Terry Mattingly, the paper's "religion writer," wrote on page 10 Christmas morning:

In a way, today's milestone also is a celebration that Trinity United Methodist is still here. The congregation membership slumped to near 1,000 in the early 1980s. Doom was in the air.

But church leaders plan to announce today that membership has hit the 2,000 mark. Boom is in the air.

Religious offerings

An entire wing of Trinity Church no longer exists. It extended north on Broadway, twice as long as the original and still remaining structure. In a story, including a photo, on March 14, 1926, following its dedication, the *Rocky* stated that with the extension Trinity "assumes a leading position in the Methodist denomination of the United States." In the same Sunday edition, the paper published its usual full page of

NEWS OF DENVER CHURCH
AND RELIGIOUS ACTIVITIES.

It included a list of 67 sermons scheduled at churches that day. At Trinity, pastor Dr. Loren M. Edwards planned to address "The Foursquare Evangel" and "The Dark Hours."

□

A Capitol Fourth of July

On the Fourth of July, 1890, as thousands of residents of the State of Colorado streamed toward the center of Denver under wicked sun, they might have breathed a huge, collective sigh of relief. After 22 years of fund shortages, political bickering, legal trials (all the way to the U.S. Supreme Court), design controversies, finance scandals and construction delays, the cornerstone was to be set that day for the state Capitol.

The celebration and program of speakers at the event took almost as long, based on the *Rocky's* report the next day. Some of the subheads on page 1:

**The Great Parade Miles in Length
and Participated in by Many
Thousands of Persons.**

**Five Miles of Tables at the Barbecue
Provide Accommodations for
60,000 Hungry Mortals.**

"Jolly Old Sol!" the lead story began. It went on about the sun for 20 lines until Mr. Sol

seemed to concentrate the whole vast radiance of his very hot beaming face on the cornerstone state of the great middle West – the state that was to lay the cornerstone of its own statehood on the national birthday in tons of mossy granite from her own eternal hills.

The parade headed towards the construction site at 10 a.m. The ritual laying of the stone at the northeast corner of the building included sealing inside a copper box full of mementos. Speech after speech proceeded until at 2:30 the crowd moved to Lincoln Park, where 300 waiters stood ready to serve roast beef that had been prepared throughout the previous night.

There were no greedy, gluttonous displays, but every man, woman and child clamored for food until they had their fill. Just think of it! Three hundred and fifty sheep, 75 calves, 237 fat steers, 13,000 loaves of bread, 3,000 pounds of cheese, 10 barrels of pickles, not to mention a few thousand gallons of lemonade.

The paper's report took an eternity to read, as well. It went on in tiny type for four pages of the 12-page edition.

Construction on the Capitol continued for four more years when it was deemed sufficiently complete to allow the governor and some employees to move in. The dome was finally leafed with gold in 1908 – 40 years after the project began.

First 'notes' column

The *Rocky's* cornerstone coverage included a number of short bits of information – notes – compiled under a small, odd subhead:

Little Crackers.

It was a howling success.
The red lemonade fiend got in his work yesterday.
The run on the beer saloons was unprecedented.
W.M. Taylor quite adds to the appearance of a mule.
Senator Tabor smiled at everyone and looked happy.

Everybody knew the pioneers when they passed.
The small boy and his fire crackers were irrepressible.
Who can estimate the crowds that lined the streets yesterday?
The secret organizations were not out in the force that was expected.
Denver's pretty girls never looked sweeter than on the glorious Fourth, 1890.

Mining nuggets, news

Colorado's residents had been afflicted with "gold fever" at least as long as the *Rocky* had been printing newspapers. By 1892, that was more than 30 years, and no where did the fever run higher than in Cripple Creek.

The claims were large, and the headlines grew larger:

CRIPPLE CREEK.
The New Gold Camp Is Making Regular Shipments.

On Feb. 28, in a special Sunday section, the *Rocky* presented its most complete report yet of the excitement surrounding the mining district that had sprung up behind Pike's Peak. The full-page front of the section included a map of the largest mines, given romantic names like the Buena Vista, Blue Bell, Independent, Ironclad, Great View, Poorman, Midnight and Morning Glory. There were elaborate drawings that depicted life in the camp – a stage arrival, a working mine, a tent meal kitchen. The main story was rich with promising details.

The Lincoln mine "has shown assays of $28 to $40 gold."

The Great View "gave an average of $35."

The Rose Maud produced "three selected sacks assayed over $2,000."

The Buena Vista shipped one carload that "gave a return of $142 per ton."

But it also explained in mineralogic terms how gold came to form in the area. It outlined the geographic extent of the mining, and it attempted to quantify its potential in realistic terms.

It was an ambitious, authoritative journalistic report.

… There were 3,660 passengers carried in and 1,336 taken out most of whom were business men and investigators. Denver, Pueblo, Aspen and Leadville capital is making a more searching examination at this time than ever before and important developments are likely to ensue.

Two months later the *Rocky* returned to Cripple Creek and produced an extensive followup report that attempted to reflect the real mining story. The Sunday, April 24 headlines:

CRIPPLE CREEK.
Results Exceeding the Fair Promise of the February Showing.

Two months is a brief period in the life of the ancient hills … but it is a period ample for mighty deeds when thousands of sturdy Western men are sending the ring and clang of their picks along the mountain side.

The story reported that in February there were 5,000 men in the Cripple Creek district. Now there were 8,000.

Cripple Creek was growing up fast. Judged by the *Rocky's* example of boots-in-the-camp reporting, so was frontier journalism. ☐

Golden day for Brown Palace

The Brown Palace Hotel marks its birthdate as Aug. 12, 1892. The *Rocky* gave a spartan headline and three columns of space on page 2 the next day in covering the first banquet – the Triennial Conclave of Knights Templar.

One hundred sixteen years later, it just doesn't seem enough.

ROYAL DEDICATION
Banquet to the Grand Encampment
in the Brown Palace
Hotel.

Magnificent Appointments That Surpass
All Others and Bewilder
the Guests.

The broad marble and onyx balcony which circles the rotunda of the hotel at the height of eight stories furnished a pleasant place wherein to chat while awaiting the signal to advance upon the enemy.

This was the evidently hungry newsman's description of the social graces leading up to dinner.

Away down at the bottom of the huge shaft the Western band of Detroit was manufacturing harmony, which rolled and thundered upward until it reverberated against the roof. On every balcony were pretty girls who were so intent upon the scene below that they were quite unconscious of the gallant templars above. The ancient knightly order has improved considerably upon the frigid and uncomfortable ruin drawn up by St. Bernard.

The great banquet hall is a splendid apartment of harmonious design about 130 feet in length and sixty feet wide, rounded at the end by a spacious alcove increasing the length by an addition of twenty-five feet.

The account goes on to describe the interior in minute detail, until –

The company being seated, attacked without more ado the following menu.

It included Little Neck clams, a Haut Sauterne, mountain trout ravigote, potatoes serpentine, filet of beef, Chateau Pontet Canet, terrapin, Golden plover barde, Nesselrode pudding, and more. Topped off by liqueurs and cigars.

The Brown Palace opened even though it still was not completed. It would be another five months, on Jan. 28, 1893, when the hotel formally opened and hosted a party given by the son of Horace Tabor and his wife. By now, the *Rocky* had a "Society" page, which covered the event.

Dying to subscribe

In 1892, the *Rocky* offered a truly unique incentive to subscribe to the newspaper – free life insurance, good for 24

hours from the date of publication. The two-column ad explaining the offer ran next to the story reporting the opening of the Brown Palace:

Will pay $500 to the legal heir or heirs of any regular subscriber of *The News* who meets death by accident while in the pursuit of ordinary avocation, provided that the subscriber so dying has upon his or her body at the time of the accident from which death occurs, this coupon, dated as above, or a copy of *The Rocky Mountain News* of current date.

The ad listed the payouts for various injuries:

$150 For the loss of two eyes
$100 For the loss of two feet
$50 For a broken ankle
$125 For the loss of one hand and one foot.

And so on.

And, sure enough, no reader could hardly dispute the legitimacy of the offer for at the bottom of the ad it listed some of its beneficiaries, right there under the words

LOSSES PAID

To the widow of Lee J. Dunham, killed while attempting to rescue little Annie Sopfe ... $500. ☐

Financial storm breaks

One of the bleakest economic periods in Colorado history took hold in 1893. Three years after the U.S. passed the Sherman Act, guaranteeing the government purchase of all the silver produced in Colorado, the law was under siege by Eastern "gold bugs" backing a single gold standard. Over three July days a dozen Denver banks failed. Fortunes were erased in a matter of hours.

Starting on July 18, 1893, *Rocky* headlines chronicled the spiral:

FELL SHORT OF CASH
By Agreement Three Savings
Banks Fail to Open Doors

The Colorado Savings bank, People's Savings bank and Rocky Mountain Dime and Dollar Savings bank assigned yesterday ... It was evident that the depositors, almost without exception, would not listen to reason or argument, and that all realized assets would be exhausted before their demands could be satisfied. Were the banks to suspend during a rush while a crowd of depositors was clamoring at the counter, scenes of disturbance might arise, and this the banks determined to avoid.

The *Rocky* attempted to provide some perspective on the crisis in an editorial:

It speaks well for the fortitude and confidence of Denver people that the shutting up of the savings banks created no unusual demand upon the national banks. If such fortitude shall continue none of the national banks can be shaken.

But the next day, three national banks and three more private banks shut their doors. The July 19 headline on page 2:

CURRENCY IS SCARCE

The financial storm broke upon Denver with full force yesterday. A few of the weaker institutions fell before it, but the solid banks stood nobly and there is every reason to believe that the worst is past. In spite of the excitement it can truthfully be said that there was nothing approaching a panic.

The newspaper now liberally used drawings and cartoons on the front page to illustrate news stories or the paper's editorial position. On July 19 it displayed a castle, stalwart against the waves of panic, washing at its foundation.

Page 2 displayed another drawing of a

bank patron at a cashier window, behind which bundles and bags of cash were stacked, a scene intended to reflect its report from the German National bank that day:

This bank has a very large number of small depositors and the crowd was consequently large. The tellers perspired as they shoved out money and kept at the work uninterruptedly. Every check was promptly paid and the quantity of boodie remaining in sight at the close was sufficient to excite the amazement of those who had drawn their money. ☐

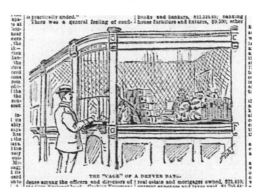

Silver loses its luster

IT IS FINISHED
Silver Completely Demon-
etized and Degraded.
A Single Gold Standard Estab-
lished by a Vote of 48 to 37.

The *Rocky's* headlines on Oct. 31, 1893, told the story. The Sherman Act had been repealed. Colorado's silver boom was over. The newspaper left little doubt of where it stood on the issue in a report laced with hyperbole and outrage:

> The hour of 7:30 on the evening of October 30, 1893, will be memorable in the annals of American congress as the hour and day when the senate of the United States, by a majority of eleven votes, abased itself before the executive and became accessory, present abetting and consenting to the greatest crime committed against American people and against civilization since the foundation of the government.

On the same front page, in the third column, two other related stories demonstrated just how inflamed the silver issue had become. The Chicago World's Fair had been called to a premature close after the assassination of Mayor Carter Harrison.

CLOSED IN SILENCE
Carter Harrison's Death Changed
The Programme of the Fair.

The first story, with a Chicago dateline, reported that the mayor had been shot by Patrick Eugene Prendergast. The murderer was later described as a deranged, unemployed Irish immigrant embittered over failing to be appointed the city's chief attorney. But the second story, with a Washington dateline, tied Prendergast to another influence:

> … The assassin had been directing messages through the mails to at least one United States senator which indicated his mind was intensely wrought up against President Cleveland. The burden of all these communications was the silver question and Prendergast disclosed he was a devotee of silver.

Joslins on the scene

On the same day, the Joslins dry goods store ran a two-column ad on page 4 selling cloaks, furs and suits. It was an early appearance by the department store that

would become a fixture in the paper's pages for nearly a century.

More classifieds

The *Rocky* classified ads for property offered:

houses from $1,050
orchards in the Grand Valley and Arizona
livestock
pastureland
 a cigar store for $175
 restaurants, a dairy, a candy store
 a 25-room German hotel for $1,000.

And there were the ever-present, ever-interesting personal ads:

MADAME DUMOND.

YOUR fortune unveiled, tells you your complete past, your entire future, how to recover lost or stolen property; she tells you how your business transactions will turn out and how to make them successful; perfect satisfaction guaranteed by mail with lock of hair. ☐

A new day for women

There was something about the West that made women independent. Maybe it was the brutal country that exacted horrible hardships upon them. Maybe it was the wide open spaces that instilled a new-found freedom in them. But in the election of 1893, against tough odds, Colorado voted to give women the right to vote. It became only the second state to do so, after Wyoming.

Thomas Patterson, publisher of the *Rocky*, did not favor voting for women. Publicly, the newspaper remained neutral. But on Nov. 9, the lead headline read:

THEY CAN VOTE
Equal Suffrage Carried by
a Large Majority.

Nearly every county in the state approved the amendment, finally passing it by a 6,000 vote margin. Pueblo was largely opposed, but Arapahoe and Boulder widely approved.

The *Rocky* reported that the Equal Suffrage Association held a spontaneous victory party on election night at its headquarters in the Opera House.

All were so happy at the result of the vote on Tuesday that a dozen candles were placed in each window and their bright lights bid all come and be happy over woman's great victory.

Among the decorations were two red, white and blue stars, bordered with gold fringe and enclosing a large letter "C" for Colorado and a large "W" for Wyoming, which, the *Rocky* wrote,

showed that two states had been redeemed and no longer placed Chinamen and women on an equal footing in regard to the ballot.

Obviously, equal rights still were not recognized for all, including in the press.

Wielding the vote

One day after the amendment passed, a page 1 headline and sub-text suggested that it wouldn't be a smooth transition:

PRACTICAL POLITICS

Governor Waite will issue a proclamation as soon as the State Canvassing Board announces the result of the election – Then women will rush to the courthouse and test the horrors of registering with complete details of age, complexion and business – After that they can go ahead and organize ward clubs for their respective parties to suit their own sweet wills.

The story went on to warn:

The ladies will soon have to begin to study up on practical politics. There is a lot more in it than going to the polls on election day. The law makes not the slightest distinction between men and women. There is no provision for separate registration offices and the women will have to step right up with the men and fight their way to the front through all the crowd and rush of registration.

'Open Book'

On the same day it reported election results the *Rocky* published on page 6 a regular boxed item that it called

The Open Book – bona fide circulation yesterday – 25,840.

The daily paper still cost 5 cents on the street.   □

Big guns lock horns

One of the more bizarre incidents in early Colorado and Denver history documented by the *Rocky* was Gov. Davis H. Waite's decision to lay siege to city hall and aim two artillery pieces at the front doors. It became known as the City Hall War.

In the style of the day, the paper illustrated the event on page 1 with rough hand drawings of the scene, complete with the waiting cannons and what appear to be citizens cheering from the rooftop of an adjacent building.

The headline on March 16, 1894:

ALL ORDERED OUT.
Entire Colorado National Guard
Put Under Arms.
GOVERNOR SUMMONS THE HORSE,
FOOT AND ARTILLERY.

The law at the time allowed the governor to appoint certain municipal officers. When Waite became dissatisfied with two of his appointees to the fire and police boards, he demanded their resignations. They refused and barricaded themselves inside city hall with provisions. Waite called out the state militia and the Chaffee Light Artillery, so the story goes:

… for the purpose of forcibly ousting Commissioners Orr and Martin and installing Commissioners Mullins and Barnes. Seven hours afterward they marched back again without having accomplished anything.

The chamber of commerce, one of the leaders of which was former *Rocky* publisher William N. Byers, was enlisted to help negotiate the standoff. The group

oscillated between the old board and the quarters of the governor, trying to make peace or secure an agreement of some kind. The gentlemen naturally were extremely excited and there was some hard language used during their visits.

The newspaper account captured the chaos and real emergency caused by the governor's action. And the theater, too.

The militia had the advantage of cannon, but there were stationed in the tower of the city hall sharp-shooters who could pick off all the gunners in five minutes. The roofs and windows of the buildings around were full of people, and on the roofs were many loose bricks which would have proven handy missiles for the deputy sheriffs who would not have hesitated to use them. As for deputies, a county official is authority for the statement that Sheriff Burchinell swore in 600, who were armed with revolvers and were men who would not stop at shooting. They were under command of the most notorious persons in the city.

Eventually, both sides agreed to arbitration and no shots were fired. □

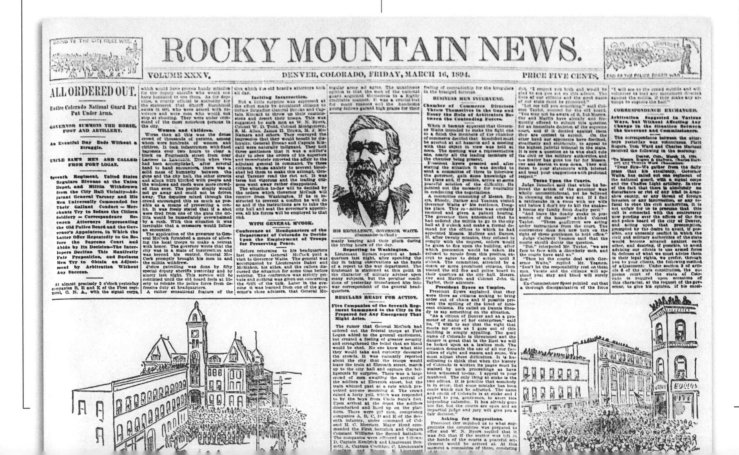

A mighty palace of ice

By the end of the 19th century, Colorado's mountains, wealth of attractions and railroad network had established the state as a place to visit and live. There was the Gold Rush. Then the Silver Boom. So on Jan. 5, 1896, when the *Rocky* devoted most of page 1 to the Ice Palace, it gave readers one more wondrous curiosity to attract interest to the state.

DENVER DAY AT THE CRYSTAL PALACE
The Ice Palace Is a Gorgeous Crea-
tion of Surpassing Mag-
nificence.

The headline, accompanied by three handsome drawings of the castle built of ice, a wildly dressed crowd ice skating inside, and its three builders riding a toboggan, sounded magical. The Ice Palace and its Crystal Carnival elevated Leadville from a mining town into a tourist attraction.

The occasion was the arrival of trainloads of visitors from Denver who came to view the spectacle.

Special to the News.
LEADVILLE, Colo., Jan. 4. – The Queen City of the Plains and the silver city of the summit clasped hands to-day under the crystal arches of the ice king's palace. With outstretched arms and portals wide the city of cloudland bade the hosts from her sister cities welcome.

In all, the paper reported that 700 "strangers" came to town aboard the Rio Grande.

Three local men – Tingley Wood, George Cook and Dr. D.H. Dougan – directed the effort to shape nearly 6,000 tons of ice into a turreted, parapeted palace 433 feet long. It was said to be the largest ice palace ever constructed. The main attraction was an ice rink 80 feet wide and 173 feet long.

A Triumph of Architecture

The spectator's first impression of the palace is its immensity and solidity. It is not a toy structure but a mighty castle. Five full acres of ground are covered.

Mining reality

On the same front page, however, across from the story that celebrated one town's mining fortune, another story reported the grim reality of digging in the mines.

EIGHT MINERS CRUSHED TO DEATH
The Men Were at Work
250 Feet Below the
Surface

Special to the News.
VICTOR, Colo., Jan. 4. – At 9:45 this morning the Anna Lee mine caved from the surface to the fifth level and eight brave and good men were in all probability crushed to death ... Fifty or more comrades of the imprisoned or dead miners are working like beavers to reach their prison or grave and hundreds more are standing idly by. ☐

The Rocky and the Mountains

The first drawn image of the Rocky Mountains to appear in the *Rocky's* page 1 "flag" – the paper's name plate – was on April 23, 1897. The occasion was the 38th anniversary of the newspaper and, apparently, its move into a grand new building at the corner of 17th and Lawrence streets.

The mountains, crowned with the sun's rays, actually were the backdrop for the bolder image of the state Capitol and surrounding structures. Also included in the flag was the paper's circulation – 23,918 daily and 31,924 on Sunday.

The mountains came and went in the flag's design throughout the paper's history, seemingly at the whim of the editor or art director at the time.

By 1906, the mountains and the skyline around the Capitol sprawled wider.

Momentarily in 1935, the mountains were removed and replaced with a large sun behind the Capitol, and the name of the paper was altered to *Denver Rocky Mountain News*.

By 1937, the mountains were back. The word "Mountain" in the paper's name appeared in a new, heavy typeface that nearly blotted out the Capitol. By the end of the year, the mountains and the Capitol had disappeared and the name was *Rocky Mountain News* again.

By 1945, the mountains returned.

By 1977, the mountains seemed to disappear for good.

Briefly in the 1990s, when management determined that dominating the Denver metro market and curtailing statewide circulation was the end-game strategy for winning the newspaper war against *The Denver Post*, the paper went back to the name *Denver Rocky Mountain News*. But no mountains.

The model for the drawings of the mountains that historically were used always included the vague image, at least, of Mount Evans, directly west of Denver. In the '90s the *Rocky* printed prototypes of a completely redesigned paper that included a photograph of the mountains in the page 1 flag. But when the designer mistakenly chose a photo of a horizon with Pikes Peak instead of Mount Evans, the publisher terminated the project.

In 2001, following the 9/11 attacks on the World Trade Center and Pentagon, a stylized version of the mountains was restored.

The paper's nickname, for as long as anyone can remember, has been *The Rocky*. It was distinctive and a proud part of the newspaper's identity for staff and residents. So was the reassuring image of the craggy peaks in the flag.

John Temple, the last editor, president and publisher, took the bold step of emphasizing the paper's familiar name and iconic mountains in an altogether new design launched Jan. 23, 2007. The new flag – on both page 1 and the paper's Internet site – printed the word *Rocky* alone on a red field followed by *"Mountain News"* overlaying a simple line drawing of its western namesakes.

The anniversary edition

The *Rocky* explained its elation over its 38th birthday in an editorial on page 4.

> … Of its record there is little need to speak. The position which it early attained and holds is the best testimonial that it has been true to the people and to justice and right. There is no other policy that will stand the test of time.
>
> At this time it is a source of pleasure that Messrs. Byers and Dailey, the founders of the paper, are still honored residents of Denver. Some of those who directed its fortunes since they crossed the plains have passed away.

To celebrate the birthday, the paper printed hand-drawn portraits of all of its staff and employees "resident in Denver," it explained.

> It would be impracticable to publish the portraits of the army of correspondents in all the cities, towns and villages of the country, whose duty is to report the news of the day.

There were 189 portraits, including four women. □

War explodes with Spain

From its very first "number," the *Rocky Mountain News* considered itself a "local" newspaper. But especially in its early years, when newspapers were usually the only source of news from elsewhere around the country – and the globe – the paper published historic headlines about events that changed the world.

One occurred on Feb. 16, 1898, half way down the front page:

CRUISER MAINE BLOWN UP
IN THE HARBOR OF HAVANA

HAVANA, Feb. 15. – At a quarter to 10 o'clock this evening a terrible explosion took place on board the United States cruiser Maine in Havana harbor. Many were killed or wounded. All the boats of the Spanish cruiser Alfonso XIII, are assisting. As yet the cause of the explosion is not apparent.

The wounded sailors of the Maine are unable to explain it. It is believed that the cruiser is totally destroyed.

The explosion shook the whole city. The windows were broken in all the houses.

Blame for the incident was quickly attached to Spain, although it never was proved to have been the cause. But the destruction of the vessel, which was a showpiece of the U.S. Navy, was a shock to America and eventually led to the Spanish-American War. The Maine was one of the first U.S. battleships to be constructed, at a cost of $2,588,000. It had been commissioned only three years earlier. Two hundred and fifty-two men died. "Remember the Maine" became the battlecry of U.S. military forces during the war.

Some historic accounts state that in the aftermath of the sinking, U.S. newspapers waged a propaganda campaign against Spain. But there was no indication of it in the *Rocky's* initial account, despite the often bombastic style of journalism at the time.

Along with the news report, the paper printed a drawing of the Maine under full steam and a telegram from Captain Charles Sigbee of the Maine:

Public opinion should be suspended till further report … Many Spanish officers, including representatives of General Blanco now with me and express sympathy.

The lead page 1 headline the same day reported the continued struggle of the "Silver Republicans" on behalf of silver interests. ☐

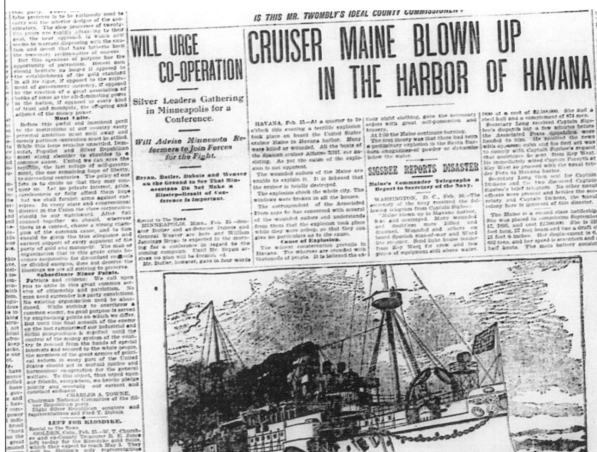

A momentous new year

The first edition of 1900 was not the first edition of the 20th century. At least not at the *Rocky Mountain News*.

The reasoning then – and even by some a century later – was that technically the century was from 1801 to 1900, because theoretically there was no "zero year." The same logic caused many to believe the whole Y2K frenzy in 2000 was a hoax, or at least one year off schedule. In 1900 the *Rocky* reasoned that the last day of the century wasn't until Dec. 31. So it saved its "turn of the century" headline until one year later.

Nevertheless, the newspaper recognized the new year in a big way in its Jan. 1, 1900, edition. The paper published a 54-page special edition that took a very boosterish look at the state of Colorado, with stories on mining, agriculture and manufacturing. As part of a grand promotion, the paper touted it as "the best paper ever printed in Colorado." It exhorted readers on page 1 to mail it around the world.

**SEND AWAY THE NEW YEAR'S NEWS
– PRICE 5 CENTS – POSTAGE 5 CENTS
Wide distribution of the New Year's News will be worth millions of dollars to Denver and the state.**

Page 1 included three drawings depicting the sales and circulation extravaganza – one showing street hawkers selling the paper, another the office of the *Rocky* with customers queued up to buy, and a third with workers loading bags of papers into mail wagons. A story followed under the unabashed headline:

A GREAT SUCCESS

The men who carried the scores of sacks from the mailing rooms to the waiting wagons felt the effects of their labors probably more than those in any other department. They strained under the heavy loads and by the time the last copy was out every one of them was ready to swear that the circulation of the paper was at the very least a million copies.

… One newsboy drew patronage by securing a Christmas tree and piling about the base of it many copies of the big paper. The tree attracted people, and once their attention was called, but few failed to purchase.

In a follow-up story Jan. 2, the *Rocky* attempted to separate itself from its city rivals:

Of all the efforts made by different publishers to get out a great newspaper, the effort of *The News* was the undisputed winner.

The paper alerted readers that remaining copies of the special edition would likely run out by the end of the week, but that it had saved the printing plates "and a second edition will be run off at any time the demand may require."

Growing circulation

By 1900, the city of Denver's population was 133,859.

On Jan. 1, the paper reported its daily circulation as 26,286 (20 percent "penetration") and Sunday as 33,659 (25 percent). It even printed its circulation, day by day, sworn to by business manager R.C. Campbell, with notary Samuel MacDonald's public seal printed with the story. The paper's share of the city's population was impressive.

The *Rocky* would hold its circulation advantage over the handful of upstart dailies for a few more years. But there were more war clouds building over Denver. The start of the newspaper war wasn't far off.

Dedications and Disasters

(Colorado Historical Society)

*Molly Brown wasn't listed among the initial survivors
saved from the Titanic. But after she and her daughter
clambered into one of the last lifeboats,
she became known as "Unsinkable."*

Rocky Mountain News

April 16, 1912

THE NEWS
ROCKY MOUNTAIN

VOL. XLII:—NO. 1. DENVER, COLORADO, TUESDAY, JANUARY 1, 1901—56 PAGES—INCLUDING COVER.—PRICE 5 CENTS. ESTABLISHED 1859.

THIS PAPER The postage on this paper is 5 cents, which must be prepaid with stamps, or the paper will be held in the postoffice. Persons who wish to send papers away may furnish lists of names to The News with 10 cents for each name and the papers will be forwarded postage paid.

HAIL TO THE TWENTIETH CENTURY

TESLA WILL TALK WITH MARS FROM PIKE'S PEAK

Great Wizard Predicts Startling Revelations in Astronomy in the Near Future.

[JA]CK CONNOR DIES A HERO'S DEATH

[Shi]ft Boss Overcome by Gas in a Vain Effort to Save the Life of a Companion.

JANUARY 1, 1901.

FATHER TIME

"KNOWLEDGE IS RECORDED EXPERIENCE."

SENATORS ARE IN HARMONIOUS MOOD

Meet to Apportion Patronage and Find They Are Not Bad Friends.

PRESIDENT HOLDS BACK SCANDALS IN CUBA

Senate Demands Report of Examiner Lawshe Into Financial Rottenness in the Island.

HUNGRY BEARS RESPONSIBLE FOR BURSTING WRIGHT'S BUBBLE

Stock Market Not Much Affected by Failure of Sixteen Brokers Who Fell Under Weight of London and Globe Stocks.

UNITES THE STREET RAILWAYS OF DETROIT

NEW CENTURY WELCOMED BY THE WHOLE WORLD

Dedicatory Services by Pope Leo —Dead Hopes Buried and People Celebrate.

JIRENE SHEAR MAY MARRY BONI CASTELLANE'S COUSIN

RUSSIAN COMMENT ON NICARAGUA CANAL TREATY

MRS. JIRENE I. SHEAR.
Who, It Is Reported, Will Marry Into Boni Castellane's F[amily]

Ringing in 20th century

The *Rocky*, following the calendar literally, believed the 20th century began on the first day of the first year – 1901. It marked the milestone with a 56-page, five-section edition that was journalistically ambitious, but just slightly bizarre.

The lead headline was big and celebratory:

HAIL TO THE TWENTIETH CENTURY

But part of the lead story ushering in the new era was a four-inch sidebar more closely resembling science fiction than journalism:

**TESLA WILL TALK
WITH MARS FROM
PIKE'S PEAK
Great Wizard Predicts Startling
Revelations in Astronomy
in the Near Future**

Special to the News.
CHICAGO, Dec. 31. – Nikola Tesla, the great electrician, writes:

"… I have observed electrical actions which have appeared inexplicable, faint and uncertain though they were, and they have given me a deep conviction and foreknowledge that before long all human beings on this globe, as one, will turn their eyes on the firmament above, with feelings of love and reverence, thrilled by the glad news:

"Brethren, we have a message from another world, unknown and remote. It reads: One. One, two, three.

"(Signed) NIKOLA TESLA."

The report continued:

Several months ago, Nikola Tesla made a journey to Colorado. He went up among the mountains, away from human habitation. There he made many experiments. His dream for years has been to ascertain if the planets are inhabited. Is it possible that in some mysterious way this electrical wizard has received a message from Mars?

Indeed, Tesla, an inventor, recently had conducted

Nikola Tesla *(Western History Collection/Denver Public Library)*

electrical experiments in Colorado Springs. One of them involved a 200-foot pole topped by a large copper sphere. Connected to the Colorado Springs Electric Company powerhouse, historical accounts state that it discharged enormous surges of energy – enough to eventually destroy the city's generator.

Tesla later would be overshadowed by rivals Guglielmo Marconi and Thomas Edison and suffer an emotional breakdown.

But for *Rocky* readers, it was an exciting start to the new century.

An omen in the sky?

The newspaper reported Denver temperatures the day before at 19 degrees below zero; the "impressive" Catholic high masses throughout the city; and – more suspicious portent? – an eery last sunset of the outgoing century:

If a Roman were in Denver yesterday he would be convinced the new century opens with a prediction of wars, pestilence and calamities. For nearly an hour before the sun sank for the last time on the nineteenth century it hung as a great ball of blood over the mountains. Such a sunset coming at that time is considered as an omen.

561 miles of paper

In its Jan. 2 edition, the *Rocky* gave details of the printing of its landmark New Year's newspaper:

Fancy one sheet of white paper thirty-nine inches broad, running from the postoffice in Denver to a point 561 miles east. That strip represents the paper used by **The News** in its New Year's edition of yesterday morning. Such a mammoth edition, so complete in reliable statistics and illustrations, had never before been issued from any office west of Chicago.

The *Rocky* printed 57,000 copies. The press run, including stops for color work, took 33 hours. ☐

A dream takes flight

First the railroad, then the automobile had become commonplace in the Rocky Mountain region. One wonders how many could have foreseen what the next piece of amazing machinery would mean to the state and the nation when they read the one-column story at the bottom of page 1 of the *Rocky* on Dec. 18, 1903:

YANKEE AIRSHIP
GOES AGAINST GALE

NORFOLK, Va., Dec. 17. – The problem of aerial flight without use of a balloon has been solved by Wilbur and Orville Wright of Dayton, Ohio.

To-day at Kitty Hawk, on the coast of North Carolina, they successfully navigated the flying machine of their own invention for three miles in the teeth of a twenty-one-mile gale and, picking their point of descent, easily landed there.

Reading the story, written in period language and a bit of awe, provides another snapshot of how exciting a time it must have been, and the role newspapers played in making it so.

The flight began from an inclined platform constructed upon a high sand hill near Kitty Hawk. There was no starting apparatus used to give momentum to the huge bird-like affair.

Gravity did the rest …

Paper promoter

The *Rocky*, along with other newspapers of the day, were well into their role as promoters for Colorado. They established a tradition

of puffing up what was viewed as good, and taking the air out of the bad.

It was commonplace now for the paper to display editorial cartoons prominently on the front page. The cartoon printed on the same day as the report of the Kitty Hawk success produced a coincidental play on words:

THE MOFFAT ROAD
AIR LINE
DENVER
TO THE COAST

The words emblazoned across the front of a steam engine busting through the Rocky Mountains campaigned for the start of work on the much-debated rail bed and tunnel under the Continental Divide.

Name that reporter

Only a month before, the U.S. had helped Panama achieve independence from Columbia. The same day, the paper also was promoting its reports from Colon under the byline Harry E. McNichol, "commissioner of *The News* in Panama." After 44 years publishing, it was one of the first uses of a formal byline in the newspaper. □

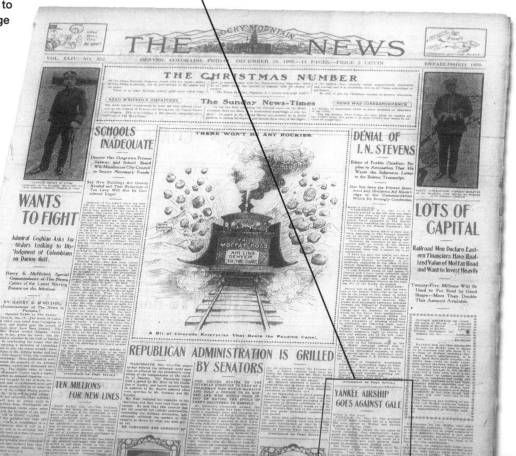

Miners' 'hell-raiser' angel

Even during the rough-and-tumble turn of the century, it wasn't often that you read reports of a 74-year-old "angel" being deported. This would be the "Miners' Angel," more famously known as "Mother" Jones.

The *Rocky's* report on March 27, 1904, that the labor crusader had been arrested in Trinidad was less of an important headline than it was an historic footnote of Mary Harris Jones' work in the labor movement in Colorado:

**UNION LEADERS ARRESTED
IN TWO MILITARY CAMPS
Mother Jones Deported From
Trinidad by Major Hill**

TRINIDAD, Colo., March 26. – A squad of militia this afternoon arrested 'Mother' Jones, William Wardjon and Joseph Paginni. They, with Adolfo Bartoldi, were sent away from the county and warned not to return. The office of I. Trovatore Italiano and the entire weekly edition of the paper were seized by order of Major Hill. The complaint is that the paper contained incendiary articles. The deported union leaders arrived at La Junta at 10 o'clock last night and went to a hotel.

… They were warned not to return to Las Animas county.

Jones, an organizer for the United Mine Workers, had come to Colorado to assist striking coal miners. Five feet, 5 inches tall with snow-white hair, her grandmotherly appearance could be deceiving. Introducing herself to an audience once, she was said to have stated:

"I'm not a humanitarian. I'm a hell-raiser."

After leaving Trinidad, she reportedly moved on to encourage strikers in the anthracite mines in Crested Butte.

Mother Jones would return to Colorado in 1913 to participate in a yearlong strike by miners. She was arrested and imprisoned twice.

Fort Collins phone service

On the front page of the same edition, a brief story was printed about the Colorado Telephone company "voluntarily" reducing the phone rates for ranches in the Fort Collins area.

"The fact that almost every ranch house in this vicinity now has a telephone in use has made it possible for the company to make the reduction," the *Rocky* reported. □

Coins begin rolling in mint

The construction of the United States Mint and dedication on Sept. 1, 1904, added another impressive structure and nationally significant landmark to the maturing core of the city of Denver. In the next day's edition, however, the *Rocky* didn't seem to treat it with great regard. There was no mention of it on page 1, and the ceremony was covered with a stiff headline and brief story on page 14, the last page of the paper.

DIRECTOR ROBERTS PRESIDES AT THE DEDICATION OF THE UNITED STATES MINT

The new United States mint, located at the corner of West Colfax avenue and Evans street (now Delaware) was formally taken possession of by government officials yesterday morning. Director of the Mint Roberts, now in Denver on his way to Washington from Alaska, was master of ceremonies at the dedication.

The exercises took place on the roof of the new building. They were simple and brief, and the new flag which will hereafter fly from the great pole on the top of the new building was raised by three veterans of the civil war.

Maybe it was the fact that the mint was another over-budget, much-delayed government project that pushed it to the back of the paper, as if to the back of everyone's minds. The site for the new mint was purchased in 1896 and construction began in 1897.

Before departing the same night on the Union Pacific, Director of the Mint Roberts prodded state officials about production.

"If Colorado will settle her strikes and get to work," he was quoted in the *Rocky*, "the output of the mint will reach $30,000,000 in gold the first year, besides $2,000,000 in silver."

Even after its dedication, the minting of coins didn't swing into full gear for nearly two years, when the mint finally began producing gold double eagles ($20) and eagles ($10) and assorted denominations of silver coins.

Still the wild frontier

Beginning in 1860, in order to handle the millions of dollars in gold and silver pouring into the city from the mines, the enterprise of Clark, Gruber & Company pressed gold coins and ingots in an office at 16th and Market streets. In 1863, that became the United States Assay Office. But even though the building was equipped with coining machinery, not a single coin was ever struck there.

Congress postponed the making of coins in Denver citing, according to one official, " ... the hostility of the Indian tribes along the routes, doubtless instigated by rebel emissaries (there being a Civil War) and bad white men."

The day on page 1

The day after the dedication of the mint, the *Rocky's* front page was almost entirely taken up by news of the quickly escalating Russo-Japan War over Korea.

RUSSIAN ARMY IN FULL FLIGHT TOWARD MUKDEN

Beneath the banner headline the paper ran side-by-side telegraph accounts of various battles from both the Russian and Japanese perspective.

The only local story on the cover was about a split in the state Republican party on the eve of primary elections for city and county of Denver offices. □

Stock show leaves chute

The *Rocky's* eight-column banner headline on page 1 on Jan. 31, 1906 marked the beginning of what would become the National Western Stock Show:

**DENVER TAKES HOLIDAY TO SEE STOCK SHOW
TWO NATIONAL BODIES OF
STOCKMEN MERGED INTO
ONE GRAND ORGANIZATION**

Two rivals of the industry, the American Stock Growers and the National Live Stock Association, had finally merged, and the city was celebrating the opening of the Western Live Stock Show, as it was called then.

The newspaper loved the idea. Another page 1 headline and story:

**All Loyal Citizens Who
Are Anxious to See
City Grow Should Go
To Today's Exhibition**

Every true blue, devoted son, native or adopted, of Denver and Colorado will be at the stock show today. The admission is free, and the men who have spent their time and money unstintedly to make this exhibition one of the best ever held anywhere urge everybody to lend their presence to the end of making the shown an absolute success. The city has declared a holiday, banks and other private enterprises will close their doors and the schools will not be in session. Everybody should be a booster.

Denver and its newspapers had been lobbying for more than a decade for such a grand show, and making it an annual affair. Only the year before, when the National Live Stock Association held its convention in the city, the *Rocky's* front page cartoon displayed a cattleman riding a horse, twirling a lasso with a key to the city at its end. The headline above it:

THE KEY IS THEIRS

A credit for the drawing was another indication of the paper's growing lust for promotion. It looked for the slightest means to tout itself over its competitors:

Drawn by George Ford Morris, the Noted Animal Painter, and E.B. Johnson of The News' Art Staff.

Stock show roots

The livestock industry was important to Denver, and the *Rocky* covered its earliest gatherings in the city. On Oct. 23, 1884, the paper reported that stockmen and the state board of agriculture met before conducting a livestock show, then known as The Fat Stock Show.

In 1898 the National Live Stock Association met in Denver and local promoters, prodding for an annual show, hosted a giant barbecue. The *Rocky* reported that hungry citizens crashed the party, though, turning it into a riot. ☐

San Francisco cataclysm

The *Rocky's* front page on April 19, 1906, shocked readers with its report of one of the greatest natural disasters in the nation's history. It also provides a historical perspective of how much journalism had improved in the 40 years since Denver's own great disaster, the flood of 1864.

The headlines carried the grim story of San Francisco's earthquake:

FLAMES ARE LICKING UP WHAT REMAINS OF THE GOLDEN GATE CITY WHERE 1,000 PERISH

FLAMES RAGE UNCHECKED AND SAN FRANCISCO HEAP OF EMBERS

The report included an amazingly detailed "birdseye view" map of the city and its condition. Long before MapQuest, drawn freehand, it zoomed in to locate well-known landmarks like Telegraph Hill, Union Square and the Palace Hotel in relation to the fire's path. Chinatown was pinpointed with the note "where 35,000 Chinamen resided." Even the original Poodle Dog Café was marked.

Secondary stories told of the scope of the earthquake, with information from Los Angeles, Santa Clara, Palo Alto, Oakland, Santa Rosa and even Reno.

Special to the News.
SAN FRANCISCO, Cal., April 18 – An earthquake at 5:16 o'clock Wednesday morning, immediately followed by fire, destroyed the business portion of San Francisco and a big part of Santa Rosa, Cal. The loss of life in San Francisco is estimated at from 200 to 1,000, with all signs indicating the latter estimate is not too much. The property loss is roughly estimated at $100,000,000.

… In San Francisco the Cliff house, which was built on solid rock, was swept into the sea. The map of the coast of San Francisco bay has been changed by the trembler.

… At Palo Alto, the magnificent Stanford university buildings were wrecked.

This edition of the *Rocky* was only 16 pages, but several were devoted to the earthquake. Another full page of coverage on page 7 led with the headline:

EARTH ROSE AND FELL WITH HEART-SICKENING MOTION

Telegraph transmission of out-of-town news photographs wasn't many years away. In the meantime, to illustrate the page, another large drawing ran which apparently *Rocky* artist Clarence Rowe, his name scrawled in one corner, was allowed to imagine. It was creative. It was believable. But it was fiction. The caption at least explained its origins:

Horror-Stricken People Fleeing for Safety – Scene Drawn From Telegraphic Description of the Frightful Panic in San Francisco Just Before the Second Earthquake Shock Broke the Water Mains.

Turning to local experts

Then as now, the Denver area claimed scientists who were considered experts at earthquake analysis. A secondary story on page 1 noted that when called upon some of these experts attributed the event to the sliding of "great masses of silt and earth down the steep declivity" of the sub-Pacific. They also thought the quake might be related to recent volcanic eruptions of Vesuvius and Sumatra. □

Chronicling first DNC

One hundred years ago, nearly to the month, the 1908 Democratic National Convention in Denver was a little different than the 2008 version.

The favorite and eventual nominee for president, William Jennings Bryan, never attended. Instead, Bryan remained at his home in Fairview, Neb., holding court in his sun room and communicating his views and platform wishes back and forth to Denver over two telegraph lines.

When the convention opened July 8 in the new Auditorium Arena, rushed to completion for the event, and Bryan's name was first uttered at the podium, the delegation broke out in a cheer that lasted one hour, 27 minutes. Then the party proceeded to drum national committee member Jim Guffey out of the convention as a rebuke to the era's politics of bossism.

The next day Bryan became the party's unanimous nomination — for the third time. Of course, he would later lose the presidency — for the third time.

Not unlike today, Denver unabashedly used its first national convention as an opportunity to trumpet the business and tourist attractions of the city and the state of Colorado. The *Rocky's* "Souvenir Convention Number (Edition)" was 32 pages, and it printed 100,000 in hopes of seeing them passed, literally, by hand, across the country.

Bryan's reaction

When news of the extraordinary demonstration for the nominee in Denver reached Bryan in Nebraska, he remarked: "You credit me with too much influence with the convention." Then he ordered that a watermelon, a gift sent to him from Texas, be cracked open to refresh the friends and journalists that packed his house.

1908 running mate

John W. Kern, a state senator from Indiana and twice the Democratic nominee for governor, became a seemingly casual choice for vice president. As the *Rocky* reported on July 11, "A conference of Democratic leaders agreed upon Kern as the most available candidate ... "

Damon Runyon

Bryan's third nomination for president was so widely expected that the next day the newspaper didn't report it as "hard news." Instead, Runyon, the legendary reporter, wrote a voluminous profile about the candidate under the banner headline:

BRYAN, MAGNETIC, VIGOROUS, PLAIN AMERICAN CITIZEN

What is he, anyhow, that the magnetism of his marvelous personality still holds the people of the United States enthralled?

Take that, Teddy

The day after the demonstration of one hour, 27 minutes for Bryan in Denver, the paper pointed out that outgoing President Teddy Roosevelt received only a 40-minute ovation at the Republican convention in Chicago.

Knight in shining armor

Bryan was dubbed with several nicknames during his political career. "The Great Commoner" and "The Boy Orator of the Platte" were the best known among them. The day after his nomination a cartoon on the editorial page of the *Rocky* pictured him as a knight in armor riding a presumably white horse. From his helmet, a huge feather waved the words: "The Plumed Knight of the West." □

Death of Geronimo

The *Rocky* reported the death of another legendary Western figure on Feb. 18, 1909. The not-so-complimentary headline and story, with a large photo, were found on page 4:

**Geronimo, Apache Scourge, Dies,
Still Bitterly Hating Palefaces
Burial of 86-Year-Old Chieftain Captured
by Gen. Miles Will Be Conducted With
Christian Ceremonies at Fort Sill**

LAWTON, Okla.. Feb. 17. – Geronimo, the noted Indian chief, died today in the hospital at the Fort Sill army post, where he has been held for twenty-two years as a prisoner of war. He died of pneumonia after two days illness.

To the last Geronimo was full of hatred for the white man … Geronimo was captured with his band at Skeleton canon, Ariz., by General Nelson A. Miles, who, with his soldiers, had pursued him for months. News of Geronimo's death was sent out from Lawton, which was named after the late Henry F. Lawton, the general who, as a member of Miles' command, led the 3,000-mile chase that resulted in the chief's surrender.

The photo of the Apache chief was apparently taken at the request of Miles, who told of Geronimo's capture in a second story:

"I got pretty well acquainted with Geronimo at the St. Louis fair, I had his picture taken. The picture shows him with a hat on. Apaches never wore head covering, not even a feather in their hair. The blanket he has over his shoulder is one I gave him."

Beneath the photo, the *Rocky* wrote the caption:

CHIEF GERONIMO, "THE RED DEVIL," WHO IS DEAD.

Death and politics

It wasn't exactly a "big news day," as they say in the business, the day Geronimo's death was reported. The front page led with these stories:

■ The issue of a warrant for the arrest of *New York World* publisher Joseph Pulitzer, charged with libeling Teddy Roosevelt;

■ A girl found beaten and lashed to the foot of a bathtub in a Chicago hotel;

■ A woman thrown from a Denver tram, who died after tramway employees delayed calling for aid.

'Short and ugly word'

In the same edition, Denver Mayor Robert Speer was attacked for a remark he made in an interview about tourist travel to California.

The "shorter and uglier word" is being applied to Mayor Speer because of his knock against Denver and Colorado … He asserted that "not one-tenth of the Eastern people who go to California see Denver and Colorado." Railroad men are emphatic in saying that the mayor didn't know what he was talking about.

"Short and ugly word" apparently was a phrase used in the day to condemn "testimony from the absolute."

Or they could have just said "bull." ☐

Duking it out over fight

It was the day after Fourth of July, 1910, a major holiday in America, and bare-knuckle boxers Jack Johnson and James J. Jeffries had provided the fireworks.

For the *Rocky,* the July 5 edition is memorable because it marked the start of one of the newspaper's enduring traditions – a sports story dominated page 1.

And as history's headlines would periodically remind readers in the coming century, this was more than just a sports story.

The buildup to the fight was rife with racial tension. Jeffries, a former undefeated heavyweight champion, came out of retirement, he said, solely to prove that a white man was superior to a Negro. Johnson, nicknamed the "Galveston Giant," was flamboyant and liked to taunt his opponents and their corners.

The *Rocky* printed two large one-column headlines of equal weight on the front page. One reported Johnson's lopsided victory in round 15; the other told of resulting riots in Illinois, New York, Georgia, Arkansas, Virginia, Missouri, Louisiana, Texas and Colorado.

The subhead over the Colorado incident:

30 HURT IN PUEBLO RIOT
[SPECIAL TO THE NEWS]

PUEBLO, Colo., July 4 – As a result of a quarrel over the outcome of the Johnson-Jeffries fight between an unidentified negro and a white man in the Bessemer park tonight a fight started that eded in a riot, participated in by five hundred persons, in which two white men were stabbed seriously in the back and twenty-five or thirty others received slight bruises from blows with sticks.

Blow-by-blow accounts of the prize fight were spread over six of eight columns on page 1 and three more pages inside. The *Rocky* had advertised before the fight in Reno, Nevada, that it would announce results round-by-round at its office, and a photo showing a solid tide of people filled half of one page. The headline and story:

Street Jammed by Thousands
To Hear News Fight Bulletins

The News bulletins of the big fight were heard yesterday by all degrees and classes, from a justice of the Colorado supreme court down to the chattering newsboys.

The paper printed a running round-by-round account, including 20 different small drawings of a black boxer and a white boxer in various punching stances to illustrate the action.

Jeffries – no, Johnson

The *Rocky* hired a popular novelist of the time named Rex Beach to write stories before the fight and cover it in Reno. The headline over Beach's prediction on the front page of the paper July 4:

JEFFRIES WILL WIN ON HIS NERVE, SAYS REX BEACH

Strangely, on July 5, beneath the page 1 headline of Johnson's triumph, one of several small subheads leading into Beach's fight story read:

Rocky Mountain News was the only newspaper to pick Johnson to win from time match was made.

Payroll plundered

On page 4 the *Rocky* ran a story from Reno estimating that $250,000 was wagered there on the fight. A few columns away on the same page, another article read:

Three sacks of gold coin containing $5,250 were taken from the safe in the business office of The News some time between 12 o'clock midnight Sunday and 6 o'clock yesterday morning.

The money was a part of The News payroll drawn from the bank on Saturday in anticipation of the usual weekly payday on Monday. Sacks containing several hundred dollars in silver coin were not touched. ☐

Denver's 'unsinkable' icon

The ship once hailed as the most unsinkable on the seas produced an unsinkable Denver legend. The headline on April 16, 1912 and one of its sub-heads:

**1,304 DIE WHEN STEAMER TITANIC
SINKS IN MID-OCEAN
Denverites Believed to
Be Aboard Ship Not
Mentioned in Report
of Persons Rescued.**

NEW YORK, April 16 – While the fate of the majority of the 2,170 persons on board the mammoth White Star liner, Titanic, which sank early yesterday on the Newfoundland banks, after a collision with an iceberg, still remains in doubt, and it is feared more than 1,300 persons were lost, a note of good cheer came from the ocean ways by wireless between 1 and 2 o'clock this morning.

It was in the shape of a wireless message from the White Star liner, Olympic, one of the vessels hovering near the scene of the disaster, flashing the news that 806 of the Titanic's passengers, mostly women and children, were being brought to port by the Cunarder Carpathia.

… A partial list of the survivors received from the Carpathia includes the names of many women of prominence who were on the steamer.

But the names of Mrs. James J. Brown (top right in the front-page picture montage), wife of the superintendent of the "Little Johnny" gold mine in Leadville, and her daughter were not among them. They also were not on the list of "Prominent Persons Believed Drowned" printed in the first day's report of the disaster.

As it turned out, Margaret Brown and her daughter, Helen, clambered into the last lifeboat to leave the doomed ship and were rescued hours later. "Unsinkable" Molly Brown would be remembered in song and on stage far more for her good luck than the good works she did later in Denver.

Again, the *Rocky* devoted pages of coverage to the tragedy. Next to a sidebar story confirming the Browns' presence on the Titanic, the paper dramatically illustrated the size of the luxury liner by standing it upright alongside other recognizable landmarks. The Titanic, 882.5 feet long, towered over the Washington Monument, the Grand Pyramid and St. Peter's Church in Rome.

The *Rocky* printed 16 stories and lists about the Titanic. Sidebars told of the wealthy passengers onboard and believed drowned – John Astor and Benjamin Guggenheim. It reported the wireless radio messages received from the Titanic and explained how Marconi's relatively new invention helped save another liner, the Republic. Another story related wireless details of bravery, impromptu religious services, hysterical acts and the separation of husbands and wives as they loaded into the lifeboats. □

Blizzard of snow, news

The *Rocky* reported the first of many "storms of the century" as more of a celebration of man over nature than a disaster on Dec. 5, 1913. Snowfall of 25.8 inches over 24 hours the day before was the most recorded since 1885.

The blizzard shut down the city and its tramway, stranded railroads and engulfed mountain towns. Eight miners and a rescue party were lost near Central City. Thousands of "pajamaless crowds" filled hotels, and the city opened the auditorium and other public buildings to shelter the homeless.

Only some of the mail and newspapers were delivered. An inside-page headline:

STORM BLOCKS
MAIL DELIVERY
Postmen Forced to Walk by
Street Car Blockade, but
Do Partial Service.
Carriers Plunge Through Drifts in
Effort to Give Service; Will
Recover Today.

The paper joined in the resourcefulness. It printed "flashlight photographs" taken that night showing a tram car blocked by a wall of snow, and a motor taxi being pulled from a drift by a horse wagon.

The most significant difference in the paper's coverage from what it would be in future years when blizzards snarled freeway traffic for hours, was its viewpoint. It reported the storm as good news. One of the main stories on page 1:

WHOLE STATE REJOICES
OVER BIG SNOW STORM
Bountiful Crops Assured by
Enormous Increase of Moisture
and Business Men Are Happy.

Millions of dollars additional wealth to Colorado were brought yesterday by the snowfall that deluged the state. It rang up the curtain on the 1914 crop outlook, revealing visions of unprecedented prosperity to every line of industry and bountiful harvest to the farmers.

A small box on page 1 offered more good news:

Anyone may have work today by applying to the Tramway company. Hundreds of men are wanted to shovel snow, and no one who wants work will be turned away.

Seven hundred and eighty men were employed by the Tramway company yesterday to clear the tracks of snow. Over 200 men found work with the city dump wagons at salaries of $3.50 a day.

Denver's worst snowstorms (then)

The list printed by the *Rocky* on Dec. 5, 1913:

April 21-23, 1885	32.1 in.
March 29-31, 1891	18.7 in.
October 20-23, 1908	23.7 in.
April 19-20, 1907	18. in.
December 4, 1913	25.8 in.

Miss Santa Claus

Despite the snowstorm, the *Rocky* promised on page 1 that "Miss Santa Claus" would be on the city streets the next day, ready to give away $100 in gold on the spot to "the one who walks boldly up to her ... and says: 'You are Miss Santa Claus of The News and The Times.'"

The winner had to possess a copy of either paper to win. It was a Christmas promotion by the two papers since the *Rocky* purchased *The Denver Times* in 1902. □

Mining camp massacre

The front page of the *Rocky Mountain News* on April 21, 1914, was all about war. Possible war between the U.S. and Mexico. And real war – with terrible casualties – between striking Colorado coal miners and the state militia.

In what became known as the Ludlow Massacre, the paper reported 13 killed in a battle between the two sides at the mining camp near Trinidad. In the end, though, 24 died in the 14-hour showdown, including two women and 11 children later found asphyxiated in a cellar beneath one of the miner's tents. Though out-numbered, the militia fired two machine guns, driving the women and children into cellars. A deserted tent burst into flames. Soon the entire camp began to burn.

> **Thirteen dead, scores injured, the Ludlow strikers' tent colony burned and hundreds of women and children homeless was the result up to midnight of one of the bloodiest battles in labor warfare in the West. Four hundred striking miners were intrenched in the hills back of Ludlow this morning awaiting daylight to wipe out 177 members of the state national guard, with whom they fought for fourteen hours yesterday.**

The paper's two-column-wide story ran the full depth of the page and jumped inside, detailing the aftermath and reinforcements that would fuel the battle into the next day.

The miners in Colorado's southern counties had been on strike since the previous September. They were demanding safer working conditions and better hours and pay. Gov. Elias Ammons sent in the state militia as a peacekeeping measure, but it didn't work out that way.

In the same story, the *Rocky* attempted to provide a reason how the gunfire erupted.

> **The cause of the clash up to late this morning had been explained only in part. It is said that on Sunday at a ball game between teams from the Ludlow camps wives of the men attacked and beat five soldiers who were watching the contest, and that in the free-for-all fight the soldiers and several of the strikers were badly beaten and bruised.**

It seemed a hollow account.

'Unsinkable' women

A secondary story to the U.S.-Mexico issue on page 1 carried the following headline:

> **WOMEN PLAN TO FIGHT**
> **IN WAR WITH MEXICO**
> **Skirted Soldiers Would Nurse if**
> **They Are Turned Down by**
> **the United States Army.**

> **Should war be carried on with Mexico, Colorado may send a regiment of women soldiers to the front.**
> **Suffrage circles were set agog yesterday by the news that Mrs. J.J. (Molly) Brown, heroine of the Titanic disaster, was on her way to Denver to organize the martially inclined women of the state for military duty, so that when the time comes they may be prepared to shoulder the rifle and fight in Mexico side by side with the men.** □

Real Estate Is Moving
And the Real Estate Page of The Rocky Mountain News—a feature of the Thursday morning paper—is the best medium through which to make deals. Get in copy early and secure position for your ad.

THE ROCKY MOUNTAIN NEWS EXTRA
COLORADO'S GREATEST NEWSPAPER

VOL LV: NO. 111. | Denver—Today Unsettled and Cloudy | DENVER, COLO., TUESDAY, APRIL 21, 1914.—16 PAGES. | Colorado—Today Rain or Snow and Colder | PRICE {Daily—2 cents on all its trains and news stands Sunday—5 cents

MEXICO WAR PLANS ARE MADE FINAL AS SENATE HOLDS UP RESOLUTION
THIRTEEN KILLED IN BATTLE AT LUDLOW; STRIKERS' TENT COLONY BURNED

12,000 TROOPS MARCH ON CAPITAL IF BLOCKADE FAILS TO MOVE HUERTA

Army and Navy Movements Are Perfected at Council of Chiefs; House Backs President in Request for Justification of Armed Force Program.

By a Staff Correspondent of the New York World and The Rocky Mountain News.
WASHINGTON, April 21.—(Tuesday)—Full congressional approval of President Wilson's program for using armed force in Mexico to put an end to insults to the American flag and the government was not decided when the senate, at 12:28 o'clock this morning, recessed until noon today. But plans for blockading the seaports of Mexico, seizing customs houses, warships, railroads and landing armed forces were brought to a point of such perfection that the American occupation is practically certain to be in effect within forty-eight hours or less.

Following President Wilson's delivery of his special message to a joint session of congress in the afternoon, the house, after spirited debate, adopted the following resolution by a vote of

SOME of the leading figures in the fourteen-hour battle at Ludlow yesterday. Above—Tent colony of strikers at Ludlow, which was burned last night. Center, left to right—Lieutenant Chase, who is hurrying with troops at Walsenburg to the scene of the fighting; and John R. Lawson. Below, left to right—Louis Tikas, leader of the tent colony, who was killed last night; and Maj. P. J. Hamrock, in command of the troops at Ludlow.

1,500 ARMED MINERS RUSHING IN TO EXTERMINATE GUARDSMEN

Fighting Rages 14 Hours and Small Force of Militia Sweeps Hills With Machine Guns to Hold Back Determined Band of Union Workers.

Thirteen dead, scores injured, the Ludlow strikers' tent colony burned and hundreds of women and children homeless was the result up to midnight of one of bloodiest battles in labor warfare ever waged in the West. Four hundred striking miners were intrenched in the hills back of Ludlow this morning awaiting daylight to wipe out members of the state national guard, with whom they fought for fourteen hours yesterday. The known dead are:
Private A. Martin of Company A, Denver.
Louis Tikas, leader of Greek strikers at Ludlow, Denver.
Injured:
Private Lewis Purcell, Colorado Springs.

EUROPE INDORSES WILSON'S ACTION

BLAST KILLS 6; WRECKS HOTEL

A park in the Rockies

Colorado acted on a passion for preserving its most cherished wild places even at a time when the state was still struggling to tame old frontiers.

The day after the dedication of Rocky Mountain National Park, the *Rocky* wrote on page 1 about the park and the efforts of outdoorsman Enos Mills to safeguard it almost as if the ceremony at Horseshoe Park had been a holy event.

New Park Dedicated,
All Nation Takes Part
JOY GROUND
FOR U.S. IS
GIVEN OVER
TO PEOPLE
By Morris Legg.

The Rocky Mountain National park was dedicated to the people of all the world for all time yesterday afternoon. Leaders in the life of the nation, the state of Colorado and the city of Denver stood with bared heads in the fine drizzle of a picturesque mountain shower as the opening exercises were observed which proclaimed this vast natural scenic wonderland open to all.

And as Enos A. Mills, pathfinder, naturalist and father of the movement to keep the land of Colorado magic inviolate for generations to come had told his part in the great work in modest manner, the clouds gathered over the distant peaks. A roll of thunder was heard and the rain came upon the gathering.

Next to it, a congratulatory message from President Woodrow Wilson ran in a box.

The lengthy story jumped to page 3 where it was accompanied by four photographs and four shorter stories. More than 2,000 attended the dedication, most of them arriving in 300 automobiles strung along the road into the park.

Mills, who lived in Estes Park and split his time between the mountains he loved and the Eastern cities where he sought to save them, was the first to speak.

"The development of great natural parks is something new. Nations have gathered to pay homage to great warships and great warriors but the nations of the future will pay honor to their natural playgrounds …"

The *Rocky's* editorial observed of Mills:

He was nature's prophet. Estes park owes to him what the Yosemite owed to John Muir.

Health warning-of-the-day

A story the same day at the bottom of page 1 told of another crusade under an eye-catching headline:

Candy Called as Great Evil to Child as Saloons

SAN FRANCISCO, Cal., Sept. 4. – Candy was declared today to be "as great an evil to the child as liquor is to the adult," in a paper by Dr. Horace L. Howe of Boston, read before the Panama-Pacific Dental congress.

"In front of almost every schoolhouse in the country there can be found a small candy store which sells cheap sweets to children … A broken-down set of teeth in children is a serious menace to them and a great handicap to their future careers."   □

Depot rises from ashes

Denver's present-day Union Station rail depot opened on Oct. 31, 1915. The event made it on the *Rocky's* page 1, but well below other headlines of the day.

NEW DEPOT ROOM WILL OPEN TODAY

The greater part of Denver's new $500,000 union station will be opened for use today. The great waiting room and ticket offices, that have been built on the street side of the great room, which is 100x110 feet, and the telegraph office, will be occupied today. The ticket offices were moved after midnight last night.

The new structure was illuminated last night for the first time. The large room, 64 feet from floor to ceiling, is most brilliantly lighted by three great electroliers that hang from the ceiling, each containing eleven 230-watt and one 400-watt light, besides twenty-eight bracket lights on the walls and three double bracket lights on top of each of the seats in the rooms, which are 22 feet long.

The story droned on about lights and gates for a few more inches on page 5, along with a photograph of the expansive waiting room that still impresses today.

Depot fire on Page 1

The original depot opened in 1881 at the same location at the foot of 17th and Wynkoop streets. But it was destroyed by fire, a debacle reported on the *Rocky's* front page on March 18, 1894, in stacked headlines.

DEPOT DESTROYED
Disastrous Midnight Fire Due to an Electric Leak.
FIRE DEPARTMENT HAMPERED BY DEFECTIVE WATER SUPPLY.

Valuable Time Wasted in Turning in an Alarm Allowed the Flames to Sweep the Full Length of the Building – An Hour After the First Alarm the Central Tower Fell, Threatening the Lives of the Firemen Working Beneath – Baggage and Express Matter Saved – Rebuilding Will Proceed Forthwith and the Almost Perfect Terminal Facilities of Denver Will Be Greatly Improved.

The one-column story was illustrated with a crude line drawing in which two firemen looked almost like stick figures. But it was a noteworthy deadline report written in the early-morning hours.

Pancho Villa in the news

On the day the new Union Station opened in 1915, the *Rocky's* banner headline reported the massing of 3,000 U.S. troops near Douglas, Arizona, as a precaution if guerilla Francisco "Pancho" Villa continued his attacks on the Mexican government recognized by the U.S. It was one of numerous border conflicts between the two nations through 1920. Five months later, after Villa led attacks into New Mexico, Brig. Gen. John J. Pershing crushed Villa's force in his "Punitive Expedition."

Also on page 1, the *Rocky* reported a major wildfire threatening Estes Park.

Pictorial 'week in review'

The paper was now printing a pictorial review of the past week's events in cartoonish style each Sunday. On Oct. 31, the subjects included women's suffrage in the U.S., local labor issues, controversy over a street arch to be built downtown, a proposed new railway loop, and Enos Mills' continuing efforts for support of national parks. □

Colorado quits the bottle

The *Rocky* safely forecast in its first edition of 1916 that it was going to be a dry year for Colorado. It was the first day of Prohibition in the state.

'DRY' YEAR IS USHERED
IN WITH MARKED QUIET
AS BARS CLOSE EARLY

Pueblo, Colorado Springs, Boulder, Cripple Creek and all the mountain and other Colorado towns went dry at midnight without ceremony. Most saloons closed doors before the final hour.

A new era confronts Colorado today. The state is dry. The most conspicuous event in the commonwealth's history has taken place.

While Denver strangely wasn't mentioned in the story's lead, it surely was included among places where booze was now banned.

Toward midnight an immense throng gathered on Curtis street and other streets in the downtown business section, tooted horns and in other ways welcomed the New Year … At the stroke of 12, saloons emptied themselves of patrons, cafes and restaurants suspended their most lucrative activity, and 1916 was greeted by an orderly, if jovial throng.

Along with six other states, Colorado passed Prohibition three years before most of the rest of the nation, led largely by a crusade of religious leaders and women voters.

It was estimated that 1,615 saloons and dramshops and 12 breweries were immediately put out of business.

Of course, the paper's story noted, Denver didn't completely dry up.

Meanwhile, the citizens who were loath to break ancient habits with the stroke of the clock were well provided. For days gurgling packages have accompanied the home-owner to the legal security of his cellar.

Dry dumb friends

Denver wasn't totally heartless when it came to weaning those creatures who were accustomed to living a lubricated lifestyle, as an inside-page story observed:

Pets of Saloon to Have Homes

Poor saloon dog! Poor saloon cat! … They have not been forgotten. Mrs. Margaret Brady, superintendent of the Dumb Friends' league, called up The News last night to announce that the home of the league at 1674 South Acoma street, would be open to all cats and dogs affected by prohibition.

… Mrs. Brady did confess that there was one gay dog among her guests whose habits were not so sober. And it is one of the gentle sex and a mother! Bearing the frivolous name of "Madame Butterfly," she is the dog of an actress and evidently acquired the bohemian ways of stage folk. When she first came to Mrs. Brady she had to have her beer every morning.

Only so dry

On Jan. 5, 1930, 14 years into Prohibition, the *Rocky* reported that Colorado had become the focus of a federal liquor trafficking investigation. Targets of the probe were Jefferson County and the "sugar moon" industry in Leadville and Trinidad. ☐

Heroes, Villains and War

*"Buffalo Bill is dead and he will sleep
the eternal sleep on top of Lookout Mountain.
His grave will look down upon the plains
where he had the adventures of his golden youth ..."*

Rocky Mountain News

Jan. 11, 1917

'Buffalo Bill' Cody rides off into sunset

Buffalo Bill found himself, as usual, among daring company on the front page of the *Rocky* the morning of Jan. 11, 1917. Between a Pueblo farmer who avenged his brother by killing his murderer, and an Indianapolis "negress" who made a fortune selling an ointment to straighten kinky hair and had purchased a prized lot on Long Island.

William F. Cody, Pony Express rider, Army scout and world showman, had died and would be buried on Golden's Lookout Mountain, the headline read:

'Pahaska' Goes to Happy Hunting Grounds After Long Fight With Death; Noted Men Express Sympathy to His Family.

Buffalo Bill is dead and he will sleep the eternal sleep on top of Lookout Mountain. His grave will look down upon the plains where he had the adventures of his golden youth. His head will lie toward the sun, his face looking proudly up to the skies of the West he loved so well. And in the stillness of the night will come the ghosts of the glorious past to gather with the mighty huntsman. The war cry of the old Sioux and the stamp of buffalo hoofs will make the motif of the choir invisible which will sing nightly for the last of the scouts.

The ground where he will lie will be hallowed ground for the youth of America. For with the passing of the picturesque figure of Buffalo Bill passed the last symbol of the West of old – the West of romance.

The obituary writer was Mildred Morris, the same woman who reported that Molly Brown intended to invade Mexico with a regiment of women.

And this was *some* obituary.

No surprise, as the paper reported, that one of the first telegrams of sympathy came from the White House:

"May I not express my sincere sympathy with you in the death of Colonel Cody?
"WOODROW WILSON."

Yep, the telegram included the question mark.

Morris omitted Cody's age; he was 71. He had been in failing health for nearly a year. "Uraemic poisoning was given as the direct cause of death," she wrote. He died in his sister's house at 2932 Lafayette St.

Robust Rocky

The *Rocky,* at the time of Cody's death, appeared in excellent health. Sunday editions were running 64 to 70 pages, stuffed with advertisements. The previous Sunday included seven pages of "Wants Ads," a "Motor Section," and a 12-page tabloid-size "Sunday Fiction Magazine." The fiction serials on Jan. 7, 1917:

- *The Son of Tarzan,* by Edgar Rice Burroughs
- Red Saunders' *Orange Blossoms*
- *The Whispering Bell*
- *Aurora of the Still Hills*
- *The Straight Girl on the Crooked Path*

The war to end all wars

WAR

The letters were 2 inches tall, as if the *Rocky* were shouting the word, warning its readers. Every headline on the front page April 6, 1917, was about the war. Except for a school ballot issue and the weather.

AMERICA ENTERS WORLD CONFLICT
Vote of House Backs Up President, 373 to 50
500,000 MEN TO BE DRAFTED IN SIX MONTHS

The lead paragraph was about Colorado:

WASHINGTON, April 6 (Friday). – Edward Keating and Benjamin C. Hilliard, Colorado members of the house of representatives, voted against the resolution declaring a state of war with Germany.

The story immediately below it was about the rest of the world:

WASHINGTON, April 6 (Friday). – Congress has declared that the United States is at war with the imperial German government ... By tonight the administration and leaders in congress will have launched upon the stupendous undertaking of preparing the nation for effective participation in the world conflict. The house leaders will take up at once the plans for raising an army of 1,000,000 men at once and the question of producing the $3,500,000,000 of revenue required by the war budget.

The names of "Fifty Congressman Who Voted 'No'" were listed by state in a box at the top of the page.

Business as usual

Surprisingly, in the next days of World War I, for such a traditionally local newspaper, there were almost no local stories related to the impending war. It was as if nothing had changed.

There was a report that some "Eastern collegiates" had begun to cancel some athletic events. But the Denver Glee Club was meeting as usual.

A large Hart Schaffner & Marx ad showed a handsomely suited gentleman above the Easter advice "Wear a cutaway next Sunday."

Ready to serve

On the day of America's war declaration, the paper included one local story on page 1 related to the coming conflict:

Civil War Captain, 80 Years Old, Leads Demonstration at Trinity Church; Colorado Organization Swept with Patriotic Fervor.

Captan John L. Boyd of the Grand Army of the Republic is nearly 80 years old and his hair is almost white, but he stood up to the full six feet of his height last night, and in the midst of his address before the citizens' patriotic mass meeting in Trinity church, turned to Governor Gunter and declared: "Your excellency, it is with pleasure that I place my service at your disposal." Scarcely had the words left his lips when, from the center of the church, there rose up a bent company of thirty-seven, aged, rheumatic, infirm – his comrades in the days of `61.

Battling enemy within

Even as the Allies gained the upper hand near the end of World War I, Colorado and America had to fight a new scourge at its own borders. A virulent strain of influenza, called the Spanish flu, because it was incorrectly believed to have started in Spain, spread from the East Coast.

The headline on the front page of the *Rocky* on Oct. 10, 1918, was alarming even though the story played at the bottom of the page and officials sounded a precautionary tone. The number of deaths in Denver due to the flu had reached 41.

**CITY TO BE SHUT
THREE WEEKS TO
CHECK EPIDEMIC
Five Additional Deaths Reported Yesterday; Scourge
Believed Under Control.**

There were approximately 500 cases in the city reported to Dr. Sharpley yesterday and he says that this death rate shows that the disease is well in hand in Denver, but that in Denver and in towns thruout the state will be for the full three weeks, the run of the disease.

Dr. William H. Sharpley was the city's manager of health.

"The closing of Denver depends wholly on the spread of the disease," said Dr. Sharpley. "It will be, naturally, absolutely necessary for the city to be closed while there is any danger. The main danger now menacing Denver is from outside towns and strangers arriving in the city from various sections of the country where the scourge is prevailing."

The newspaper printed a list of the cities where public meeting places, including schools, churches, theaters, pool halls and lodge rooms were suspended: Colorado Springs, Boulder, Golden, Pueblo, Sterling, Fort Morgan, Delta, La Junta, Rocky Ford, Florence, Gunnison, Walsenburg.

Another headline on page 7 warned of an even more innocent source of the disease:

**Cleanliness Is Urged
At All Soda Fountains**

"A great many soda fountains maintain a small collection of glasses practically hidden beneath the counter or slab, where the germs of the town are pooled and re-distributed," a federal official cautioned. "There is no more effective way for people in a city or village to exchange germs than is maintained by a great number of drug stores."

On Nov. 15, 1918, the *Rocky* reported there were only two deaths in Denver from Spanish flu over the past 24 hours. The report of new infected cases in the same period was down to 264.

The worst of the epidemic was over in the city. But nearly 8,000 died in Colorado before the disease was controlled.

Behind on Liberty Loans

The headline at the top of a full-page ad on page 5 of the *Rocky* Oct. 10, 1918, put it bluntly:

SHORT!

Denver's quota for purchasing Liberty Loans, government-backed bonds to support the Allied cause in World War I, was nearly $18 million and the city was $6.5 million short. The Denver loan committee was urging – no, demanding – that citizens double what they had already given.

As for those deliberate slackers who have plenty of means but have been trying to get by for only fifty dollars, this committee herewith serves notice that after this week they will be handled without gloves. □

Celebrating war's end

Maybe it was Colorado's doubt or reticence over the war, reflected by the *Rocky Mountain News* at the start, that limited the amount of initial local coverage. That definitely wasn't the case the day the newspaper told its readers:

THE WAR IS OVER

Newspapers normally don't like to print type in multi-column widths because it is difficult to read. But the *Rocky* couldn't resist in the joy of the moment. The lead of the main story ran a full eight columns wide (one of only two occasions I found in all of my research):

By Associated Press.
WASHINGTON, Nov. 11, Monday. – The world war will end this morning at 6 o'clock Washington time, 11 o'clock Paris time. The armistice was signed by the German representatives at 5:01 o'clock Paris time.

… The announcement was made verbally by an official of the state department in this form: "The armistice has been signed …" The terms of the armistice, it was announced, will not be made public until later. Military men here, however, regard it as certain that they include: Immediate retirement of the German military forces from France, Belgium and Alsace-Lorraine. Disarming and demobilization of the German armies …

And the party began around the world, Denver included:

DENVER GOES MAD
WITH WORD TRUCE
HAS BEEN SIGNED
Thousands Parade; Streets
Jammed as Crowd Revels
In Wild Celebration.

As the bombs from The News, the shrill of factory whistles and church bells tolled the glad tidings of the end of the world's war at 12:45 o'clock this morning, sleeping Denver arose from its lethargy, rubbed its eyes, swarmed onto the streets and joined in a glorious saturnalia of noise, joy and enthusiasm.
… Denver went wild.

And there was this announcement in bold type at the bottom of page 1:

Mayor Mills at 3 o'clock this morning authorized The News to announce a holiday all day today with all flags flying.

The celebration continued into Nov. 12 with this lead local story:

Thousands Throng Streets for 24 Hours in Greatest Celebration of Century in Commemoration of World's Freedom

Next to the story the paper ran a three-column cartoon showing a relieved Uncle Sam pulling on his coat of stars with the quote in a bubble: "Well, now I'll get back to business!"

Grave news

On an inside page, the *Rocky* reported the city's grave diggers had apologetically gone on a one-day "strike" to join the city party:

All funerals scheduled for Fairmount and Riverside cemeteries yesterday were forced into postponement because of the fact that all the grave diggers abandoned their work and joined the celebration in the downtown district. Before quitting their jobs of the day, however, they notified officials at the cemetery that they would offer their services free when it came to dig a final resting place for the ex-kaiser. ☐

'The Manassa Mauler'

For some years the *Rocky* had printed a growing "sporting" section. It began with a focus on boxing and horse racing. A 1913 edition included football, baseball, billiards, polo and pistol shooting, and a tradition of printing "motor news" – a new model or a big race, it didn't matter – had begun.

But on July 5, 1919, Colorado had its first legitimate, home-grown, big-time world champion. Jack Dempsey, born in Manassa, Colorado, took the heavyweight title from Jess Willard in a lopsided fight. Once again, boxing was front-page news:

Willard Quits Cold to Better Man, Says Dickerson
JESS, OUTCLASSED, GOES
DOWN IN DEFEAT BEFORE
JACK'S TERRIFIC HITTING

"Dickerson" was Emerson W. Dickerson, one of two reporters the paper sent to cover the fight in Toledo, Ohio. Even then, sportswriters were given a long leash and editorial license.

TOLEDO, Ohio, July 4. – Pitiful best describes Willard's efforts before quitting to Dempsey in the third round of the championship fight today. Willard did not make one move even suggestive of championship class. His left hand, with the reach advantage possessed by holding it out straight, might as well have been chained to his side.

Practically every blow Dempsey started landed where it was aimed, and as most of them were aimed towards Willard's jaws, it was like landing on a punching bag.

The story jumped to page 8 and the rest of the day's sports news. There were 12 more stories about the fight. None of them mentioned what Dempsey's overall record was after his victory (55-5-8 with 5 no-decisions). Forty-six of his wins were by knockout, while he had only been KO'd once himself, by Fireman Jim Flynn.

One story reported that Willard's wife, who had never attended one of his bouts before, watched her husband get beaten up and then announce his retirement.

"I am sorry that Jess was beaten," Mrs. Willard was quoted, "but I can truthfully say I am happy that he's no longer champion."

After his pounding of Willard, Dempsey became known as "the Manassa Mauler" for the rest of his career. But in nearly a full page of coverage, the nickname was not given to him by the *Rocky*. In fact, the paper listed Dempsey as being born in a different Colorado town.

If the two reporters had given him his sobriquet, he would have been "the Salida Mauler."

Titanic champion

In the same edition Dempsey's victory was reported, another Colorado legend reappeared, on the back page, with a photo larger than the new champion's:

Titanic Survivor Again Famed

Mrs. James J. Brown, Denver woman heroine of the Titanic disaster, again becomes famous, according to officials of life insurance companies of New York, who declare she is the most heavily insured woman in this country. She had five large endowment policies in force … These policies, they said, according to a dispatch to The News last night from Newport, were drawn in favor of her children.

The story did not report the value of the policies nor any estimated wealth of Molly Brown. □

Hell and high water

The news couldn't have been worse for the people of Pueblo, the morning of June 4, 1921, and it wasn't much better for Denver, Boulder, Lafayette and beyond.

It had rained for three days when the Arkansas River crested a mile wide and 12 feet deep around Pueblo the night before. Beneath a large, black banner headline, the *Rocky* told the story:

FATE OF SCORES IN SMELTER CITY UNKNOWN, DAMAGE IS PLACED AT $4,000,000; BIG FIRE BREAKS OUT

Cloudbursts in Colorado early yesterday morning and late yesterday afternoon caused the loss of at least four lives and possibly many more; enormous damage in all parts of the state; flooding cities and towns; interrupting railroad and wire communications, and inundating thousands of acres of rich farming land.

… Pueblo's business district is under water and all communication with the city ceased shortly after midnight.

Another story told of about 300 automobiles stranded by deep water between Denver and Boulder:

They passed the night perched in their cars, marooned beside the floodswept road, or shared the hospitality of farmers and townspeople along the road, who threw open their houses to care for the stormbound autoists.

The grim toll mounted in story after story:

■ In Sterling, one mother and her child were swept away and drowned in Pawnee Creek. Her two other children were missing and, the *Rocky* reported, "The entire city of Sterling is threatened."

■ In Lafayette, homes were swept away and hundreds of cattle drowned when Coal Creek overflowed.

■ In Louisville, a two-story brick building weakened by the rain collapsed, 10 minutes after more than a dozen people escaped.

■ In Marshall, cracks in the Farmers Reservoir dam raised fears it could collapse and flood the town. Plans were made "to explode bombs as signals to the people" if the dam gave way.

■ In Colorado Springs, the city lost electric power and some homes on lower streets had flooding up to three feet.

The next day

On June 5 the front page of the *Rocky* was again filled with reports of the flood disaster. In a small box near the top of the page, the paper announced it had begun a relief collection:

FOR STRICKEN PUEBLO

Good Samaritans of Denver Join With The Rocky Mountain News and The Denver Times in Relief Fund For Sufferers.

The paper named the first five contributors, who together donated $190. The paper pledged $1,000.

That day martial law was declared in Pueblo. In the end, the flood would claim more than 100 lives. □

A deal to divide the waters

The Colorado River Compact established the "Law of the River," as it is still known in the West. Indeed, the agreement is probably more important and more valuable today than it was when the *Rocky Mountain News* announced it on page 1 on Nov. 25, 1922. But even then it commanded capital letters and serious regard. Beneath the banner:

PACT ASSURES
DEVELOPMENT
OF VAST REGION

SANTA FE, N.M., Nov. 24. – In the historic Ben Hur room of the old Palace of the Governors in Santa Fe, and upon the lapboard upon which General Lew Wallace wrote most of his manuscript, representatives of seven states at 6:13 o'clock tonight signed a compact to secure the expeditious agricultural and industrial development of the Colorado river basin, the storage of its waters and the protection of life and property from flood.

The states signatory to this compact, the first of its kind in America, are Arizona, California, Colorado, Nevada, New Mexico, Utah and Wyoming.

… The treaty seeks to provide for the "equitable division and apportionment of the use of the waters of the Colorado river system to establish the relative importance of different beneficial uses of water, to promote interstate comity and to remove causes of present and future controversies."

It took only two days for California to lodge the first challenge to the agreement. Numerous objections, negotiations and compromises shaped the flow of Colorado's preeminent resource for years to come. In 1973, Colorado Gov. John Love even threatened to try and nullify the compact if states continued to dip deeper into the Colorado.

But the Law of the River remains the law of the land.

'If You Don't Know'

The *Rocky* was now running several daily columns under mostly self-evident titles like Little Benny's Notebook, Tonsils and Their Ills, and Jesus, The Friend of Sinners. And one other, in what may be the first question-and-answer column run by the paper.

Some offerings on Nov. 18, 1922, from:

If You Don't Know
ASK THE NEWS

Q. Is the actress, Julia Marlowe, an American? – A.G.P.
A. Julia Marlow, whose real name was Sarah Frances Frost, was born in Caldeck, Cumberlandshire, England, Aug. 12, 1870, and was brought to this country by her parents in 1875.

Q. What is polygyny? – C.W.
A. Polygyny, popularly called polygamy, is the scientific name for a common form of marriage in barbaric and lower civilization, in which one man is united with several women.

Q. Is alcohol and tobacco bad for a tuberculosis patient? – T.C.
A. The public health service says that alcoholic liquors are always harmful to such a patient, even when taken in moderation. The effects of tobacco are so different in different cases that no general rule can be laid down. ☐

The great mint robbery

Six days before Christmas, 1922, the *Rocky's* page 1 lead story had all the elements of a bestseller – the robbery of $200,000 from the U.S. Mint; a shootout and getaway in downtown Denver; and the alluring notion that the "queen" of a bandit gang might somehow be involved.

A banner with four sidebar stories blared the story on page 1:

OUTLAWS COVER UP TRAIL IN DASH FOR OPEN COUNTRY WITH FORTUNE IN PLUNDER

Bloody Fingerprints on Stock of Shotgun Have No Duplicates in Bertillon Records of Police Department; Eva Lewis is Questioned; First Arrest Proves Fruitless.

While federal and county officers watched all roads throughout Colorado and neighboring states and officers of the law were sharpening their wits in effort to checkmate the fugitives, the four bandits who robbed a United States mint at 10:30 o'clock yesterday morning and killed Charles T. Linton, a guard, were still at liberty late last night, and the searchers frankly admitted that they were without clews.

The 63-word first paragraph was only the beginning of breathless coverage that would continue for days. The paper printed eight stories the first day after the robbery.

Four masked "desperadoes" in a black touring car with curtains drawn pulled in front of the West Colfax Avenue entrance to the mint alongside a truck from the federal reserve bank.

"I heard a shot, then several. Then the general alarm going in the mint," superintendent Robert Grant told reporters after. "Every man picked up a rifle and rushed to the door."

But Linton was shot, dying, and the robbers had grabbed the 50 packages of $5 bills the guards had been transferring from the mint into the truck.

"I understand that the bandit car drove up just as our men had re-entered the mint," Grant said. "It was nicely timed and the bandits evidently had followed the bank truck from Arapahoe street."

Ironically, reporters might have had a front-row seat to the robbery in later years as the *Rocky* would occupy the office building across Delaware Street from the mint.

The photo on page 1 was of a disconsolate-looking Eva Lewis. She had been released from prison only two months earlier after serving four years for her association with a gang that killed four law enforcement officers in Denver and Colorado Springs over two days in 1918. Though Lewis apparently took part in robbing a couple in a nightclub and then stranding them in the countryside and wasn't involved in the killing spree, the *Rocky* dubbed her the "Former Queen of Bandits."

Police questioned Lewis about the mint robbery, but she was quickly cleared.

The next day police offered a reward of $10,000 "for the capture of the gang, dead or alive."

Eighteen days later, the shot-up getaway car was found in a Denver garage. Sitting inside was the frozen body of one robber injured in the shootout. A portion of the money, $80,000, was eventually recovered in Minnesota. Then in 1934, Denver police announced that five men and two women had been linked to the robbery, but no names were released. Police said all of the suspects were either dead or in prison for other crimes.

No one was ever charged in the heist. □

Klan rises, only to fall

KKK.

The acronym summons a visceral response of disgust and disapproval from most Coloradans today. One might add disbelief, as well, at the influence the not-so-secret Ku Klux Klan wielded in the state early in the 20th century.

On Nov. 6, 1924, the *Rocky* delivered the results of the state election in which Klansmen Rice Means and Clarence J. Morley won the offices of U.S. senator and governor, and another Klan contributor, Lawrence Phipps, was re-elected U.S. senator. In addition, according to *Colorado: A History of the Centennial State,* members of the hate organization were selected for lieutenant governor, auditor, attorney general, secretary of state and a Supreme Court justice. But the Klan wasn't mentioned in any of the *Rocky's* election-results stories that day.

The Klan's stranglehold on influence in the state Republican party leading up to the election was well documented. A front-page headline on Nov. 11, 1923:

Gov. Clarence J. Morley

FIERY CROSSES
ERECTED HERE
ARE TORN DOWN

Eleven huge fiery crosses erected and set burning last night in various parts of the city by the Denver Ku Klux Klan were torn down by anti-klan factions soon after they had been put up.

Shortly after 9 o'clock the first burning cross was reported. It had been placed on the steps of the state capitol, and stood twenty feet high. A few moments later crosses were reported burning at prominent places of vantage in Cheesman park, City park, Washington park, at Twenty-third and Welton streets, Inspiration point, East Sixth avenue and Garfield street, Grasshopper hill, the Country club golf links and at street intersections in Park hill and Valverde.

On page 5, Sept. 23, 1923:

COLORADO KLANSMEN
HOLD HUGE INITIATION

Hundreds of white-robed members of the Ku Klux Klan met on the summit of Castle mountain, east of Golden, Colo., last night in what was believed to be the largest meeting ever conducted by the organization in the state. Among the many white-robed figures were seen more than 150 men in citizen's clothing, who were believed to be initiates.

... The meeting was preceded by an advertisement which appeared in Denver newspapers several days last week, reading as follows:

"Ku Klux Klan Members: Obtain immediate instructions from your secretary or other known klansmen. By order Exalted Cyclops, Denver Klan No.1."

The 1924 election, however, marked the pinnacle of the Klan's power in Colorado. The inability to forge legislation and internal politics doomed the Klan.

Give peace a contest

In the years after World War I, America struggled with its role in world politics. Presidents and citizens agonized over the perils of isolationism. On the same day in 1923 that the *Rocky* reported crosses burning in its city, it announced the close of a nationwide contest it joined in promoting to present the American Peace Award. A prize of $100,000 was to be presented in New York to the author of the "best practicable plan by which the United States may co-operate with other nations to achieve and preserve the peace of the world."

The *Rocky* received 302 entries, averaging 3,500 words. The most popular strategies, the paper reported, supported "Christianity, a superstate and a universal language ... Total disarmament, a world court and equal distribution of life's necessities also have a large number of advocates." □

Lindbergh flies Atlantic

The *Rocky* turned over page 1 to "Lucky Lindbergh" on May 22, 1927. The Sunday front page, recognizing Capt. Charles Lindbergh's solo transatlantic flight, the first from New York to Paris, carried four stories, the pilot's flight log, and five drawings depicting the event.

Thousands Trample Each Other in Eagerness to Welcome Young American Flier as He Grounds on Le Bourget Field; 200 Congratulatory Cables Given Him as He Starts for Hotel

LE BOURGET FIELD, France, May 21. – Capt. Charles Lindbergh arrived here today from New York by air, collapsed at the controls of his craft a moment after it stopped and recovered in time to say to the crowd which lifted man and machine to their shoulders:

"So this is Paris. I did it—"

His time was 33 hours and 30 minutes. He arrived at 5:21 p.m., eastern daylight time, without a light on his plane and with his energy fast ebbing. Men, women and children were injured in the welcoming rush by 30,000 people. Barriers were smashed and discipline went for naught when the crowd charged.

Later reports estimated the crowd at 100,000. The 25-year-old Lindbergh was indeed a world hero. When he landed the "Spirit of St. Louis" monoplane, he won the $25,000 purse for the stunt. Days before, he made a daring one-stop flight from California to New York to out-maneuver other fliers seeking the prize.

Favorite son-pilot

Everyone rushed to capitalize on Lindbergh's feat, including the *Rocky.*

In the same Sunday edition, the paper reported it had uncovered the dismantled plane that Lindbergh had flown throughout Colorado only months before as part of a flying circus. The paper reprinted a photo of the plane being paraded aboard a truck through the streets of Denver, sporting a sign:

"LUCKY" LINDBERGH'S DENVER PLANE
USED HERE BY HIM IN AUG-SEPT. 1926
Read the NEWS

On page 2, a Denver-based airplane builder, Alexander Aircraft, printed a letter apparently written by Lindbergh in an ad endorsing its Eaglerock model:

"I have never felt as though I could trust implicitly in any new production commercial ship until I had the pleasure of piloting this Eaglerock," the airman is quoted. "I climbed in doubtful and climbed out convert."

In Paris, the *Rocky* reported, scores of French aviators came to the airfield simply to touch the wings of Lindbergh's craft for good luck.

The name game

The *Rocky's* stories of the famous flight referred to Lindbergh with no less than four nicknames: The Flyin' Mailman, Lone Wolf of Air, Lucky Lindbergh and The Flying Fool. □

Rails under the Rockies

The *Rocky's* lead story on Feb. 27, 1928 paid tribute to one of Colorado's great enduring industrial projects and the man who lost a fortune trying to build it. Beneath the banner headline, a secondary headline read:

Celebration at Portal Marked by Simplicity; Courage of David Moffat Revered as First Passenger Train Goes Under Divide

The Moffat tunnel was opened to passenger traffic yesterday with a brief ceremony under a blue Colorado sky.

… While the courage and foresight of David Moffat, originator of the tunnel plan, was revered by the celebration, more in evidence was the import of a tremendous commercial future for Colorado.

In the mid-1860s David Moffat was cashier at First National Bank of Denver. He became bank president in 1880 and went on to invest in Colorado mining, real estate, farmland and railroads. He invested – and lost – everything attempting to build a direct route – the Moffat Road – from Denver to Salt Lake City. Two bores traveling six miles under James Peak wouldn't be completed until 17 years after Moffat died.

The first steam locomotive to make the trip, No. 200, left the Denver railyards at 8:20 in the morning, arrived at the east portal for the dedication at 1 p.m., and emerged from the west portal at 2:20. The dark ride under James Peak lasted 19 minutes. The paper's coverage included several photographs of grim-faced men in topcoats and wide-brimmed hats at the two mouths of the tunnel. The photos filled the fronts of the *Rocky's* two sections – the paper was up to 18 pages.

Live on KOA

Adding to the tunnel christening, KOA radio station broadcast the events from the east portal.

Reception in Denver was declared to be perfect, with even the sound of an engine pump, several feet from the "Mike" being audible. Denver learned that the first train was entering the tunnel when six bombs were fired from the roof of The NEWSpapers building.

Causing a flap

On the same day, a much smaller story nevertheless was deemed worthy of page 1:

Flappers Impudent
Little Snips, Says
Spinster, Age 105

United Press
CHICAGO, Feb. 26. – Flappers are impudent little snips, and they, with their gin and cigarets, should be in jail, according to Miss Mary Hogan, a spinster.

"I have no objection to their smoking as long as they do it privately," Miss Hogan said as she puffed on her corncob pipe. "I wouldn't think of smoking my pipe in company."

She predicted the flapper would pass out of existence in a few years. □

Blows to economy, paper

It became known as Black Thursday when the stock market crashed on Oct. 24, 1929. It was still in free fall when the market re-opened the following Monday. The *Rocky's* headline the next day on page 1:

WALL ST. LOSES 10 BILLION IN NEW BEAR RAID
LEADING STOCKS
COLLAPSE UNDER
HEAVY POUNDING

NEW YORK, Oct. 28. – All the wealth of New York banks was unable today to check another tremendous wave of liquidation on the stock exchange.

… The Dow-Jones industrial average broke 38.33 points and the railroad average 10.91 points, the largest break in history.

Under the circumstances, the paper's front page cartoon didn't seem funny at all – a "man on the street" gazing with envy at a speculator rising in a hot air balloon, then in the second panel watching with satisfaction as he plummeted to earth.

The mood in Denver's financial district wasn't any more positive.

Speculative excitement swept Seventeenth Street yesterday as Denver investors suffered in the collapse of stock prices that caught Wall Street and the nation.

… All groups of stocks suffered, in varying degree … The oils, held in larger blocks by Denver investors, closed with net declines for the day, tho these were less extreme in most cases than the losses of more volatile market leaders.

Hard times for the *Rocky*

The market crash coincided with a bleak period in the history of the *Rocky Mountain News.*

Scripps-Howard, the Cincinnati-based newspaper owner, had purchased the *News-Times* in 1926 for $750,000. The company's lighthouse logo, playing off the slogan "Give light and the people will find their own way," now occupied the upper left corner of the front page. Circulation was 30,000 versus 160,000 for its rival, *The Denver Post*. Scripps poured more than $3 million into the paper in an attempt to drive *The Post* out of business, and Sunday circulation briefly rose to 100,000 by 1928. But after the expensive "newspaper war" the two papers called a truce. The *Rocky*

folded its afternoon paper; *The Post* killed its morning edition, and paid the *Rocky* $250,000.

The next 15 years saw the *Rocky* and its circulation slip into decline.

Turning to entertainment

Motion pictures were growing in popularity, and advertisements for them were beginning to fill inside pages. At the time of the stock market crash, Mae West was starring in *Diamond Lil,* Joan Crawford was out in *Our Modern Maidens,* and Gary Cooper had filmed "all talking, all outdoors" and was set to open in *The Virginian.*

In Sports, Colorado College was still playing football; Denver University was still playing the University of Colorado; and a new young reporter was writing the column "As Curley Grieve Sees It." □

Legal booze begins flowing again

Denver and Colorado didn't binge any more lustily the night Prohibition was repealed than it did the night it became law, 17 years earlier.

When liquor once again became legal, the *Rocky* reported on Dec. 6, 1933, citizens did not immediately start boozing, partly because there weren't vast stores available.

Legal Goods Mostly in Warehouses as Big Day Arrives
IT'S SMART TO BE LEGAL

(By United Press)

The death of prohibition was being toasted tonight largely with the same illegal liquor used to flout the 18th amendment's existence.

Officials ruled that bonded liquor in warehouses could not be removed for distribution to wholesalers and in turn to retailers, until Utah formally ratified repeal ... There were only about 3,000,000 gallons of rectified liquor on hand on which taxes had been paid.

Utah ratified the law later the same night, which the paper did report.

The lead news story was accompanied by a boxed message from President Franklin Roosevelt appealing to Americans to responsibly exercise their regained right to drink.

The "smart" slogan was a slightly altered version of one advocated by the Anti-Saloon League – "Make It Smart to Be Legal." The paper adopted its slogan, printing it with nearly every repeal story, to bolster its editorial position that Denver's new liquor code must truly make it possible to legally buy a drink.

From the *Rocky's* editorial:

> So for the administration to merely say that no speakeasies would be permitted without at the same time indicating there would be a chance for thirst to be slaked lawfully, would be as foolish as the bone-dry announcement of federal officials while the 18th amendment was in effect.

Inside, the paper reported the toll of the "noble experiment":

- 3,765 persons now serving federal prison sentences for prohibition violations;
- 79 law enforcement officers and 179 civilians killed;
- 45,549 deaths due to alcoholism from 1920 to 1932.

A lofty celebration

The "smart" slogan even found its way into an unlikely repeal-related story inside the paper – on the society page:

SOCIETY TOPLOFTIES GREET RETURN OF LEGAL LIQUOR

If it's smart to be legal, society went ultra-smart in a big way last night ... The cream of Denver's toplofties gathered in the Silver Glade ballroom of the Cosmopolitan Hotel and raised glasses – many of them – to the lifting of the lid thru which only surreptitious moisture bubbled during the past 17 years.

The Junior League held its first gala of the season to raise funds for its welfare projects.

Familiar number

The top of each page of the *Rocky* now carried the paper's main phone number, which it would use for years to come:

KEystone 3333

'Diamond' edition a cut above

One of the most remarkable editions of the *Rocky Mountain News* – the Diamond Jubilee edition on the eve of its 75th birthday – was published at a low ebb in the paper's history. From 100,000 circulation in 1928, the proud paper slipped to 33,421 daily by 1934.

But the Jubilee edition was a journalistic masterpiece, and its color pages hung framed in the newspaper's offices on the day it closed. It is the only edition in the paper's historic archive that occupies its own single microfilm roll.

The special Sunday paper was printed in 15 sections. Five of them were graced by original, themed color drawings intended to depict the progress of Denver and Colorado – the arrival of settlers on the Indians' plains; the printing of the first *Rocky* alongside Cherry Creek; development of transportation and industry; society's inventions and achievements; and a futuristic skyline including airliners flying over the city.

The headlines were a little over-the-top, too:

Shower of Congratulatory Messages Received From Prominent Citizens and Former Members of Staff in All Parts of the U.S.

The only graphic image on the front page was a signed letter from President Franklin Roosevelt with his photo overprinted. His letter was addressed to the *Rocky's* editor, Charles E. Lounsbury:

> "My dear Mr. Lounsbury:
> "I have just learned that on April twenty-second the Rocky Mountain News of Denver will celebrate the seventy-fifth anniversary of its founding.
> "It is interesting to note how the growth of this newspaper parallels the growth of the City of Denver and how each has sided in the development of the other."

A reception was held in the paper's second-floor business office. Searchlights played off the office windows over-

looking Welton Street. A musical program was presented. Congratulatory ads filled the next day's pages. The public was invited to an unveiling on Sunday of a State Historical Society bronze tablet to be mounted on the Market Street bridge at the exact site of the *Rocky's* original printing office.

One inside page carried congratulatory messages from numerous city and state officials, accompanied by their photos; only one was a woman, Secretary of Labor Francis Perkins.

The lead editorial in that edition ended as follows:

> For three-quarters of a century The News has attempted to keep the pledge of (founder) William N. Byers to the people of this community. As for the future – the covenant he made still stands.

Relief effort

The then-familiar NRA box had taken up residence in the *Rocky's* flag on page 1, right next to the Scripps-Howard lighthouse. The National Recovery Administration had been launched only a year earlier as part of Roosevelt's "New Deal" to help pull the country out of the Great Depression. The paper included the NRA slogan on page 1: "We do our part."

Funny business

A long line of editors at the *Rocky* learned to choose carefully when tampering with the comics section, knowing how loyal readers are to their favorite strips. Throughout the paper's history it has promoted the comics, and it wasn't shy about it in 1934. Across the top of the section:

The Greatest Comic Section in America

It wasn't an idle boast. The Sunday edition printed 40 comics in full color over 20 pages. In the Jubilee edition, many of the comic characters were specially drawn to wish the newspaper congratulations on the anniversary.

"Kaga!" – or, "Hail!" – a breech-clothed Tarzan proclaimed, in whatever language Tarzan spoke. □

The death of 'Baby Doe'

If there was another iconic grand dame of Denver to match Molly Brown it was Elizabeth "Baby Doe" Tabor. When she was found frozen to death in a rough mining shack next to the silver mine her dying husband swore her to safeguard years before, she once again stole *Rocky* headlines on page 1:

One-Time Queen of Colorado's Silver Empire Faithful to Last to Horace Tabor's Parting Injunction

They found the body of the faithful Baby Doe Tabor in her Leadville miner's shanty yesterday.

Her lonely vigil at the Matchless Mine is ended. But, to the death, the proud Elizabeth McCourt Tabor … had kept the deathbed trust of her late husband, Senator H.A.W. Tabor, to "guard the Matchless."

Two neighbors, Tom French, a miner, and Sue Bonney, broke into the crude board shanty on Fryer Hill yesterday afternoon to learn why Mrs. Tabor had not been about for several days.

They found her on the floor of the one-room shanty, frozen to death … Tattered remnants of a wardrobe which once made her the best-dressed woman in the West covered her body.

Baby Doe was believed to be 81. The blonde beauty arrived on the Denver social scene and the pages of the city newspapers when Tabor, elected lieutenant governor in 1878, took her as his mistress. After divorcing his first wife, the austere Augusta, he married Baby Doe in 1883 with President Chester Arthur in attendance. Tabor served only one month in the U.S. Senate, filling the term of Henry Teller.

The fortune Tabor dug from Colorado's silver mines, once estimated at $11 million by his biographers, made him the state's richest man. He built Denver's Tabor Grand Opera House and the Tabor Grand Hotel in Leadville. But he lost nearly all of it in the great silver purge before he died in 1899.

"Hold on to the Matchless, never let it go," Tabor reportedly whispered to his young wife from his deathbed.

Baby Doe, whose husband presented her with a $4,000 diamond once owned by the queen of Spain, moved to Leadville, where she lived for a quarter of a century in the shack near the mine. When she lost title to the mine, the company that foreclosed allowed her to continue her watch and live in its shadow.

The day after

Even in death, Baby Doe held Denver's attention captive. The next day's *Rocky* bannered preparations for her funeral in an even larger headline:

DYNAMITE BLASTS GRAVE IN FROZEN SOIL FOR BODY OF BABY DOE TABOR

The ground in Leadville was still frozen five feet deep.

Beneath the headline the paper printed three photos of a child – Baby Doe's daughter, Rose May Echo, who died more than a decade earlier in a fire in a cheap rooming house in Chicago. The girl was known as Silver Dollar Tabor, a name supposedly given her by William Jennings Bryan. ☐

All downhill from here

Pinpointing the day or the edition when skiing and winter sports burst onto the front page, or became Colorado's trademark, is as risky as predicting the first snowfall of winter.

In 1887, Crested Butte and Gunnison were staging rudimentary downhill skiing competitions. Miners had been sliding out of the foothills into Denver for years, so had early mailmen. One of the earliest stories in the *Rocky* reporting a skiing feat appeared on March 10, 1919, after Anders Haugen ski jumped 213 feet in Dillon to set a world record.

But in a story printed Feb. 8, 1924, the newspaper stamped a Norwegian immigrant to America as the man responsible for establishing the sport in the state. The headline on page 4, above a story written by a skiing enthusiast named Dr. Menefree R. Howard:

Carl Howelson Is Called Daddy of Colorado Skiing

To Carl Howelson must be given the credit as the "daddy" of ski sport in Colorado, and the queer part of it is that Carl is a bachelor.

... Carl came to Denver about 1910 and engaged in the contracting business. He was not happy unless he spent a great deal of the winter time on skis. At this time no ski clubs were known in Colorado, but almost as soon as he arrived he began looking around for good skiing places. About a year later he went over to Hot Sulphur Springs, and by his encouragement there was organized a ski club.

... Ski sport really started in Colorado after the big snow in 1914. At that time skiing was forced on many of the residents of Denver as a necessity. The writer's first experience on skis was on four feet of snow at Seventeenth and Curtis streets.

It wasn't long before the sport stormed the state.

Hot Sulphur Springs became a hotbed for ski jumping. Howelson staged the first winter carnival in Steamboat Springs in 1914. Clubs like the Colorado Mountain Club, the Arlbergs and the Eskimos flocked to ski on Genesee Mountain west of Denver in the early 1920s. With the open-

ing of the Moffat Tunnel in 1928, Denver skiers enjoyed easy transportation to ski Berthoud Pass and slopes right outside the west portal with which the city would soon have a close connection.

One of the first mentions of skiing on page 1 was the morning of Aug. 21, 1938:

Forest Service Grants City Huge Ski Area

Denver's drive to turn the Western Slope into a winter sports paradise was given a boost by Uncle Sam yesterday.

The U.S. Forest Service granted the city permission to take over a 6,400-acre tract to provide fun and comfort for skiers and tobogganers.

Denver, of course, continues to own Winter Park ski resort today.

Winter money-maker

It wasn't long before countless operations, including the *Rocky,* figured out that skiing was big business. By 1937, the newspaper was publishing annual winter recreation sections of up to 12 pages, and growing. The special section on Jan. 31 that year featured a cover of classic winter art, pieces of which would be dug out of archives and reprinted for years if not decades to come.

One story in the section was mandatory reading for the Denver ski set, under the headline:

Schuss! Here's What to Say on the Snow Train

Deeper in the news

Strangely, the larger skiing grew, the more skiers traveling to Colorado, the more accessible the sport became, the deeper in the *Rocky* editors seemed to bury it.

From Winter Park on page 1 in 1938, coverage of the opening of the Aspen ski area in 1947 was relegated to inside pages, although the paper wrote articles for three days; when Vail was dedicated Jan. 26, 1963, the next day the paper carried a three-paragraph brief on page 58 of the Sports section. □

Red Rocks formation

The page 1 photo captures the dramatically lighted stone walls of Red Rocks amphitheatre, while below them thousands of black and white faces appear to be bobbing on a dark, undulating sea. But they were all listening raptly to Helen Jepson, not Madonna. And this was June 16, 1941, not 2009.

It made for one of the most dramatic of any *Rocky Mountain News* front pages. The occasion was the dedication of what was to become one of Denver's most beloved parks, with an international convention of Rotarians in attendance. Referred to at different periods in its history as Mount Morrison, Theater of the Red Rocks and Red Rocks Amphitheatre, it would be known all over the world for its beauty, acoustics and distinctiveness. From reporter Robert L. Perkin's opening night story:

> A Rotarian crowd of nearly 9,000 persons, gleaned from the cities and towns of the world, last night dedicated Denver's awe-inspiring Theater of the Red Rocks in a setting like something from a Wagnerian dream.
>
> Floodlights of red and white, blue and green played on the angles and curves of the massive red sandstone formations to give the dedication, opening mass meeting of the 32d annual convention of Rotary International, an eerie magnificence.
>
> … The crowd, oblivious to the sprinkle, massed in the bowl formed by Ship Rock and Creation Rock

silent as the rocks themselves and heard the first fifenote of the Denver Municipal Orchestra and the last trilling syllable of the songs of Helen Jepson, Metropolitan Opera singer and star of the program.

More than 12,000 Rotarians attended the convention and the *Rocky* gave the event front-page treatment daily. The previous day's edition used Rotary's easily recognizable geared wheel logo, with mugshots of leading officers and delegates filling the holes in the wheel, as its main graphic on page 1.

The men behind Red Rocks

John Brisben Walker, a noted journalist, editor, manufacturer and farmer from Pennsylvania, fell in love with Colorado and purchased 4,000 acres of red sandstone land west of Denver in 1906 and named it Garden of the Titans.

In 1910, the *Rocky* ran a two-column ad calling all "Denver Music Lovers" to attend "the first concert test of the acoustic qualities of the great natural auditorium … in which the most delicate notes of a violin will reach every part." Round-trip tickets to the park aboard the Colorado & Southern Railway sold for 60 cents. Ferulo's band from Lakeside Park played.

Walker later sold the land to Denver and in 1935, George E. Cranmer, Denver's manager of parks and improvements, used an army of unemployed men to finally build the amphitheatre.

Denver worshippers didn't greet the sunrise at the first Easter Sunday service until 1947.

'Roving Reporter' Ernie Pyle

The same day in 1941 that the *Rocky* reported Red Rocks' dedication, the newspaper began promoting a book of dispatches written by Ernie Pyle, who was making a name for himself as the Scripps newspapers' "Roving Reporter." The book was a collection of stories Pyle filed from England and provided his personal perspective of Britain's fight in the days before America entered World War II.

Included were Pyle's "description of London on the night it was 'ringed and stabbed by fire.' His first shocked glimpse of Londoners sprawled by the hundreds on a shelter floor."

The *Rocky* sold the book for 50 cents a copy. □

Plunging into world war

The *Rocky* tried to keep up with the collision of history-changing world events the night of Dec. 7, 1941, and into the next day with five "WAR EXTRA" editions.

In a 24-hour period, Japan attacked Pearl Harbor and virtually obliterated the U.S. Pacific fleet; U.S.-held Wake Island, Guam and the Philippines were under attack; an American ship only 1,300 miles west of San Francisco was sunk; and on Dec. 8, President Roosevelt told the nation it was entering another world war, the paper reported.

The United States probably will enter the second World War today with formal declarations of hostilities not only against Japan but also Tokyo's Axis allies – Germany and Italy.

Aroused by savage Japanese surprise attacks Sunday on the Hawaiian Islands, the Philippines, Guam and probably Wake and Midway, many observers believed that Congress was ready for a full plunge into the great world conflict.

Japan's declaration of war against the United States and Great Britain came two hours and 55 minutes after Japanese planes spread death and destruction in Honolulu and Pearl Harbor at 7:35 a.m. Hawaiian time (11:05 p.m., MST Sunday).

It seemed a much more restrained and somber *Rocky* than the one that announced the start of the first World War 24 years earlier. Reports that Japan had flown heavy bombers far beyond their range to return home, warned readers the enemy would sacrifice everything for its cause.

The paper included far more stories about the local impact of the war. Inside headlines carried an ominous tone of next-door immediacy:

Denver FBI Men Go on
24-Hour Emergency Duty.
No Order Received Here
To Round Up Japanese Aliens
As in Other Cities, Says Head

11,000 Colorado Men
To Be Drafted by June 1

Denver Men
Rush to Join
Fight on Japs

Men who pleaded with tears in their eyes that their advanced years be waived and their services accepted, men with false teeth and men who swore they were "about 30" though their hair was gray, were among scores who yesterday swarmed Denver recruiting offices.

Police and fire units in Denver were assigned to 24-hour protection against sabotage at more than 20 "vulnerable spots" like the Denver Ordnance Plant; another yard in the middle of the country where hulls for 24 naval ships would be pre-fabricated; and railroads, dams and electrical utilities.

The paper ran the first two pages of what would become scores in the days and months ahead, filled with mug shots of soldiers, sailors and fighting men under the headline:

These Denverites Fighting Japanese Aggression in the Pacific

Inside, the *Rocky* also printed some of the first transmitted news photos from Hawaii and Washington, credited to *Rocky Mountain News-Acme Telephoto*. However, it would be another day before the awful scope of Pearl Harbor's disaster would be printed in the Rocky Mountains. □

To get bigger, Rocky shrinks

As Denver entered the 1940s, the *Rocky Mountain News* was in decline. Circulation had slipped to nearly 30,000. Owner Scripps-Howard vowed something had to be done to make it bigger.

The answer was to make it smaller.

Jack Howard, son of board chairman Roy Howard, convinced the company to give him one chance to save Colorado's oldest newspaper. He named Jack Foster as editor. Foster printed more popular comics, added new features like complete radio listings, and directed staff to more aggressively report local stories.

Then H.W. "Bill" Hailey, who was named the paper's business manager in 1941, had an idea: change the size of the paper to a smaller tabloid. His reasoning was it would be easier for readers to handle, advertisers would receive better display on the smaller pages, and with the war-time paper shortage it would use less newsprint.

On Monday, April 13, 1942, the *Rocky's* first tab-sized front page carried only three headlines and one photo. The page 1 banner headline reported how the Russian army had blunted a German attack. Beneath it, in a bold box, the paper re-invented itself:

**HERE
WE ARE!**

At 7:30 last night the first edition of this modern-tempo newspaper rolled from the presses, and a new era in Western journalism began. As Denver has moved into the war effort, so has The Rocky Mountain News moved into an accelerated form reflective of the tremendous currents surging within the heart of this nation.

… We shall try – and will – do better.

The 40-page edition included two editorial pages, four pages of sports, and one full page of comics with others anchored in regular sections.

There was a report from "The Roving Reporter" in Silver City, New Mexico, who very soon would become an indispensable war correspondent embraced by the entire nation – Ernie Pyle.

The paper announced the start of a new Sunday section coming – PARADE, a 32-page "picture magazine." The radio log included the hour-by-hour programming of five local stations – KLZ, KVOD, KOA, KFEL and KMVR.

The *Rocky* also launched a different daily edition strategy. An army of "street boys and dealers" began selling the "Blue Streak Edition" by 8 p.m. And an early home edition featured short, off-beat stories. The April 13 early front page included stories about two young boys whose hands were "burned" when they were handed dry ice by a street peddler, a Kerry blue terrier that had been named top dog by the Col-

orado Kennel Club, and the swearing in of 4,000 air raid wardens in Hollywood, Calif., among them movie director Cecil B. DeMille.

Secret weapon

The new, smaller *Rocky* tabloid was an instant success. Five months later, daily circulation had shot up to 48,200 and Sunday hit 53,500. It would continue to rise.

Halfway inside the paper, readers discovered one of the most popular and enduring features for years to come – a new column called "Dear Mrs. Mayfield." On April 13, without any photo, she introduced herself:

Have you any personal problem that is troubling you? Has the war complicated your life so that sometimes it seems you just can't figure things out? Write to Mrs. Molly Mayfield of The Rocky Mountain News. Mrs. Mayfield will give you the benefit of her wide experience, and she will keep your name confidential.

Unknown to readers, Mrs. Mayfield was Frankie Foster, the editor's wife. Her advice column for the forlorn and lovelorn would become the model for the Dear Abbys and Ann Landerses of the future. □

Stunned farewell to FDR

Franklin Delano Roosevelt was no stranger to Denver and Colorado. His first notable visit was in 1932, as a presidential candidate, when the special train he traveled in pulled into Union Station and he was driven up 17th Street through a crowd the *Rocky* estimated at 30,000.

On several of his visits he took the drive over Trail Ridge Road into Rocky Mountain National Park, a trip his friends said was one of his favorites. In 1936, when Fitzsimons General Hospital was in danger of being closed, President Roosevelt toured the facility and made Colorado a promise:

"There will be a Fitzsimons General Hospital as long as I am President of the United States."

His presidency lasted 13 years before he died suddenly while resting in Warm Springs, Ga., where he often retreated for relief of the paralysis that struck him at age 39. His death took Colorado and the nation by surprise, as the exclamation point in the paper's headline reflected.

Franklin Roosevelt, right, campaigns in Denver for the presidency on Sept. 15, 1932, accompanied by Colorado Gov. William Adams. *(Harry Rhoades/Rocky Mountain News)*

WASHINGTON, April 12. – (UP) – President Franklin D. Roosevelt died suddenly of a cerebral hemorrhage at 4:35 p.m. (EWT) today (2:45 p.m. Denver time) and Harry S. Truman was sworn in at 7:08 p.m. (5:08 p.m. Denver time) as the 32d president of the United States.

Mr. Roosevelt, the first man ever to serve more than two terms as president, died in "the Little White House" at Warm Springs, Ga., as armies he helped to muster drove toward final victory over Nazi Germany.

EWT was the abbreviation for Eastern War Time, used from 1942-1945. It was equivalent to year round Eastern Daylight Time. The *Rocky's* conversion of time from 4:35 to 2:45 was an apparent typo in the original story.

The newspaper carried numerous stories about FDR, many with local angles. One, under the byline of Sam Lusky, who would later start one of Denver's leading public relations firms, reported the reaction of David Wallace, a Denver resident and the brother of Mrs. Truman.

Stories included reaction from Colorado leaders and "the man on the street." An editorial cartoon showed the earth with the label "United Nations" and a giant black ribbon tied around it. Department stores such as May Co. and Neusteter's ran special ads of sympathy and announced they would close during the hours of FDR's funeral.

Death hits Denver hard

One brief story on an inside page captured the shock of Roosevelt's death:

It was 4:50 p.m.

News was received at the Max Cook Sporting Goods store at 1608 Glenarm pl. that "The President of the United States is dead." The customers looked at each other and started for the door. Some of the clerks went too.

"Stop him," the cashier cried out, but the customer was gone. He had left his change from a $20 bill on the counter.

Bad news travels slowly

News of Roosevelt's death overwhelmed Denver's telephone system, another inside story reported. For 30 to 40 minutes after word reached Denver many callers were unable to get numbers through the switchboard. It was the greatest overload the system ever experienced, according to the Mountain States Telephone and Telegraph Co. □

Rocky Mountain News

80TH YEAR NO. 103 — DENVER, COLO., FRIDAY, APRIL 13, 1945

FINAL HOME — PRICE 5 CENTS

ROOSEVELT IS DEAD!
Dies in Warm Springs; Truman Takes the Oath

Deaths of a devil, a hero

Adolf Hitler's death, later to be determined a suicide, was treated by the *Rocky* as the major story it was, but also as another step toward ending the fighting in Europe.

LONDON, May 1. – (UP) – The German radio said tonight that Adolf Hitler died this afternoon, "fighting till his last breath," in his Reichschancellery command post in battle-enshrouded Berlin after naming Grand Adm. Karl Doenitz, navy commander-in-chief, to succeed him.

Doenitz at once pledged himself to continue the war "against Bolshevism," but said he would fight America and Britain only "in as far and so long" as they hindered the fight against Russia.

There was still suspicion whether Hitler was really dead. Amidst speculation that the fighting could end any day, the Allies immediately demanded the body of Germany's führer as a condition of surrender.

Doenitz's rise to power was based on the noteriety he gained by devising Germany's infamous "Wolf Pack" submarine tactics.

The end of the European campaign was believed to be

Ernie Pyle

imminent. On an inside page, an Associated Press story said even Truman was hinting at it.

White House newsmen, anxious over war developments, asked him: "Are we safe to go home for the night?"

The President smiled and said he couldn't answer that. When he had left last night, the President had assured reporters they were safe to go home for the evening.

The typewriter soldier

Only two weeks earlier, an American hero of the war had been killed – Ernie Pyle, the Pulitzer Prize-winning war correspondent for Scripps-Howard, which owned the *Rocky*. In a column in the same edition, one of Pyle's friends, newsman Lee G. Miller, wrote that someone should pen a book about Pyle, whose specialty had been chronicling the life of the everyday G.I. Years later, Miller would write the book *An Ernie Pyle Album – Indiana to Ie Shima*. Ie Shima was the Pacific island where Pyle was killed by Japanese machine-gun fire.

Looking ahead to baseball

On the same day that Hitler's demise was reported, the paper's young sports columnist, Chester "Chet" Nelson, wrote a column entitled "Better Denver Baseball."

Several of the local citizens interested in baseball have gotten together and organized a municipal baseball association. ... Any way you look at their efforts you must agree that the good game of baseball will be benefited both this summer and in the summers to come.

Denver already had minor league baseball. In the years to come, Nelson would be one of those who clamored for a major league team in the city. He probably never imagined it would take 48 years. □

Germany surrenders

The news scoop that Germany had unconditionally surrendered in World War II was greeted with celebration all over the world, and with the start of a little war between the Associated Press and Allied Supreme Headquarters.

One day earlier, AP bureau chief Edward Kennedy filed the unauthorized report of the surrender from Reims, France. The Allies issued a statement that did not deny the AP story. Then Allied command promptly withdrew AP's filing privileges throughout Europe, which became part of the VE Day story in the Rocky:

> Allied Supreme Headquarters "authorizes correspondents at 4:45 p.m. Paris time to state that (it) has made nowhere any official statement for publication up to that hour concerning complete surrender of all German armed forces in Europe and no story to that effect is authorized."
>
> Allied command "subsequently announced that AP's filing privileges for the entire Europe theater had been suspended."

The *Rocky* reported the quarrel in a United Press story on page 1 alongside the big news:

> WASHINGTON, May 7. – (UP) – The White House announced tonight that President Truman "confidently expects" to make a radio announcement to the nation at 9 a.m. EWT tomorrow (7 a.m. Denver time) – presumably the long-awaited proclamation that VE-Day is here.

Inside, the newspaper printed AP's original story and below it a report that Roy W. Howard, head of the *Rocky's* parent company, Scripps-Howard Newspapers, had protested AP's suspension in a letter to President Truman. Then, a third story:

AP Suspension From (European Theater) Lifted

> PARIS, May 7. – (AP) – A supreme headquarters order suspending filing facilities of the Associated Press in the European theater was lifted tonight except as it applied to Edward Kennedy, chief of the AP's Western Front staff, who sent the Reims dispatch

telling of Germany's unconditional surrender.

Eventually, everyone decided they had bigger things to do.

Hungry to celebrate

War restrictions on nighttime lighting and horse racing were quickly removed in Denver, and there was hope more gasoline and tires would soon become available. But there was still one gnawing national shortage: food.

Downtown office workers looking to celebrate VE Day swarmed lunch counters and restaurants, which were still under rationing, the paper reported:

> Most restaurants and short order shops were closed, as well as the taverns. There just wasn't enough food to go around, no matter how thin you sliced it ... By dinner time, the situation was worse. Signs began going up in lunch stand windows, "We are out of food."

Pulitzer-winning rabbit

On VE Day, there was also a party in Denver over a rabbit.

Mary Coyle Chase, a former *Rocky* reporter and society editor, learned she had won a Pulitzer Prize for writing the Broadway hit play *Harvey* about a friendly man who enjoyed a few drinks and his 6-foot invisible rabbit. Chase said her father had told her *Harvey* would be a success.

"He bet me a carton of cigarets against a box of cigars it would win the Pulitzer Prize."

VE Day perspectives

The paper ran a short "man on the street" story about Victory in Europe Day with a crazy cross-section of reaction:

> Ed Minteer, managing editor, Rocky Mountain News: "There are too many Yanks graves in Europe, too much fighting to be done against the Japs for any celebration now. Rather, we should rededicate on this day all our efforts toward final victory."
>
> Dennis Rockwell, six: "I think it's good. Otherwise there are a lot of guys I know who might get shot." □

Day the world changed

The stunning attack and awful destruction of the first atomic bomb on Hiroshima were felt in Denver and Colorado.

The morning of Aug. 8, 1945, the *Rocky* offered readers all it could about the unbelievable new force unleashed on the world, from every point of view. The headlines from countless stories:

Einstein Can Explain
New Bomb, but Won't

VATICAN PRESS OFFICE
FROWNS ON 'A' BOMB

New Bomb Will Shorten
War, Says Man in Street

Atomic Discoveries
Are Likely to Spur
Mining in Colorado

The paper's lead editorial, attempted to put it in perspective:

> Colorado has contributed largely of its brains and its treasures in the development of atomic power that is destined to play such a large part in the future of mankind.

The editorial went on, in a reserved yet boastful tone, to credit scientists from the University of Denver, University of Colorado and the School of Mines for their role in the development. It even suggested the state of Colorado might take some pride in giving up the uranium found beneath its mountains.

> Now the treasure of this once remote part of the world becomes a means of ending the most terrible war in history – and, we hope, of assuring peace in the future.
>
> Once again it is proved that there is no remote part of the world any more.

If it had hit Denver

The newspaper, in trying to describe the force of the atomic bomb, provided several comparisons. Equal to an air raid by 2,000 B-29 bombers. Three times the devastation that Superfortress bombers caused in an attack three months earlier on Hiroshima that burned 1.3 square miles of the city. If such a bomb hit Denver, the paper reported, it would completely destroy

> A district from Broadway to Steel st. and from E. Colfax to E. Alameda ave. Or, an area about one and one-half as big as the entire down-town business district.

War-time want ads

The everyday realities of World War II were evident in the farthest corners of the daily newspaper. "Help Wanted – Women" ads, due to the lack of available men, were numerous and quaint:

> SODA fountain help of all kinds: salad table girls, steam table girls, and fountain girls, good hours, good salary; meals and uniforms furnished. Apply – Mr. Riley, Republic Drug Co., 1600 Tremont.

The ads also sometimes reflected the social realities of the time:

> **COLORED MAID**
> Steady Job, Apply

Rocky Mountain News

86TH YEAR: NO. 220 Published every morning by Denver Publishing Co. DENVER, COLO, WEDNESDAY, AUG. 8, 1945

FINAL
HOME
★ ★ ★ ★
WEATHER
Continued
PRICE 5 CENTS

60 PERCENT OF HIROSHIMA IS WIPED OUT

Atomic Bomb Destroys 5 Major Targets

THE PILOT

GUAM, Wednesday, Aug. 8. — (UP) — The first atomic bomb dropped on Hiroshima completely destroyed an area of four and one-tenth square miles — 60 percent of the city's built-up area.

It wiped out five major industrial targets with a tremendous blast which obliterated the city in a cloud of boiling smoke and flame.

This history-making announcement by Gen. Carl A. Spaatz, commander of the Strategic Air Forces, gave the news that had been anxiously awaited for more than 24 hours. The single atomic bomb had wiped out more than half

Japan as a grim warning of the fate in store for Nippon, had already described the moment when the bomb exploded.

The men aboard the plane exclaimed as one: "My God!"

What had been Hiroshima going about its business at 9:15 o'clock of a sunny morning went up in a mountain of dust-filled smoke, black at the base, towering into a plume of white at 40,000 feet.

Here at Guam this morning, reporting the results to Gen. Carl A. Spaatz and Gen. Curtis E. LeMay, were Pilot Paul W. Tibbets Jr., Miami, Fla., and navy Capt. William

Notice to Hirohito

By United Press

Fukuoka, approximately the same size as Hiroshima, was hit last June 20 by Superfortresses which dropped nearly 1000

A scourge descends

Nearly 30 years after the "Spanish flu" shut down Denver and the *Rocky* ran the story announcing city closures at the bottom of page 1, the newspaper wouldn't commit the same blunder with its second major public health crisis.

The headline on Sept. 12, 1946, was in 2-inch type and ran three lines deep.

Denver's public and parochial schools will not re-open Monday as scheduled because of continuance of the statewide polio epidemic.

Two weeks before, school openings were delayed after a national conference about the disease.

The decision to delay the reopening was prompted by the reporting of 16 new polio cases throughout the state yesterday. The upsurge brought to 659 the total number of cases in the state since Jan. 1. The disease has claimed the lives of 38 persons during the period.

... Attention of the (health) department was focused on a report from Pueblo which listed eight new cases ... Pueblo County came under the polio spotlight when State Fair officials refused to heed orders to ban children from attendance at the fair.

In Denver, the disease for the first time struck a young woman employed as a physiotherapist at Children's Hospital. Two new cases were reported in Denver yesterday, raising the city total for the year to 210. Fifteen Denver persons have died of the disease during the period.

Only the month before, in the peak heat of summer, Denver had closed all city beaches and swimming pools due to the rise in cases of infantile paralysis. The story announcing the closures included another ominous development that would creep through science and history nationwide for decades to come.

The U.S. Public Health Service

... also disclosed that a quantity of the powerful insecticide, DDT, now owned by the state will be used in

Denver within the next two weeks in areas where insects, believed chiefly responsible for spread of the disease, are most prevalent.

One of the first areas considered for spraying would be the Stockyards district, which had shown the highest incidence of polio cases that year.

However, the next day's *Rocky* ran a story stating the spraying of DDT would begin that very day.

Finally, the day came when the paper ran this headline:

First Polio-Free Year Recorded In Denver

But it wouldn't appear in print until December, 1961.

Nylons return

In the same *Rocky* edition Aug. 22, 1945, in which Denver and Colorado health officials called for a unified strategy to combat polio in an inside-page story, two other stories filled page 1. Douglas MacArthur was taking over the occupation of Japan. And this:

Oh, Glory Be, Nylon Will Cover Milady's Calves by Thanksgiving!

The second story was accompanied by a photo of five bare-legged women from the knees down.

WASHINGTON, Aug. 21. – (UPI) – Nylon and rayon were given back to the women tonight and nylon stockings may be on sale by Thanksgiving.

Both fabrics were freed of all controls except for one technicality blocking the immediate use of nylon for hosiery. War Production Board officials said this formality will be ironed out promptly ... Rayon, principal component of wartime stockings, has been used during the war for synthetic tires, parachutes, nurses' uniforms.

... The women already have been assured of the return of coveted two-way stretch girdles, cotton dresses and other items which made the wartime row hard to hoe.

Again, the wire service's wording. □

Emily Griffith's mysterious death

Among the calamities and deaths of Colorado's well-known heroines – Mother Jones, Molly Brown, Baby Doe Tabor – none was more tragic than that of Emily Griffith. On June 20, 1947, the *Rocky* reported in 2-inch type in its "Sunrise Edition" the murder of the quiet, retired Denver educator whose famed Opportunity School gave adults a second chance at life.

Griffith, 67, and her invalid sister were both found shot in the head in the Pinecliffe cabin where Emily had retired to care for Florence on a Denver Public Schools pension of $40 per month.

A second story inside the paper, by reporter Betty Caldwell, ran beneath the headline:

Emily Griffith Made an Idea Into an Institution

She was Emily Griffith, the woman who brought to Denver and the world the new idea of a second chance in education for the men and women who needed it most. Though her achievements brought her personal fame, her goals never changed. Her ambition always was to rise not from the ranks, but with them.

As a young teacher in a poor Denver neighborhood in 1913 and 1914, Griffith came to believe the parents of her students needed further education just as badly. She convinced DPS authorities and business leaders who helped her start the Opportunity School. Expected enrollment when the school doors opened at 14th and Welton streets in 1916 was 200; actual Board of Education records show 2,389 had applied. From its beginning, Griffith's school was free and a part of DPS.

The immediate murder suspect was Fred Wright Lundy, a 61-year-old friend who built the Griffiths' cabin and drove them on errands. His motive was strangely believed to be one of mercy, wrote Pasquale Marranzino on page 1:

Lundy on many occasions had expressed grief over the "martyr" life which Emily had spent in caring for her sister. On occasion, he expressed the sentiment that he would "rather see them dead than the way they are living."

Lundy disappeared after leaving a suicide note. A witness reported seeing a man matching his description hopping a train headed for Denver the afternoon of the murders. Lundy's body was later found, shot in the head, in a deep pool near Pinecliffe.

Mysterious Molly Mayfield

The column "Dear Mrs. Mayfield" in the *Rocky* continued to captivate readers. In the same edition that reported the Griffiths' deaths, though, the writer printed a creepy letter:

DEAR MRS. MAYFIELD:
There is a group of us here in Loveland that have heard arguments about you. They say Mrs. Mayfield died a few years ago and her husband writes the column now, but as we are a curious group, would like for you to answer us soon and tell us the truth.
GROUP

DEAR GROUP:
Your letter gave me the creeps. And with some effort I am trying to refrain from saying that the reports of my death are greatly exaggerated. Anyway, I'm delighted to report to you that there has been only one Mrs. Mayfield from the time I wrote the first column on April 13, 1942, and that I, and I only, am
MOLLY MAYFIELD

She was also Frankie Foster, the editor's wife. □

Rocky Mountain News

DENVER, COLO., FRIDAY, JUNE 20, 1947

HOME FINAL
PRICE 5 CENTS

'MERCY' MOTIVE IN KILLING OF EMILY GRIFFITH

EMILY GRIFFITH—Her Last Picture

By PASQUALE MARRANZINO
Rocky Mountain News Writer
Copyright 1947, by The Denver Publishing Co.

PINECLIFFE, June 19.—Boulder County sheriff's officers and Denver police tonight speculated that the bizarre double slaying of Emily Griffith, famed Denver educator, and her invalid sister, Florence, might prove to be mercy killings.

Piecing together a handful of meager clues, the officers instituted a nation-wide search for kindly, quiet, 61-year-old Fred Wright Lundy, who 20 years ago taught under Emily Griffith in the world-famous Opportunity School she founded.

Lack of Motives Baffling

Baffled by a lack of motives for the shocking slayings, officers theorized that the recluse and inventor had taken the lives of the aged sisters with whom he had been in almost constant company in this mountain hamlet for the past 13 years.

Neighbors and friends of the sisters and Lundy pointed out that Florence Griffith in the past year had become an increasingly heavy burden in the life of Emily Griffith. She had been in ill health for many years and recently had shown signs of failing fast.

Felt Emily Was 'Martyr'

Lundy, they said, on many occasions had expressed grief over the "martyr" life which Emily had spent in caring for her sister. On occasions he expressed the sentiment that he would rather "see them dead than the way they are living," Dick Griffith, petroleum geologist and a nephew of the Griffith sisters, asserted that he believed "Fred decided it

(Continued on Page 5)

My Memories of Emily Griffith
By Her Closest Friend for 30 Years
FRANCES WAYNE ....Page 14

First Murder Scene Pictures
—A full page on Page 16

Magnificent Obsession
—The Story of Emily Griffith's Grand Idea on Page 6

Tunneling for tomorrow

The report of the passage of the Taft-Hartley Labor Bill on the front page of the *Rocky* on June 24, 1947, marked a historic piece of legislation that reined in organized labor in the U.S. for the first time in 12 years.

Then there was the 15-year-old kid's shootout with cops in Massachusetts, and the 51st anniversary of two Denver brothers' bicycle trip to San Francisco, both stories dramatically pictured. Word that three men had been injured near Granby while working on "Big Tom" – the Colorado-Big Thompson water project – was worrisome.

But for Coloradans, perhaps the most significant news of the day almost went undetected at the bottom of page 1.

In the smallest type, read the headline:

First Water in Adams Tunnel, Page 15.

Staff writer Betty Caldwell's account inside did the story justice.

ESTES PARK, June 23. – Life-giving water, Colorado's most vital natural resource, today flowed for the first time from the headwaters of the Colorado River on the Western Slope through the Alva B. Adams Tunnel to the fertile farm lands of northeastern Colorado.

The initial flow of water, a highlight of ceremonies dedicating the newly completed tunnel, marked the climax of more than a decade of planning and construction for the first major trans-mountain diversion of irrigation water.

At 11:16 a.m. Governor (Lee) Knous turned a valve releasing water at the Grand Lake Portal of the Adams Tunnel … Three hours later, water emerged from the 13-mile bore.

In 1947, it was the longest irrigation tunnel in the world. It was posthumously named after the U.S. senator who pushed the federal project in Washington.

It took nearly 10 more years to finish the entire C-BT project. In simplest terms, it gathers snowmelt from four Western Slope dams, pumps it through Granby and Shadow Mountain reservoirs into Grand Lake, which is drained by the Adams Tunnel. Originally built for agricultural purposes, today it serves multiple power, storage and recreation demands for more than 29 cities and towns.

Tunnel rat

The Adams Tunnel was drilled from both sides of the Rockies directly beneath Hallett Peak. On June 11, 1944, the *Rocky* reported the exciting moments when the east and west bores met. NBC Radio actually broadcast the final blast live to the nation.

"This is as great a moment for the West as it was for the nation when the Panama Canal was cut through," the

paper quoted Asst. Secretary of the Interior Oscar Chapman. The reporter was the editor of the paper, Jack Foster.

With these words … drove home the switch and a series of explosions at the tunnel head a quarter-mile distant sent a howling wind through the bore. Immediately, the mucking crew moved in and began battling their way through the smoke.

But water wasn't the first sign of life to traverse the tunnel. Wrote Foster:

Presently a grinning head appeared through the whirling clouds. It was that of Howard Costee, who operates a mucking machine. He had come through from the Grand Lake side … he was the first man through.

The prime of Mrs. Mayfield

That June, Foster's star columnist (and wife), Molly Mayfield, continued to report surprising details about Denver doings in her column, Dear Mrs. Mayfield:

Note to CHECKER CAB DRIVER: Sorry I snubbed you June 16 about 11:30 a.m. on 16th and Glenarm. I'm the girl in the white dress and big black hat. Call me KE 9073, apt. 209, after 6 p.m.

Editor's note: KE 9073 was the lady's phone number, in case anyone still wants to try. □

General given the boot

The *Rocky's* page 1 headline the day after Army hero Gen. Douglas MacArthur was relieved of all military duties by President Harry Truman is one of the largest ever printed by the newspaper. It was only the second time in 92 years of publication that I found the story lead printed full-page width; the first was the report that World War I was over.

The layout reflected the nation's shock at seeing one of its boldest soldiers yanked back to earth for disagreeing with his president's foreign policy in the Far East. MacArthur helped drive the Japanese out of the Pacific. He declined political overtures to make him a presidential candidate, opting instead to be named Supreme Commander of U.N. Forces in Korea. And as Supreme Commander for Allied Powers in Japan, he had ruled over the former enemy nation for the past five years as a virtual emperor.

But MacArthur was on record as wishing to wage a more vigorous war in Asia than the ongoing Korean conflict. The outspoken general said the West was fighting Europe's battles in the Far East; recommended bombing Red Chinese bases in Manchuria; and supported turning loose Nationalist Chinese troops, possibly to establish a second front on the mainland.

America wasn't used to seeing its military leaders duke it out in public.

"Not now, not now," the United Press story reported as MacArthur's reaction when asked about his discharge by Truman.

The *Rocky* carried a short story inside that reported angry phone calls it had received after the president's announcement. The story seemed to reflect the common news desk view that such reaction is usually one-sided.

Indicative of the attitude of Denverites, none of the calls expressed pleasure at the firing. Most of the calls came from World War II veterans:

Al Peterson of Denver read the text of a telegram he had composed to President Truman: "For the benefit of our country, please get out of office."

A different beetle

It's the pine bark beetle that is decimating Colorado forests today. In the same edition as MacArthur's firing, the paper reported the state was losing an equally destructive war to another bug then – the spruce bark beetle. Colorado congressman Wayne Aspinall was fighting to continue a federal control program started a year earlier. If ended, he predicted, forest losses would cost the state $400 million.

Sounds familiar

On the same day, the *Rocky* reported that California Eastern Airways was seeking approval from the Civil Aeronautics Board for a new fare for Denver-to-New York flights – $65.30.

"That type of transportation is different from existing airlines," the paper's Washington correspondent wrote, "in that it eliminates the luxury features of air travel and utilizes cargo space for passengers."

To make the flights financially viable, Cal Eastern proposed eliminating meals, pillows, blankets and beverages, and carrying 73 passengers. Most current flights sold 44 seats.

Oh, and the average flight time for the trip would increase from eight hours, 35 minutes to 10 hours, 25 minutes.

The story ended by reporting that although a CAB examiner recommended against the service, "most of the board members ... seemed to be in favor." □

Unnerving revelation

Denver and Colorado profited enormously from the post-war building of the Rocky Mountain Arsenal, which got underway in 1942. Twelve years later, though, when readers uncurled their *Rocky* on the morning of March 20, 1954, they might have received a shock.

The headline was scary enough. The photo of an arsenal worker encased in a rubber suit, hood and gloves made it all too real.

The copyrighted story made it sound as if no one knew before what was going on at the secured 20,000-acre site northeast of the city.

Denver's Rocky Mountain Arsenal is making the deadliest weapon known to man – the lethal nerve gas or G-gas – the Rocky Mountain News learned in Washington Friday.

Major Gen. E.F. Bullene, chief chemical officer for the Army, unveiled the awesome secret about the Arsenal for the first time.

The story went on to describe in six paragraphs of horrid portent just how deadly the gas was. The type was set in six different fonts and sizes, as if to emphasize its seriousness, or importance.

So deadly is a tiny drop of the liquid from which the gas is made that it will kill a man in 30 seconds.

The gas from a single bomb the size of a quart fruit jar could kill every living thing within a cubic mile, depending upon wind and weather conditions.

It never has been used in warfare. Tests on animals indicate it will kill upon contact with any exposed flesh, by breathing, or swallowing.

A tiny drop of the gas in its liquid form on the back of a man's hand will paralyze his nerves instantly and deaden his brain in a few seconds.

Death will follow in 30 seconds.

With certain weather conditions, seven tons of bombs dropped from a bomber could kill every living thing within 100 square miles.

You get the picture.

A second headline and story inside carried scant reassurance:

**Arsenal Officials Assure Denver
There's No Possibility of Danger**

Less than two months after the *Rocky's* story appeared, another story reported:

**70 Mild Nerve Gas Cases
Revealed
At Arsenal in Army Doctors'
Report**

After the Arsenal was finally closed in the 1990s, it took more than 10 years and $2 billion to clean up.

Long-eared alarm system

As part of the *Rocky's* big scoop about the Arsenal in 1954, it included a photo from somewhere inside the military facility of a cage holding two bunnies. Two large ducts vented directly into the cage. The Army used an updated version of the "canary in the mineshaft" as part of its gas-detection safety system. ☐

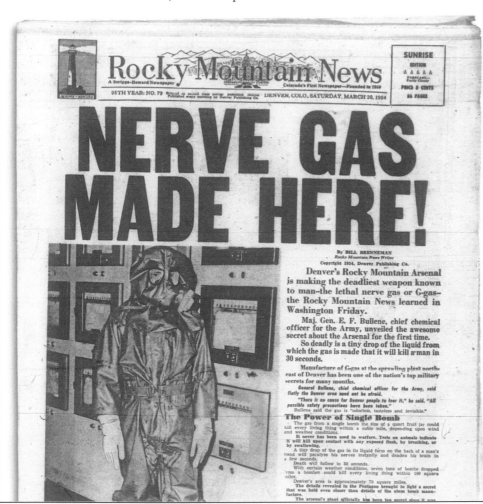

Landing an academy

The *Rocky's* fat headline on page 1 on June 25, 1954, left no doubt the newspaper and Colorado thought building the U.S. Air Force Academy in the state was a good thing. It wouldn't be many years before newspapers across the country shed the use of the promotional "we" in print. But it was still journalistically acceptable in the post-war '50s.

The celebratory photo on page 1 included generals and captains of Colorado Springs flashing the victory sign. Inside, state business and civic leaders predicted that construction of the academy would result in "the biggest boom in Colorado's history."

The lead story ran the full width of page 3:

> The Air Force officially adopted Colorado as its home Thursday when Air Sec. Harold E. Talbott chose Colorado Springs as the site of the nation's air academy.
>
> The multi-million dollar academy, with an estimated payroll of $1.5 to $2 million monthly, will be constructed near the base of lofty 14,100-foot Pikes Peak.

Colorado Springs was chosen over Lake Geneva, Wisconsin, and Alton, Illinois. For a time, a Denver site near Buckley Field was in the running, but the day the selection board visited the two sites they had a gorgeous day in Colorado Springs, but ran into a blizzard in Denver. Another controversy arose: Earlier in the year, renowned architect Frank Lloyd Wright withdrew from the national contest to design the new academy.

While construction began on the academy's new site, its first class was enrolled July 11, 1955, at a temporary facility at Lowry Air Force Base. The *Rocky's* page 1 headline:

Air Academy Is Born
Air Cadets Gaze at Their Future

A proud new tradition was born at Denver's Lowry Air Force Monday as the nation dedicated its first new service academy in more than 100 years.

High-level military and civilian dignitaries bade "happy landings" to the first class of 306 fledglings. A mighty armada of jet fighters and bombers thundered overhead in salute. The President of the United States (Eisenhower) sent best wishes. Precision honor guards from West Point and Annapolis marched by in a ceremonial welcome to their new comrades-in-arms.

Ground-breaking

In the same edition that the *Rocky* marked the dedication of the academy, it reported groundbreaking for the new Lakeside Shopping Center, and a motion picture re-release in local theaters – *The Wizard of Oz.*

Dressed to wilt

Finally, the day of the first formal review of cadets at the Air Force Academy in Colorado Springs arrived. Sept. 1, 1958, was a blazing day in the high 80 degrees. Twelve cadets fainted and dropped during the ceremony. The *Rocky's* photo of the formal review on page 5 the next day showed rows and rows of cadets standing at parade-rest in starched dress whites, while at their feet several stricken classmates lay like soggy piles of laundry. □

Colorado's air terror

Before baggage inspection.

Before X-ray machines and body wands.

Before warnings not to leave carry-on bags unattended.

Before 9/11.

There was John Gilbert Graham.

The only news more shocking than the explosion of United Flight 629 over Longmont on Nov. 1, killing all 44 people aboard the DC-6B, was the dispassionate confession by Graham two weeks later that he blew up the plane to collect his mother's flight insurance of $37,500.

The *Rocky's* front page on Nov. 15 showed a handsome young man, eyes staring downward, being led away in handcuffs.

PLANE DYNAMITING
IS CONFESSED!

A young Denver drivein operator admitted Monday he tied 25 sticks of dynamite together to make the bomb that exploded a United Air Lines plane near Longmont Nov. 1.

... The tall, muscular youth (23) told how he fashioned a dynamite bomb, of maneuvering his family so that he could hide the death device in his mother's suitcase, and of how he dawdled over dinner at Stapleton Field until word of the crash came.

Before placing the bomb in the suitcase, reporter David Stolberg wrote,

Graham said he set the bomb to explode in 90 minutes, the maximum time allowed him by the timing device.

Graham did not reply when asked whether he felt remorse over the deaths of the 43 persons whose lives were lost with his mother's in the flaming crash.

The next day, in a copyrighted story, the *Rocky* revealed another twist to the Graham puzzle. Lakewood neighbors told the FBI that Graham said he had hidden a surprise Christmas gift, a jewelry-making tool – his mother made costume jewelry – in her suitcase.

Graham was described two days after the crash as being despondent "for failing to make his mother's last hours happy by not giving her the present before she left Denver."

'Solution to the Air Crash'

This was the headline over a *Rocky* editorial the day after Graham's confession. The unnamed writer could not know the ominous portent his commentary carried:

We doubt that the general public ever would stand for the opening or inspection of luggage. And anything short of that would hardly detect any sort of explosives.

... Fortunately, this tragedy has been solved. We find it difficult to believe that it could – or would likely – be repeated.

Digging deeper

Scrape beneath the surface of any historic newspaper and you are bound to turn up a few nuggets. Such was the case in 1955:

The May Co. was selling professional Geiger counters for $149.50.

Evelyn "$50,000 Treasure Chest" West, "the world's greatest G-string artist," was performing at the Tropics on Morrison Road.

And in Sports, Paul Smith, an up-and-coming Denver lightweight who had won his last six fights, was to be the opponent when a well-known local boxer – Rodolfo "Corky" Gonzales – attempted a comeback in a few days at Mammoth Gardens. Before the end of the year, Gonzales would retire from boxing to enter the ring of political activism. □

Rocky Mountain News

96TH YEAR: NO. 319   DENVER, COLO., TUESDAY, NOV. 15, 1955

PLANE DYNAMITING IS CONFESSED!
Denver Youth Gives Details on Killing Mother and 43 Others for Her Insurance
—MORE PHOTOS AND STORIES ON PAGES 3, 5, 8, 11, 13, 14, 32, 34 AND 35

Subdued debut for Broncos

There was no front-page photo screaming of blue and orange on Aug. 15, 1959.

There was no front-page mention at all.

There was barely any mention at all the day the Denver Broncos were born.

Deep inside the *Rocky*, on page 47, the second page of Sports carried a 5-inch wire service filler about some upstart football league.

It's Official! Denver in New Grid Loop

CHICAGO, Aug. 14 – (UPI) – A second professional football league, to be called the American Football League, was officially formed Friday night and franchises were announced for six cities.

Lamar Hunt of Dallas announced that teams would be formed in Dallas, Houston, Minneapolis-St. Paul, Denver, New York and Los Angeles.

… The Denver franchise was represented by Robert Howsam of Rocky Mountain Empire Sports, Inc., owner of the Denver baseball team.

If it had been 20 years later, when the NFL Broncos were headed for their first Super Bowl, the page 1 stories of 1959 – a bank robbery suspect arrested; Eisenhower signing a labor bill, and a Little Britches Rodeo photo – would have been banished to the inside pages.

The Broncos would become big news in Denver and Colorado, of course. A franchise worth hundreds of millions of dollars, national television audiences and – after almost every game – the front page of the *Rocky*.

But in 1959, things were different. One hundred years after its first edition, you could still buy the newspaper for only a nickel.

How long ago ...

On the same day, the top Sports story reported the Baltimore Colts' annual demolition of the College All-Stars 29-0 in the 26th fall exhibition before the start of pro and college football seasons.

CHICAGO, Aug. 14 – (AP) – The cunning passing arm of Johnny Unitas and the massive power of the Baltimore Colts overwhelmed the College All-Stars.

A crowd of 70,000 that included Vice President Richard M. Nixon sat in awe at the mid-season form shown by the Colts, the 1958 National Football League champions.

In not too many years, as injuries to players became too risky and TV ratings all-powerful, the pro-college game was discontinued.

TV listings

Both the *Rocky* and rival *Post* now carried full daily television lists of programs. Aug. 15 was a Saturday, which meant a morning of *Howdy Doody, Ruff & Reddy* and *Mighty Mouse,* and an afternoon of baseball, baseball and baseball until pro wrestling and *The Lone Ranger* broke things up.

Channel 7, then KLZ-TV, had an unbeatable evening lineup of *Have Gun, Will Travel, Gunsmoke, The Phil Silvers Show* and *Burns and Allen. The Silvers Show,* though, with the egg-headed Sgt. Bilko, had lost popularity and would be cancelled at the end of the season.

Of the four TV stations on air, only one, KOA Channel 4, had a 10 p.m. newscast. At 9:55, KBTV Channel 9 would interrupt *Movie Masterpiece* for five minutes of weather, than go back to the movie.

The last listing of the night was at 1:15 a.m. *When I Led 3 Lives* was over, the late-night viewing crowd had only the channel pie and black-and-white snow to watch until church services in the morning. ☐

The Coors kidnapping

The story was every hard-core newsman's dream, every crime reader's fantasy, and every wealthy family's nightmare.

Adolph Coors III
Feared Kidnapped!

The *Rocky's* page 1 headline the morning of Feb. 10, 1960, was hard to imagine. The crime was easy to believe. The reigning king of a storied brewing and textiles fortune and one of Colorado's most famous families, was missing, and the story would enthrall readers for the next seven months.

By Al Nakkula
Rocky Mountain News
Writer

Adolph (Ad) Coors III, millionaire head of the Adolph Coors Co. in Golden, disappeared mysteriously Tuesday while en route to work.

… Coors' car, its motor still running, was found abandoned on a tiny wooden bridge across Turkey Creek, just two miles north of the missing man's home near Morrison.

Blood stains were found on the side of the road near the car and splattered on the bridge railing.

The front-page photo by longtime staff photographer Dick Davis showed three members of the Jefferson County Sheriff's Mounted Posse riding horses over the bridge. A section of railing had been removed by investigators to perform lab tests on blood stains. The photo is historic for at least two reasons: First, that they still had posses then, and second, it must have been the last crime scene where any journalist was allowed closer than a mile.

The next day presented the next headline in the story, the next piece of the puzzle:

Coors Offers
Ransom for Son

"They have something I want to buy – my son," said Adolph Coors II, as he boarded a plane in Honolulu Wednesday to return to Denver to negotiate with kidnappers.

The third day and headline after the disappearance of "Ad" Coors, who was 44 and said to be allergic to beer:

3 Suspects Sought
In Coors Mystery

The headlines continued into March, when Joseph Corbett Jr., a former Fulbright scholar, became the 127th fugitive named on the FBI's Ten Most Wanted list. The charge was unlawful flight in 1955 from a Chino, California, prison where he had been confined for murder. Then it was learned that Corbett had lived in Denver since 1956, but that he had suddenly packed his belongings and fled his Pearl Street apartment early the morning after Coors disappeared. Corbett drove a yellow Mercury, which was later found burning in a dump near Atlantic City, New Jersey.

The mystery remained just that until Sept. 14 when a target shooter hiking the hills in an area known as Devil's Head south of Sedalia found a skeleton and clothing that was later identified as belonging to Coors. He had been shot twice in the back in an apparent botched kidnapping. The Coors family had received a ransom demand for $500,000.

Corbett was finally arrested in Vancouver, B.C., in October. He was convicted for the murder of "Ad" Coors and sentenced to life imprisonment. Corbett was paroled in 1978. He committed suicide in his Denver apartment in 2009.

A reporter's reporter

In the 1950s and '60s, if the *Rocky* had a major crime story, Al Nakkula's byline was usually at the top of it. A colleague once grudgingly admitted, "he's the best crime reporter in the city."

The son of Finnish immigrants, he was irascible, versatile, grumpy and irreverent. He owned a nasally voice that regularly squawked from below a pinched nose and horned-rim glasses and was impossible not to pick out of the noisy newsroom.

In addition to leading the reporting on the Coors kidnapping, "Nak" dogged Denver's largest police department scandal which led to the arrest and conviction of more than 40 officers. The first national journalism award for police reporting was named after him and a plaque still hung in his honor in the newsroom the day the paper closed. ☐

Tragedy's echoes linger

The saga of Colorado's worst traffic accident in history needed to be told twice.

The first report began in the *Rocky* on Dec. 15, 1961, the day after 20 children died when a train traveling 79 miles per hour smashed through a school bus in the Weld County community of Auburn. The front-page photo showed the mangled bus and dozens of onlookers milling about on the nearby train tracks.

EVANS, Colo., Dec. 14 – Authorities quizzed Duane R. Harms, youthful bus driver, for three hours Thursday in an attempt to pinpoint the cause of a tragic accident which transformed an isolated railroad crossing into a scene of carnage.

Harms, 23, was the man at the wheel of a Greeley school bus when a Denver-bound Union Pacific streamliner chopped the vehicle in half, killing 20 of the 37 occupants.

Under oath, Harms told everything in a 22-page sworn statement which covered his every action from supper Wednesday, to his sleep and awakening and his moves until the moment of impact.

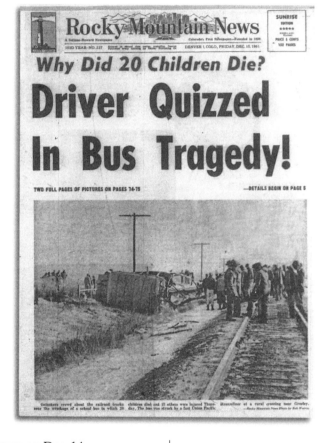

The lead headline and story focused on the driver – the "second-day story" – probably because the tragedy occurred early in the morning, in time for the *Rocky's* afternoon competitor, *The Denver Post,* to print its story on Dec. 14.

The *Rocky* printed the names and ages – from 6 to 13 – of the children who died. Five families lost two children. Inside the paper, 13 pages of coverage were devoted to the accident, including two pages of photos of the scene and of injured children in their hospital beds.

One story inside attempted to unravel clues to the crash:

**Last Few Seconds
Before Tragic
Crash Recounted**

GREELEY, Dec. 14 – "I thought the bus was stopping. To my surprise I saw him come on. The bus windows weren't clear, but I could see children inside. I yelled to Mr. Sommers, 'I hope he stops. There's children in that bus.'"

Slowly, in a low voice, Melvin C. Swanson, fireman on the Union Pacific's City of Denver, told of the last few seconds before the collision of the train and school bus near Evans, Colo., Thursday morning.

On the same page, another story is printed beneath a photo of two beautiful, stony-eyed young girls:

**Hand of Death Brushed
Evans Girls**

GREELEY, Dec. 14 – "Daddy scolded us because we overslept and missed the school bus.

"But he's not mad anymore."

In this way, 13-year-old Colleen Yetter explained the simple stroke of fate which kept her and her blond-haired younger sister, LaDean, 6, off the ill-fated school bus which carried 20 of her classmates to their death Thursday.

The school bus crash filled page 1 for three days.

'The Crossing'

Forty-six years after that fateful day, in January of 2007, the *Rocky* published the second telling of the school bus crash. Reporter Kevin Vaughan set out to write a series honoring the victims, but also recounting how the tragedy changed and reshaped the lives of Duane Harms and the Yetter sisters and the many other family members and witnesses touched by the event. Vaughan and photographer Chris Schneider conducted interviews with survivors now spread across the country.

The result was a 33-part series called "The Crossing." And, demonstrating how the *Rocky* and journalism changed during the same time, the project included a powerful Internet and video component produced by the *Rocky's* Interactive Media team.

"The Crossing" was a finalist for the Pulitzer Prize.

Squaring off over nukes

It was called "the week that shook the world."

There probably was not a march of brick-sized headlines across the front pages of the world's newspapers to match it until September 2001.

The standoff between the United States and the USSR, between American President John F. Kennedy and Soviet Premier Nikita Khrushchev, over the buildup of Soviet missiles in Cuba, began on Oct. 23, 1962, in the *Rocky*.

> WASHINGTON, Oct. 22 – President Kennedy Monday night clamped a naval blockade on Cuba, United Press International reported.
>
> He said Soviet missiles and other offensive weapons had turned the island into an armed camp capable of hurling destruction into the heart of America.
>
> At the same time, the President warned Russia that the United States would respond with an attack on the Soviet Union if a nuclear missile is launched from Cuba against this nation or any other country in the Western Hemisphere.

The paper devoted 13 pages the first day of the story, including the complete text of Kennedy's warning. Local man-on-the-street interviews strongly supported the President's actions. The parade of page 1 banners continued:

(Oct. 25) RED SHIPS TURN OFF

Some Soviet vessels sailing toward Cuba change course, even as Cuban housewives empty food stores.

(Oct. 26) ADLAI RIPS ZORIN AT UN

U.S. Ambassador Adlai Stevenson displays photos of Soviet missile bases in Cuba before the United Nations.

(Oct. 27) MISSILE KO DEADLINE!
'Matter of Hours or Days'

The U.S. sets a deadline of less than one week for the Soviet Union to begin dismantling the missile bases or it will take action against them.

(Oct. 28) JFK Says Reds Hint At Missile Removal

Kennedy says a proposal from Khrushchev indicates the basis for a negotiated settlement of the crisis.

(Oct. 29) World Tension Eases As Nikita Gives In

> WASHINGTON, Oct. 28 – Nikita Khrushchev Sunday agreed to tear down his Cuban missile bases under United Nations inspection, UPI reported.
>
> President Kennedy called his action a "statesmanlike" move that helped pull the world back from the brink of war.

Don't touch my football

The Cuban missile crisis gripped the world's attention. Or at least most of it. On Sunday, Oct. 28, the hopeful news that Khrushchev might relent was played lower on page 1, leaving room for the traditional box of college football scores.

Journalism takes day off

On the same Sunday, the *Rocky* chose page 5, where all week tense news of the standoff had been well reported with the use of military photos and maps, for a shabby piece of work. At the top of the local news page, in a four-column photo, a staff photographer staged a deer head behind the steering wheel of an automobile, with a rifle seemingly aimed out the driver's window. Two local hunters joined in the fun, posing as if they were draped over both front fenders in the classic 1920s transport of dead game. Beneath the photo ran this caption:

> Fed up with the slaughter of his fellow Colorado mule deer, this big buck decided to take matters into its own hands and go after some hunters. From the looks of things, he did right well. His bag includes Harold Koinzan, 45, at left, of 3310 W. Wesley ave., and John M. Davis, 30, of 1685 S. Mabry way. Both men believe the hunters have had things their own way too long.

It was a case of tired, old, weekend journalism. The paper could have served its readers better. ☐

Rocky Mountain News

A Scripps-Howard Newspaper

Colorado's First Newspaper—Founded in 1859

SUNRISE
EDITION
★★★★★
FORECAST
Fair
PRICE 5 CENTS
104 PAGES

105TH YEAR: No. 215 — Published every morning by Denver Publishing Co. Entered as second class matter postoffice, Denver — DENVER 1, COLO. SATURDAY, NOV. 23, 1963

PRESIDENT IS SLAIN

Suspect Held

DALLAS, Nov. 22 — (UPI) — President Kennedy was assassinated Friday.

A sniper's shot mortally wounded the 35th President of the United States as he rode in an open car through a crowd of a quarter million in downtown Dallas.

The 46-year-old President died in Parkland Hospital at approximately 1 p.m. (noon Denver time).

Funeral rites for Mr. Kennedy were set for Monday.

Lyndon B. Johnson was sworn as President at 2:39 p.m. (1:39 p.m. Denver time).

Oath Aboard Plane

The swearing-in ceremony took place aboard the presidential plane. The oath was administered by a woman federal judge. Then the plane, carrying the new President of the United States, the body of the late President and Mrs. Jacqueline Kennedy, the widow, roared off to Washington.

The prime suspect was a man who was cornered and seized in a movie theater in the Oak Cliff section soon after the assassination.

The man was identified as Lee H. Oswald, chairman of a Fair Play for Cuba Committee.

Oswald once sought citizenship in Russia. He was charged with the President's murder.

Mr. Johnson was in the same cavalcade but a number of cars behind Mr. Kennedy. He was not hurt.

Texas Gov. John B. Connally, sitting across from Mr. Kennedy in the bubbletop presidential limousine, its bullet-proof glass lowered, was hit in the chest. He was reported in good condition Friday night after surgery.

Mrs. Jacqueline Kennedy was riding beside her husband. She was not hurt. She screamed as he toppled over on the seat and then cradled her husband's head in her arms as he was sped, dying, to the hospital.

Mrs. Nellie Connally, the governor's wife, also was in the limousine. She was not injured.

Caught off Guard

Secret Service men and motorcycle police escorts were caught off guard by the swiftness of the treacherous attack. They unlimbered automatic rifles and pistols, but too late.

The limousine sped off to Parkland Hospital where 10 doctors fought, in vain, to save the President's life. He was administered final anointing and then died after spending two years, 10 months and

(Continued on Page 5)

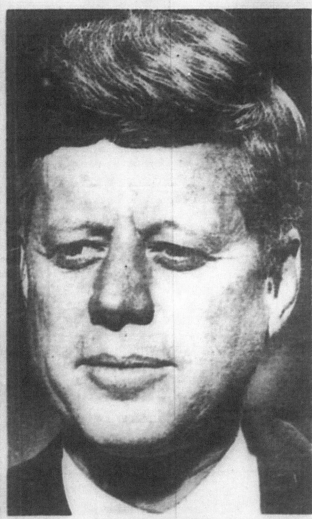

This picture of President Kennedy was taken by Bill Perry, Rocky Mountain News photographer, on Sept. 25, 1963, when Mr. Kennedy visited Laramie, Wyo.

John Fitzgerald Kennedy
May 29, 1917—Nov. 22, 1963

LBJ Is Sworn In

'Where were you when ... ?'

For at least two generations of Americans, the memory of his death will always be the answer to the question:

"Where were you when ... ?"

Few who read the *Rocky's* page 1 headline the morning of Nov. 23, 1963, will ever forget it, nor the terse five-word lead of the story:

**PRESIDENT
IS SLAIN
Suspect Held**

DALLAS, Nov. 22 – (UPI) – President Kennedy was assassinated Friday.

A sniper's shot mortally wounded the 35th President of the United States as he rode in an open car through a crowd of a quarter million in downtown Dallas.

John F. Kennedy was shot by Lee Harvey Oswald, although conspiracy theories still flourish today. Texas Gov. John Connally, sitting across from the President in the limousine, was also shot and wounded.

The *Rocky* that day was 104 pages. Classified ads took up 32 pages. Of the 72 remaining, 11 pages carried coverage of the assassination, plus the full-page condolence ad run by the May D&F department store chain. American Furniture Co. ran a similar ad the next day and announced its stores would remain closed Sunday and Monday, when Kennedy was to be buried. The lead local story began:

Colorado went into mourning Friday as the news of President Kennedy's assassination stunned the state.

Bells tolled ... flags were lowered to half staff ... entertainment events were called off. But the men who ordered these things, and the men who did them, acted largely like automatons, doing what had to be done, but stunned by the enormity of the act that made it necessary.

A sidebar reported that Denver firemen had to save three people who suffered apparent heart attacks when they learned that the president had died.

Al Nakkula and Dick Davis, the same reporter and photographer who covered the kidnap-murder of Adolph Coors III, were assigned to record reaction in downtown Denver. Nakkula started with the newsroom.

All we did was look at each other dumbfounded, as we waited for the (wire service) machines to give out their messages in jerking, spluttering stops of broken paragraphs and sentences as the first story was pieced together.

... The atmosphere of dismay and bewilderment hung over the city room even as editors gathered to organize personnel.

Customers and employees in the downtown May D&F store huddle around black-and-white televisions on display to hear the first news of President Kennedy's death. *(Dick Davis/Rocky Mountain News)*

The next top-played wire story reported that Soviet Premier Nikita Khrushchev was rushing by train back to Moscow.

The *Rocky* reprinted an essay written by JFK the previous year for a Scripps-Howard Newspapers series entitled "Americans in Action."

Sports events were hurriedly postponed the next day's Air Force-Colorado football game, Sunday's Broncos-Raiders game, state AAA high school football playoffs, the Regis-Pueblo Catholic game for the Colorado Catholic High School championship. The college and pro cancellations resulted in the *Rocky's* hallowed $250 weekly football contest being postponed a week, as well.

Jack Foster, editor of the paper, wrote a special op-ed piece:

Grief is a growing thing. It does not come all at once, but step by step.

It begins with unbelief. The President has been shot, they say.

The President of what?

The President of the United States.

Oh, no. ☐

Rocky Mountain News

A Scripps-Howard Newspaper

Reg. U S Pat. Off.

Colorado's First Newspaper—Founded in 1859

SUNRISE EDITION
★★★★
Partly Cloudy

5¢

106TH YEAR: NO. 127 — Second class postage paid at Denver, Colorado. Published every morning by Denver Publishing Co. — DENVER 1, COLO., THURSDAY, AUG. 27, 1964

144 PAGES

Picks Humphrey as Running Mate

Johnson Nominated; Flies to Convention

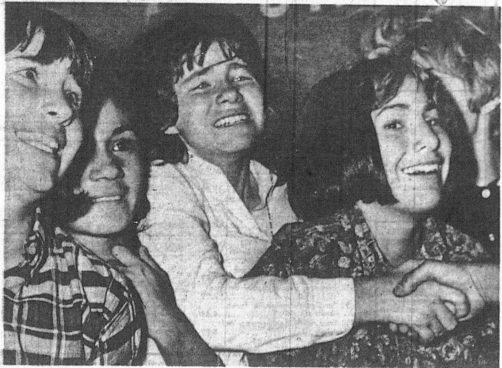

Tears From a Young Beatle Fan

2 Beatle Picture Pages: 118, 119

—STORY, PICTURE ON PAGE 5

Tears stream down the face of Jonna Scott, 14, of Lamar, third from left, as she stands among the crowd of 5000 persons that gathered outside the Brown Palace Hotel Wednesday at 17th st. and Tremont pl. to greet the Beatles. The tears were prompted because the 9th-grader feared she would not be able to see her favorite Beatle, Paul McCartney. The girl was disappointed because the quartet was taken in a rear door of the hotel to avoid the mob.

—Rocky Mountain News Photo by Bill Peery.

—STORY ON PAGE 3

More Convention Stories on 8, 10, 11, 14, 28, 30, 44, 46, 48, 50, 66, 82, 84 and 97

Hurricane postpones Titan shot page 5

Viet Nam mob kills 4 in hospital page 58

Unplanned Changes Push Way Into LBJ's Script

By the staff of the Scripps-Howard Newspapers

ATLANTIC CITY, Aug. 26 — President Johnson held the strings of this puppet show, but another force gave it a life of its own.

Plan for the convention did not call for sweeping changes in party structure. Forces building up for years took over and pushed it that way.

Plan called for unity, conciliation. Not for decision finally made — after years of agonizing hesitation—to come down on the side of Negro voting in Southern party affairs.

There was nothing in the script about loyalty oaths —but the whole convention took one and voted to make it a pre-condition for seating delegates four years from now.

Mr. Johnson said no floor fight, and there was none. Mr. Johnson didn't want militant Southerners, spoiling for a scrap, evicted and they weren't.

But the fact, clear and evident, that Negroes were winning an emotional victory here brought about unplanned changes that could be as far-reaching as any ordered by the Supreme Court.

PRETTY GIRLS dispense soft drinks here free to reporters and delegates as they did at San Francisco. At GOP convention, all the girls were white. At this one, many are Negro.

SEN. EDMUND MUSKIE (D-Maine) got first word that his vice presidential boomlet was dead

(Concluded on Page 3)

Going helter-skelter

The *Rocky's* concert review the day after the Beatles' only show in Denver was brief but warm – like the Fab Four's performance.

Beatles Rock
Happy Fans
By Ralph Veatch
Rocky Mountain News Writer

The Beatles, whom some have called "the greatest thing to hit America since cotton candy," rocked and socked through a musical review Wednesday night at Red Rocks Amphitheater, and more than 9000 young people ate it up, you might say, as they shrieked almost nonstop through a tuneful half hour performance.

There was no cute letter grade or row of stars to rate the act. Just 13 inches of restraint, back on page 102, with a 2-inch filler at the bottom, about a fire in New York, because the review didn't completely fill its allotted hole.

The unsung hero of the group is Ringo Starr, the hard-working drummer-boy. He's often been touted as a presidential candidate of the young folk. He should win everyone's vote for his 100 percent strong rhythmic performance.

... About the only untoward event, if it was that, was the intermittent shower of jelly beans which the crowd threw onstage. But, undaunted, the British foursome played on.

The Beatles, who professed an especial interest in singing at Red Rocks, proved by their performance that the early reports were not idle publicity. The Beatles really poured it on and the energetic audience poured it right back.

Talk about Penny Lane

Seats at Red Rocks for the Beatles cost $6.50. Again ...

George Harrison, John Lennon and Ringo Starr, all wearing matching western-style vests, join Paul McCartney at a pre-concert press conference at Red Rocks. Publicist Derek Taylor is in the background.
(Ken Mausolf/Denver Theatres & Arenas)

that's 6 dollars and 50 cents. Promoter Verne Byers had wanted to book the show at Denver University Stadium, where he could sell 2,000 more seats, but the Beatles wanted Red Rocks.

Page 1 warning

The morning of the concert, the *Rocky* took the high road and printed an unusual editorial message, boxed on page 1, that sounded like the bun-haired teacher wagging her finger at unruly students.

Attention!
Teenagers of Denver

Teenagers of Denver, you have the opportunity of attracting worldwide attention today!

... But don't be rowdies. Don't throw things. Don't try to smuggle beer or liquor into Red Rocks Theater. Don't kick and elbow. Gird on the self-discipline that is the mark of a true American citizen.

In every city where the Beatles have landed they have been met by crushing mobs. Teenage girls have fainted ... Show your heroes, the Beatles, that in Denver teenagers are different.

A crowd of 10,000 screaming fans lined a fence for two miles bordering Stapleton Airfield when the Beatles landed. Six girls were taken to Denver General Hospital for injuries. Five thousand more fans awaited the British pop group outside the Brown Palace hotel.

LBJ's ticket to ride

The *Rocky's* lead story on page 1 the day after the Beatles' concert was Lyndon Johnson's nomination as the Democratic candidate for president and his choice of Hubert Humphrey for vice president. □

Last of 'Big Three' mourned

Another giant of world history had fallen, the *Rocky's* page 1 banner on Jan. 24, 1965, announced.

LONDON, Jan. 24 – (AP) – Sir Winston Churchill, Britain's man of the century, lost his last battle Saturday.

The 90-year-old statesman, last of the Allied big three of World War II, died at 8 a.m. London time (1 a.m. Denver time) in his London home, 28 Hyde Park Gate, 10 days after suffering a stroke.

Strokes also carried away President Franklin D. Roosevelt and Joseph Stalin, wartime comrades with whom Churchill lived his finest hour in the immense struggle against the Axis powers.

… John F. Kennedy, in welcoming him to honorary U.S. citizenship, called Churchill "The most honorable man to walk the stage of human history in the time in which we live."

It was the biggest news on a busy news day.

Badge No. 50-51

Beneath the banner headline honoring one hero on page 1, the paper printed a Denver widow's ode to another. Three days earlier, Police Patrolman Paul Major was shot and killed in the line of duty. His wife, Dorothy, wrote the life story behind Badge No. 50-51 and presented it to her minister. With her permission, the *Rocky* reprinted it.

The wild blue yonder

For the first time in its brief 10-year history, the Air Force Academy was embroiled in a cheating scandal, the paper reported on page 5.

Eugene M. Zuckert, U.S. Air Force secretary, said in Washington Saturday that "at least 100" cadets at the Air Force Academy near Colorado Springs are involved in the current classroom cheating scandal.

Individual cadets brushed aside questions about the investigation, but a spokesman for the Academy said, "They are disturbed and embarrassed about this. They aren't saying much, but I know they want any cadets who have violated the honor code to clear out."

Eventually, more than 30 of those found to be involved were varsity football players.

Deeper and deeper

On a page deep inside the newspaper, an AP story told of the increasing infiltration of North Vietnamese fighters through Laos into South Vietnam. A second story reported the death of the 350th American in the conflict.

Further into the paper, on the editorial page, the *Rocky* attempted to analyze what had gone wrong with the U.S. strategy in Southeast Asia beneath the headline:

Why Are We Losing in Viet Nam

Of course we are not winning the war in Viet Nam! And here's why:

Through infiltration from North Viet Nam and recruitment of peasants from the South, the Communists are building up faster than government forces and U.S. help.

… THE MOST IMPORTANT THING FOR US TO DO IS TO PERSEVERE.

We should not pull out of this highly important yet relatively "cheap" and "little" war.

It would take many years and many lives before this view would change. ☐

Writing the storm out

Coloradans are used to severe weather. No one is prepared for immensely destructive, killer weather, though.

Over five days in 1965, the state felt it all. The *Rocky's* front page on June 19, 1965, began to count the toll after the South Platte River inundated the city of Denver:

21 Are Dead In Flood;
$102 Million Damage

The normally tame river, swollen by rains, overflowed its banks, washed out 26 major bridges and eventually caused $300 million damage.

The paper carried a small boxed notice on page 5 for readers:

If Your Paper Is Late,
Don't Blame Your Carrier

The day before, the front-page photo showed a swamp of cars, trailers and timber washed up against the West Alameda bridge. The South Platte flows horizontally from top to bottom of the photo – over the Valley Highway (I-25).

Inside the June 18 edition, the paper's Washington correspondent, Dan Thomasson, reported that President Lyndon Johnson was following news of the flood.

WASHINGTON, June 17 – President Johnson said Thursday he will make "all the resources of the United States" available to the distressed people of Colorado.

The President personally assured The Rocky Mountain News he is keeping close watch on the situation through his Office of Emergency Planning.

The *Rocky* and *Post* had their own problems, and the two newspapers helped each other publish during the flood.

Denver's two daily newspapers, vigorous rivals in the normal competition for news and advertising, co-operated early Thursday to bring flood coverage to Denver residents.

When all power went off at The Rocky Mountain News plant shortly before midnight Wednesday, the rival Denver Post offered its facilities to get out the paper.

When the Post (still an afternoon paper) lost its power the next morning, The News returned the offer, but it turned out to be not necessary.

Appearing on the same page, Amter's Fashions ran an ad for women's swimsuits.

The day before, the *Rocky's* page 1 story reported evacuations up and down the river.

Residents of Sedalia, Louviers and South Platte River sections of Denver, Littleton and Englewood were evacuated at the dinner hour Wednesday as a 20-foot wall of water roared down the river in the wake of a series of tornadoes which swirled out of the Central Rockies earlier in the afternoon.

In its June 16 edition, the paper reported storms pummeling Colorado, Wyoming and Nebraska.

The storm coverage that began on June 15 was bleak enough. The page 1 headline:

Tornado Strikes
West of Loveland

Beneath the banner a photo looked down on what had been a residential street in the northern Colorado town, but now more closely resembled a kindling yard.

Playing catch-up

Always at the mercy of late-night weather and power failures, the *Rocky's* sports section had plenty to tell fans after it couldn't produce its full report the night of June 16. The next day, it tried to recover in its typically breezy, loose style.

Late breaking sports stories which went by the boards when the flood – an unscheduled event – put an end to type-setting at 11:47 p.m. Wednesday included a U.S. record Twin Quin of $12,790 at Cloverleaf (dog track) and a 13-inning, 4-1, win by the Denver Bears at Salt Lake City.

Ed. April 5, 1968. Denver, Colo. —ROCKY MOUN

Rocky Mountain News

A Scripps-Howard Newspaper

Reg. U.S. Pat. Off.

Colorado's First Newspaper—Founded in 1859

109TH YEAR, NO. 349 — Second class postage paid at Denver, Colorado. Published every morning by Denver Publishing Co.

DENVER, COLORADO 80201, FRI., APRIL 5, 1968

HOME
FINAL
★★★
FORECAST:
Warmer

10c
128 PAGES

Fatal Shooting Delays LBJ's Trip to Hawaii

Memphis Assassin Slays Dr. Martin Luther King

Racial Violence Flares in Several Cities

ROCKY MOUNTAIN NEWS PHOTO BY MEL SCHIELTZ

Dr. Martin Luther King Jr. in meditative pose.

Picture taken last May when Dr. King visited Denver.

MORE ON KING ON PAGES 3, 5, 8, 16, 32, 56, 96, 97

MEMPHIS, April 4—(UPI)—Dr. Martin Luther King Jr., who walked with death in his nonviolent battle for racial freedom, was slain by a white sniper Thursday on the balcony of his motel.

The 39-year-old Nobel Peace Prize winner's assassination swept the nation like a shock wave and violence erupted in some areas.

Rioting broke out in Memphis. Two policemen were shot and National Guard troops and highway patrolmen were called in.

Violence Flares

Violence also erupted in New York's Harlem and Brooklyn, in Oakland, Calif., Washington, D.C., Raleigh, N.C., Birmingham, Ala., Miami, Fla., Jackson, Miss., Boston, Mass. and Hartford, Conn. There was looting, window-smashing and rock-throwing in several of these areas.

Police issued a bulletin for a young white man in dark clothes who dashed out of a building across the street from the Lorraine Motel, where King was

'The King Assassination,' an editorial on Page 56.

killed. He dropped a Browning automatic rifle on the sidewalk and fled in a car. But Police Chief Frank Holloman said: "We have no definite lead we can report at this time regarding the assailant."

President Johnson appeared on nationwide television to announce he had postponed his trip to Honolulu because of the slaying. He asked "every citizen to stay away from the violence that struck Dr. King."

Guardsmen Recalled

But three hours after King's death was announced, Holloman went on television in Memphis to report "rioting has broken out in parts of the city. Looting is rampant. The National Guard is coming back into town," he said.

He referred to the 4000 troops called out after last week's rioting in Memphis. The guardsmen were sent home earlier this week. National Guard planes were fanning out over the state to pick up massive contingents of riot-trained highway patrolmen.

(Concluded on Page 3)

UPI TELEPHOTO

Atlanta, Ga., Mayor Ivan Allen Jr. holds umbrella over Mrs. Martin Luther King Jr. She had started to fly to Memphis but changed her mind when she learned her husband had died of his wound.

News Sports Writer Dies in Auto Crash

STORIES ON PAGES
20 AND 88

'A time of sorrow, fear'

Sadness and frustration gripped the nation with the news that the Rev. Martin Luther King Jr. had been assassinated. Once again, the *Rocky* and other newspapers served as the grim messengers.

MEMPHIS, April 4 – (UPI) – Dr. Martin Luther King Jr., who walked with death in his nonviolent battle for racial freedom, was slain by a white sniper Thursday on the balcony of his motel.

The 39-year-old Nobel Peace Prize winner's assassination swept the nation like a shock wave and violence erupted in some areas.

Rioting broke out in Memphis. Two policemen were shot and National Guard troops and highway patrolmen were called in.

Violence also erupted in New York's Harlem and Brooklyn, in Oakland, Calif., Washington, D.C., Raleigh, N.C., Birmingham, Ala., Miami, Fla., Jackson, Miss., Boston, Mass. and Hartford, Conn. There was looting, window-smashing and rock-throwing in several of these areas.

Rev. Martin Luther King, Jr., right, talks with Rev. L. Sylvester Odom during a 1964 visit to Denver. *(Bob Talkin/Rocky Mountain News)*

A young-looking white man in dark clothing had been seen running from a building across the street from the Lorraine Motel, where King was killed. He dropped a Browning automatic rifle on the sidewalk and fled in a car.

In the years since his death, many stories of King's foreboding about being killed have surfaced. *Rocky* readers read one of the first accounts in the first day's coverage. George Brown, a state senator from Denver, became a close friend of King's during his visits to Denver.

Brown told The News he and Dr. King had discussed the possibility of Dr. King's being murdered

when the civil rights leader came here last May for a speech at the University of Denver.

"He felt his time might come," said Brown, a Negro who is chairman of the board of Denver Opportunity.

If it did come, Dr. King hoped it would trigger a wave of indignation so that people of good would band together, seeking an end to the racial evils against which he had long fought, said Brown.

Memphis paper offers reward

The *Rocky's* front-page story the next day announced that a $25,000 reward for information leading to the arrest and conviction of King's murderer had been offered by Memphis' largest newspaper, *The Commercial Appeal*. The Memphis paper was owned by the same company as the *Rocky,* Scripps-Howard, which added another $25,000 to the reward.

It would be two months before James Earl Ray was arrested and eventually convicted of King's assassination.

Edward Kennedy speaks out

The same day, Sen. Edward Kennedy, brother of the slain president, delivered an impassioned speech in Denver.

Kennedy lashed out at "haters" and those who allow haters to operate by wearing their "own personal blinders." He described "a time of sorrow and a time of fear" in the nation and said violence – since the advocate of non-violence was killed in Memphis – cannot be tolerated.

"How many good men must we give before we finally face the fact that the weakness in our society is a weakness in ourselves?" ☐

Another Kennedy falls

For the third time in five years – the second time in two months – a U.S. leader had been gunned down. Sen. Robert Kennedy was in critical condition after being shot in the head in Los Angeles, even as he took command of the California Democratic primary close to midnight.

The *Rocky,* and every other morning newspaper across the country, scrambled to tear apart already-closed editions and rush an Associated Press story into the June 5 paper.

LOS ANGELES, June 5 – Sen. Robert F. Kennedy, brother of the assassinated President John F. Kennedy, was shot in the head twice early Wednesday by a gunman whose bullets turned a scene of political triumph into one of shock and confusion.

Three others also were wounded.

Frank Mankiewicz, his press secretary, said Kennedy's condition was "stable."

"He is breathing well and has a good heart," he told newsmen. "I do not think he is conscious."

A curly haired man, about 25 and of Latin appearance, was seized immediately as he brandished a small pistol.

The shooting occurred as Kennedy finished a victory speech after surging ahead of Sen. Eugene McCarthy in the California Democratic presidential primary.

The *Rocky* ran a small photo of Kennedy alongside another of Rafer Johnson, the Olympic decathlon champion and Kennedy supporter who was credited with capturing Sirhan Bishara Sirhan in the Ambassador Hotel, where Kennedy was shot.

In the early-morning hours, to change the front page as quickly as possible, editors cut the earlier lead story on the primary results to a single column. The results showed Kennedy with 266,186 votes to Eugene McCarthy's 218,832. California Gov. Ronald Reagan, who did not seek the Republican nomination but ran unopposed on the ballot, received 179,827 votes.

No one would ever know what might have happened in a presidential race between Kennedy and Richard Nixon, the eventual GOP nominee. The *Rocky's* page 1 headline on June 7:

Kennedy to Be Buried
Beside Slain Brother

NEW YORK, June 6 – (UPI) – Robert F. Kennedy joined his brother in an assassin's death Thursday, and mourners began the long journey with the body toward its resting place beside the late President Kennedy in Arlington Cemetery.

Only two months earlier, Dr. Martin Luther King had been killed in Memphis.

Denver headquarters closed

The *Rocky* sent the intrepid Al Nakkula to cover the closing of Kennedy's campaign headquarters in the Denham Building in Denver. There he found a janitor scraping black lettering off the glass door of Room 314. It read: "Kennedy for President."

Life is interrupted

For Robert Walters of Russell, Kansas, June 6 was the best day in all his 14 years. He was named champion of the annual Scripps-Howard National Spelling Bee in Washington D.C. The original spelling bee schedule called for he and his family to take sight-seeing tours of the nation's capitol, but that had all changed now, as a story deep in the *Rocky* explained.

The scheduled itinerary was completely disrupted by the assassination of Sen. Robert F. Kennedy and the continuing disputes emanating from Resurrection City. Scripps-Howard officials have wisely avoided taking the spellers and their escorts into areas which present potential danger. This is graphically illustrated by the special security guards present during the spelldown and riding the sight-seeing buses. □

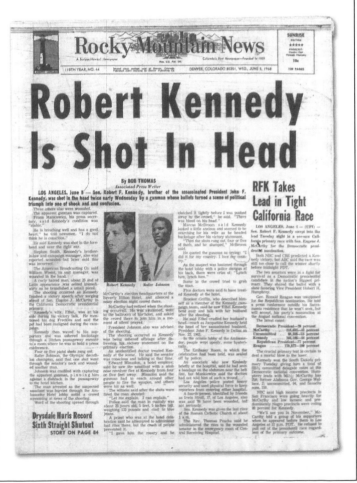

Poverty meets its match

In the pages of the *Rocky*, Rodolfo "Corky" Gonzales was a hero and a villain, one of the founders of the Chicano Movement and a legendary rebel-rouser. He was a larger, more significant figure than any single story ever printed about him.

He was a boxer, a poet, a political activist and a leader. March 21, 1969, wasn't the first time his name appeared on page 1, after he slugged a police officer during a protest at Denver West High School. His life was often in the headlines. As the paper reported:

> Several hundred West High School students fought with police on the front steps of the school Thursday after walking out of classes in protest over alleged racial slurs by a teacher.
>
> A television newsman and a student were hospitalized because of injuries during the fight and at least 26 persons were arrested, including Crusade for Justice director Rudolph "Corky" Gonzales. Gonzales later was released on bond on the simple assault charge.
>
> ... The crowd of students in front of the police building grew to about 100 in the afternoon, their ranks joined by members of the SDS (Students for a Democratic Society) from the University of Colorado.
>
> ... The crowd chanted "We Want Corky."

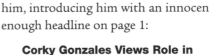

Rocky Mountain News

West High School Students and Police Fight
Two Persons Are Hospitalized and 26 More Arrested

ARSENAL LAND REPORTED RELEASED TO DENVER
ICC Examiner Approves Largest Railroad Merger---Page 80

Crusade for Justice was Gonzales' creation and was in the forefront of a national struggle for Chicano civil rights.

Days later, Gonzales convened the first Chicano youth conference, attended by many future Chicano activists. The *Rocky* printed only a 6-inch short advancing the conference and did not cover it. One of the factors may have been the death of former President Eisenhower on March 28, which dominated newspapers for more than a week.

However, significantly, during the conference the paper devoted nearly two full pages up front to a story headlined:

Economics Is Pertinent
Root of Hispano Problem

The West High incident led to the story. Gonzales was mentioned only briefly in an attempt to bring his role into focus:

> The leadership of Corky Gonzales is oft-debated. Does he represent the feelings of the Hispanos or is he a demagogue?

Gonzales later wrote the epic Hispanic poem *Yo Soy Joaquin (I Am Joaquin)* and became a key figure in the national La Raza Unida Party. When he died of organ failure in 2005, he was aptly remembered as "the fist" of the Chicano Movement.

Charisma compounded

Years before, Denver recognized Gonzales' leadership qualities. City officials just weren't sure how to tap them. In 1965, at age 37, he was already director of the Neighborhood Youth Corps when he was also named chairman of Denver's War on Poverty (DWOP), a struggling program. On Sept. 29 the *Rocky* profiled him, introducing him with an innocent enough headline on page 1:

Corky Gonzales Views Role in
Poverty Program

The reporter started the story inside like Gonzales the boxer coming out of his corner in the first round:

> "I'm an agitator and a troublemaker. That's my reputation, and that's what I'm going to be. They didn't buy me when they put me in this job."
>
> ... The typical occupant of such a position as chairman of Denver's War on Poverty shuns involvement in picketing and demonstrations like the plague.
>
> But Gonzales is unabashedly a man of the streets. That's where the people are; that's where the action is; that's where he'll make a good part of his battle.

Seven months later he was removed as head of the Neighborhood Youth Corps.

Street success

In a sidebar to the interview, Gonzales cited a bizarre example of the effectiveness of Denver's War on Poverty:

> "There was this fellow who'd been in the Training Home at Ridge. We tried a number of ways to get him a job, but it looked pretty hopeless – he couldn't read or write. I finally used some muscle and got him a job on a city work gang.
>
> "I met him on the street the other day. He was wearing a new suit like the Beatles. He had a little money in his pocket, and a 6-pack in the icebox at home. We did the job against poverty for him."

Golf, trout lured Ike

Dwight D. Eisenhower left his mark on the world, to be sure. But he quite literally left it on Colorado – on the fireplace mantle of the Brown Palace suite where he pinged a golf ball off it during one of his many vacations spent in the state.

The *Rocky* had many tales to tell about the former president when it printed news March 29, 1969, that "Ike" had died after several heart attacks.

LONDON (AP) – Comrades-in-arms as well as leaders of nations whose forces fought under him and against him extolled Dwight D. Eisenhower Friday as a man who guided the liberation of Europe in World War II and helped calm a jittery postwar world.

"I am very distressed," said Field Marshall Lord Montgomery, the British ground commander under Ike in the war. "I want to be left alone now." He and Ike had their differences during the war.

… For the great and the small, the passing of Eisenhower summoned up memories of the great events of peace and war in the 1940s and 1950s. One way or another, Eisenhower was involved in most of them.

The paper carried the expected military and political tributes earned by a great man, stories that filled 14 pages.

But it was the small, human remembrances of the time he spent in Colorado that make the *Rocky's* coverage still worth reading today.

His wife, Mamie Doud Eisenhower, grew up on Lafayette Street in Denver, and the couple married at Fort Logan. Relatives, golf and trout always lured him back.

His favorite fishing spot was St. Louis Creek just outside Fraser. The town's Cozens Ranch museum still holds rooms full of Eisenhower memorabilia. The day after Ike died, reporter Don Lyle wrote:

The President was given Colorado fishing license number one in 1953 and has received it every year since.

… The people of Fraser never did quite get used to the outlandishly-dresssed posse of reporters who, pretending they were Westerners, rode out to the ranch daily for press conferences and to check Ike's fishing luck.

That year Eddie Eldridge, Ike's Rocky Mountain News carrier, got a thank you note for fine service from the President.

Eisenhower's Colorado vacation in 1955 looked like it was off to a great start after a round of golf at his favorite course, Cherry Hills Country Club. He and club pro Ralph "Rip" Arnold stopped for lunch and headed out for another round that ended after one hole "in a shock which left the nation and most of the World holding its breath," Lyle wrote. Ike suffered one of his heart attacks and he spent the next 48 days in a wheelchair recuperating.

Years later, the President said he might have retired in Colorado had it not been for his health and doctors' fears for him living at altitude. Continued Lyle:

Ike's last visit to Colorado was a sad one, too. On June 3, 1966, he came back to Denver to transfer the body of his first son, Doud Dwight Eisenhower (who died of scarlet fever), from the Doud family plot at Fairmount to the Eisenhower plot in Abilene.

Eisenhower's legacy lives throughout the state. During his presidency the Air Force Academy opened (with a golf course named in his honor) and the Blue River water dispute settled. He gave his name to a Colorado Golf Association scholarship fund for young, needy golfers. After his death, the Eisenhower Tunnel under the Continental Divide would carry millions of skiers and tourists into the mountains he loved. □

'One giant leap for mankind'

America loves its heroes. So when astronaut Neil Armstrong thrilled the world by becoming the first human to set foot on the moon, the *Rocky* tried to produce a newspaper to match his feat.

Editions of July 21, 1969, were declared "Moon Landing Sunrise Extras." And beneath the page 1 headline, in a box, the paper claimed:

**First Colorado Newspaper
On Great Moon Triumph;
You'll Want to Preserve
This Historic Edition**

The Denver Post was still an afternoon paper, and the *Rocky* went to press earlier than any other morning newspaper in the state, so it probably was the first to print the story.

The Associated Press lead was a model of brevity and history:

HOUSTON (AP) – Two Americans landed and walked on the moon Sunday, the first human beings on its alien soil.

They planted their nation's flag and talked to their President (Nixon) on earth by radio-telephone.

Millions on their home planet 240,000 miles away watched on television as they saluted the flag, and scouted the lunar surface.

Ads out of this world

Denver's department stores had been pouncing on historic events with solemn or honorary ads since at least 1945 when President Franklin Roosevelt died. But they out-did themselves the day after humans walked on the moon.

On page 2, May D&F (later Foleys, now Macy's) designed a full-page ad showing a young boy, head upward, searching the skies.

On page 4, upscale Neusteter's ran a rough drawing of the spacecraft on the surface of the moon with Earth over the horizon, and the words: "And now ... man begins to decode the secret of time."

On page 21, another full-page ad appeared with the cartoon character Snoopy floating in space asking, his words in a bubble: "Where's the May D&F."

Maybe they sold more bedsheets.

Drama on Earth

The day before, the *Rocky's* page 1 banner heralded Apollo 11's successful moon orbit and prepared readers for the much-anticipated landing. But the second headline on the cover reported another story that Americans would whisper about for years to come:

**Sen. Kennedy Misses
Death in Auto Wreck
Young Woman Passenger Killed**

Alongside the story ran photos of Sen. Edward Kennedy and Mary Jo Kopechne.

EDGARTOWN, MARTHA'S VINEYARD, Mass (UPI) – A car driven by Sen. Edward M. Kennedy plunged off a narrow bridge into a pond early Saturday, killing a pretty blonde secretary who was riding with him.

Kennedy, who escaped from the car, said he made a futile attempt to rescue Mary Jo Kopechne, 29, diving repeatedly into the 10-foot saltwater pond before wandering away from the scene in a daze. □

Air tragedy in Rockies

It was another story of tragedy, and the morning of Oct. 3, 1970, the *Rocky* did its job again acting as messenger, mourner and questioner.

A twin-engine airliner carrying at least 40 persons, most of them football players and officials of Wichita State University, crashed and burned high on the east slope of the Continental Divide north of Loveland Pass at 1:14 p.m. Friday.

... It was believed to be the nation's worst air tragedy involving a sports team.

The plane, with registration number N464M, was one of two Martin aircraft carrying the Wichita State football team to Logan, Utah, for a Saturday game against Utah State University. The second plane, with 39 persons aboard, landed safely in Logan, where its passengers were immediately taken to a motel and given sedation.

Witnesses on the ground said the Martin 404 aircraft appeared to labor to gain enough altitude to cross the Divide. The plane crashed at 11,000 feet; the Divide directly west of the crash rose to more than 13,000 feet.

'I didn't do anything'

Carl Hilliard was already a veteran Associated Press reporter in Colorado when the Wichita State plane went down and he rushed to the scene. In nearby Bakerville, he found a shaken witness.

Bob Lincoln, 32, a black, bull-shouldered construction electrician, curled his hands around a beer in a roadside tavern about five miles from where a Wichita State University plane crashed Friday afternoon, killing many of those aboard.

"I said to the guy who told us – 'Hey, that's my school. I'm going up there,'" Lincoln said.

Lincoln said he had attended Wichita State in 1957 and also played football there. He and a handful of others who were working on the Eisenhower Tunnel scrambled to the crash site. They found there was little they could do. They covered one victim they found who had been thrown from the plane.

"We went up there to help – in any way – if we could," Lincoln told Hilliard. "There was nothing alive in that plane. We found a shoulder pad, and a helmet. I think a jersey, and a football shoe.

"Don't use my name," he said. "I didn't do anything. I just used to go to school there."

Sports news

The *Rocky* devoted 12 pages of coverage to the Wichita State crash, but the only mention of it in the Sports section was a brief, bland wire story that chronicled past air tragedies involving sports figures.

The lead Sports story was the naming of former Denver Bears manager Billy Martin to manage the Detroit Tigers. Quarterback Joe Kapp, who the year before had led the Minnesota Vikings to the NFL championship but was sitting out the current season as a free agent, signed with the Boston Patriots. The NFL finally had merged with the upstart AFL, but Kapp's move to the American Football Conference team was still regarded as a defection. ☐

Rocky Mountain News

FINAL

Football craft plunges, burns on Loveland Pass

29 are feared dead in crash of plane

FULL PAGE OF PHOTOS ON PAGE 8; MORE PICTURES AND STORIES ON PAGES 5, 6, 10, 12, 20, 24, 38, 76, 83 AND 87

Plane carrying Wichita State University football players burns after crash in Dry Gulch Creek near Loveland Pass.

Colorado spurns Olympics

The 1972 election in Colorado sent shock waves from Denver across the country, and around the world.

The state helped elect Richard Nixon as the 37th president.

It launched the political career of Rep. Patricia Schroeder.

It swept Floyd Haskell, a former Republican, into the U.S. Senate as a Democrat.

It installed Dale Tooley as the city's district attorney.

It killed the state's long-sought hosting of the 1976 Winter Olympics.

And it thrust State Rep. Richard Lamm, who would go on to become a three-term governor, onto the national stage as the man who drove a ski pole through the heart of the Olympics.

Inside the election edition of Nov. 8, 1972, the Olympics story was written by Richard O'Reilly, the news reporter who covered the business and politics of Denver's bid from the start.

Colorado voters reject
1976 Winter Olympics

Colorado voters sent the 1976 Winter Olympics in search of a new home Tuesday,

Anti-Olympics forces viewed the vote as the beginning of a new era in which politicians will be more attuned to limiting population growth and reordering priorities for spending tax funds.

Olympic proponents saw the vote as a misguided effort which will have serious future repercussions for the state.

Only two years before, when Denver beat out Sion, Switzerland, for the Games, the *Rocky's* page 1 banner on May 13, 1970, captured the excitement:

Jubilant Denver is winner in
1976 bid for winter Olympics

The defeat of the Games really was a referendum on growth and spending in Colorado. A *Rocky* editorial the next day summed up reaction:

We believed in the Olympics for Colorado and endorsed it from the start, although raising serious questions about the manner in which planning was being carried out. Given the size of the vote against further Olympic spending, we are grateful this matter was brought before the people. They have spoken emphatically, we abide by their decision and consider the Olympic debate settled.

Nevertheless, Beaver Creek resort, the proposed site for some of the alpine events, was still built, and the I-70 corridor is choked today beyond anyone's dire predictions in 1972.

To this day, committees form to resurrect Denver as a site for future Olympics. Without fail, echoes of the state's decision in '72 can be heard.

"I think with this we'll just have to say we won't have the 1976 Winter Olympics," Mayor William H. McNichols Jr. said after the election. "The IOC (International Olympic Committee) will give them to someone else. In my opinion, they will never come to this country. After you go and get it, and then have a country reject it, it would be very surprising to me if they ever put them back in the United States." □

Under the mountains

Not even a woman walking inside it could stop the opening of the Eisenhower-Johnson Tunnel in 1973. Millions have passed through since.

Four months before the first bore was completed, the headline and photo on the front page of the *Rocky* told the bizarre story on Nov. 10, 1972.

60 men walk out as woman enters highway tunnel

GEORGETOWN (UPI) – Janet P. Bonnema, wearing miner's coveralls, a grin and a hard hat, walked into a tunnel through the Rocky Mountains Thursday to defy a superstition that women underground are bad luck. Sixty men walked off the job.

"Get out of here!" yelled a workman inside the mile-long $67 million Eisenhower Memorial Tunnel.

"You buy it and I will!" Janet shouted back, hitching up her coveralls. She had been kept out of the highway tunnel two years because of superstitious miners.

Most of the workers returned after the 33-year-old engineering technician finished her tour that came two days after Colorado voters approved a constitutional amendment giving equal rights to women.

... Janet entered the tunnel with a wave and a grin at the guard who had barred her for two years.

Bonnema had to file a $100,000 sexual discrimination suit against her employer, the Colorado Highway Department, to gain entrance. More from the story:

But W.K. McLaughlin, project manager for Straight Creek Contractors, Inc., which is building the tunnel said the superstition is no myth.

"It's no joke," he said. "Some years ago I took my wife into a tunnel we were working on in Climax (Colo.). The next day a man got killed."

Two years before, the highway department had hired Bonnema by mail and addressed her hiring letter to "Mr. Janet P. Bonnema."

The tunnel project was well known, of course, to Coloradans and the nation's truckers, who for decades had braved the steep, often icy 10-mile drive over Loveland Pass to reach Summit County. When it opened on March 8, 1973, it carried traffic in one lane in each direction. It would be another six years before the second bore, named after former governor and U.S. Sen. Edwin C. Johnson, opened two more lanes.

Red-faced dedication

On dedication day, Gov. John Love drove a limousine through the tunnel as the honorary "first driver." Except he wasn't really the first. That distinction went to a maverick nightrider who was arrested the previous October for his joyride.

After Love passed through, legislators, lobbyists and journalists boarded buses to make the 1.7-mile drive. Within minutes the inside of the entire tunnel shimmered with the mirage-like effect of photochemical smog. The tunnel superintendent later explained that the 16 mammoth ventilation fans hadn't been turned on in deference to the dedication ceremonies.

On second thought ...

The Colorado Highway Commission initially planned to close Loveland Pass during the winter once the Johnson bore opened Dec. 22, 1979, to save the cost of snow plowing. But Winter Park, Steamboat Springs and other towns successfully lobbied against the idea, fearing restrictions on trucking hazardous material through the tunnel would reroute more loads over Berthoud Pass and through their communities.

Today, with the Eisenhower Tunnel choked with winter ski traffic and talk of a new tunnel, more and more drivers are using the pass and going home the old-fashioned route.

War ends in Vietnam

The *Rocky* of Jan. 24, 1973, gave readers what America, for years, had been clamoring for – the end of the Vietnam War.

WASHINGTON (AP) – Agreement has been reached to end the Vietnam War – the longest in America's history – with a cease-fire effective Saturday night and complete U.S. withdrawal coinciding with release of all war prisoners, President Nixon told the nation Tuesday night.

Nixon said it is a just and fair peace – an honorable way to end a nightmarish, decade-long war that left nearly 350,000 Americans killed and wounded and caused an unprecedented upheaval at home.

The *Rocky's* coverage seemed to reflect the nation's mood: spare, cheerless, reserved. There weren't a lot of local reaction stories or pages of celebratory coverage.

Colorado demonstrations

May, 1970, marked some of the largest Vietnam War protests ever on U.S. college campuses. Two demonstrations and an act of violence on Colorado campuses took over the front page for days.

In the first week of May, four students were killed at Kent State University during a protest. By the end of the week, thousands of students had gathered on campuses in Boulder and Denver.

(May 8) 10,000 join march at CU

The accompanying photo was of CU President Frederick Thieme, appearing stunned and concerned as he looked over a sea of young faces. On the same day, some 300 students erected a plywood and canvas campsite they named "Woodstock West" on two quadrangles at DU.

(May 9) Two campus buildings at CSU are swept by flames

A fire, later found to be arson, destroyed Colorado State's 93-year-old Old Main building and another structure used by the campus ROTC. Beneath the banner headline a photo showed more than 1,000 CU faculty members, with arms thrust upward, voting support of their students against the war.

(May 12) *Governor weighs decision on sending troops to DU*

Announcement of a decision on whether the National Guard will be called to restore order on the University of Denver campus will be made Tuesday, a spokesman for the governor's office said after a late night meeting between Gov. (John) Love, Police Chief George Seaton and Colorado National Guard Adjutant General Joe C. Moffitt.

The next day – the same day the *Rocky* reported Denver had won the 1976 Winter Olympics – the second-play headline on page 1:

Gov. Love pleads for peace on campus

DU students had re-erected Woodstock West. But troops were never called in and ultimately a confrontation was averted.

'Cold type' and hot ads

In the '70s, most of the newspaper industry converted from impression printing with lead type to photo imaging pages upon which stories and ads were pasted as "cold type." The printers who performed the paste-up voluntarily assumed another unassigned, yet not discouraged duty – spontaneously hand-drawing lacy underwear on some of the women appearing in ads for Denver's growing X-rated movie and live show trade. Some of the printers were offended by the revealing ads; others simply enjoyed dabbling as the Lace Police. □

All the president's men

The beginning of the end, as it appeared in the *Rocky*, was a quiet, three-column story on page 9 the day after Father's Day, June 19, 1972:

Nixon re-election aide cited in Dem unit burglary probe

WASHINGTON (UPI) – President Nixon's re-election campaign committee admitted Sunday one of its employees was involved in a break-in at Democratic national headquarters.

The infamous location wasn't named until the 10th paragraph of the 13-paragraph story – the Watergate Apartments.

The investigation, of course, reached warp speed faster than you can say Captain Kirk. The blockbuster headline and story in the *Rocky* came on May 1, 1973:

WASHINGTON (UPI) – Vowing there will be "no whitewash at the White House," President Nixon Monday night told the nation he personally accepts responsibility for the Watergate case.

In an emotional 27-minute radio and television speech, just a few hours after accepting the resignations of Attorney General Richard G. Kleindienst and three close White House aides, Nixon said he had been misled by advisers about high-level involvement in the Watergate affair.

He said the "easiest course" would be to blame his subordinates, but that it would be "the cowardly thing to do."

Nixon fired John Dean, special counsel to the President, and in addition to Kleindienst, accepted the resignations of H.R. Haldeman, his chief of staff, and John Erlichman, chief domestic affairs adviser. Eventually, all would be convicted of crimes.

Three weeks later, the page 1 headline in the *Rocky*:

Nixon admits ordering aides to limit probe of Watergate

On July 31, 1974, two years after the break-in, Watergate was on page 1 again:

Impeachment resolution sent to House

WASHINGTON (UPI) – The House Judiciary Committee narrowly approved a third impeachment charge against President Nixon Tuesday – for defying Watergate tapes subpoenas – and ended six days of historic debate by sending to the full House a resolution that Nixon be stripped of his office.

... Senate leaders, anticipating impeachment by the House, already were mapping plans for a televised trial of the President this fall. Nixon is the first president since 1868 and only the second in U.S. history to face impeachment.

Congress knew history was still in motion. It just didn't know the direction it was headed.

This won't sit well

On Jan. 23, 1974, a local story interrupted the daily march of Watergate headlines across page 1:

$10 million and no seating

It seems that when Denver voters approved the $10 million bond issue to build McNichols Sports Arena, no funds were included for the 17,200 permanent seats. The arena was part of Denver's bid for the 1976 Winter Olympics when the bond issue was approved, and the city was expecting federal funds to pay for the seats. Colorado turned the Olympics away, of course, in 1972.

The oversight was brought to light in a weekly City Council meeting.

Nation puts on the brakes

In the Jan. 25, 1974, edition of the paper, readers were reminded that most of Colorado soon would be driving the state's 9,100 miles of highways at a maximum of 55 miles per hour. Gov. John Vanderhoof made it law by signing the first bill in the 1974 legislative session. Road crews were beginning to post the speed-limit signs and enforcement would begin in about 10 days. □

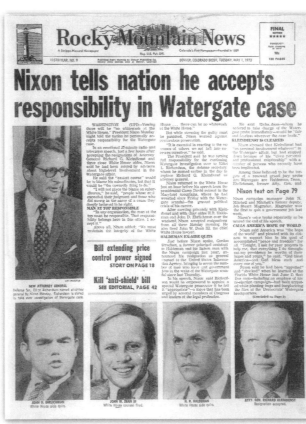

A president resigned to his fate

The events of late summer, 1974, resulted in a truly historic front page in every newspaper in America on Aug. 9. And, surely, one of the most tragically embarrassing moments in history. The *Rocky's* page 1 story, edited from wire services:

WASHINGTON – President Nixon resigned Thursday night, telling the nation he acted to help heal the wounds of Watergate and to give America "a full-time president" in Gerald Ford.

As he became the first man to resign the highest office, Nixon urged Americans to rally behind Ford, who will assume the powers of the presidency at noon Friday (10 a.m. Denver time).

That is the effective hour of the resignation Nixon said was personally abhorrent, but necessary in the national interest.

Stories and photos covered 14 pages including the entire text of both Nixon's televised resignation speech and Ford's following address to the nation.

Former Colorado governor John Love, who resigned as the nation's first energy czar after six months with the Nixon administration, was quoted in one of the lead stories: "I feel like a man who lost my reservation on the Titanic."

The *Rocky* gathered reaction from citizens found in Duffy's Tavern, May D&F's old downtown department store, the men's grill at the Denver Country Club and bars across the city.

A photo page presented a gallery of Nixon moments – waving with Spiro Agnew, bantering with Nikita Khrushchev, toasting with Chou En-lai, and walking the San Clemente beach alone, wearing his presidential windbreaker.

One Associated Press story speculated that Colorado would very soon have another president as a regular visitor.

VAIL (AP) – This ski resort town in the heart of the Rocky Mountains may become "Winter White House" as Vice President Gerald Ford takes over the presidency.

Ford has been a familiar sight on the ski slopes each winter, especially at Christmas time, since he bought a $50,000 condominium for his family in 1970.

Bumped by history

Some Denver television viewers were particularly incensed over Nixon's address, the *Rocky* reported. The speech interrupted popular serials *Kung Fu, Streets of San Francisco, Here's Lucy, The Dick Van Dyke Show,* and – oh my god! – a World Football League game between the Hawaii Hawaiians and the Jacksonville Sharks.

"I tell them they're going to get commentary until 11 because that's what ABC is giving us," Mrs. Esther Gregg, the switchboard operator at Channel 9 told the paper. "But these 'Kung Fu' people aren't satisfied when you tell them it's cancelled for the night."

Ads of the times

In the same edition, Montgomery Ward was still selling sewing machines for $59.88. And a Lionel Richie look-alike showed off Afro "permanents" for $19.95.

At the movies

It may not have been a good year for presidents, but it was for movie-goers. The *Rocky* was running large display ads for *Death Wish, Chinatown,* the re-release of *Night of the Iguana* and *Doctor Zhivago* and – not to be missed – Disney's *Herbie Rides Again.* □

Big Thompson flood

Once again in the high desert, water was everywhere on Aug. 2, 1976.

On page 1 of the *Rocky*, beneath the photo of a broken, washed-out U.S. highway 34 by veteran photographer Bill Peery, a secondary headline said the unimaginable:

U.S. 34 west of Loveland is no more

LOVELAND – At least 56 persons were dead and hundreds injured or trapped on steep slopes and in mud-bound cars late Sunday, after a flash flood swept through 30 miles of canyons Saturday night between Loveland and Estes Park.

… A total of 500 persons were evacuated Sunday from the flood-ravaged area. A group of 42 persons reported stranded at the town of Glen Haven were to be airlifted out of the area late Sunday or early Monday, the state patrol said.

In one of those quirks of infamous journalism, not until the 10th paragraph did the lead story on page 5 name the flooded river.

Survivors told of a surge of water in the Big Thompson River and its north fork that ranged from "a wall six to eight feet tall" to "a steady rise that took everything with it – cars, houses, everything."

The flash flood hit between 8:30 p.m. and 10 p.m. Saturday night following a violent thunderstorm centered in the high country a few miles east of the Continental Divide.

The news wasn't any better in the next day's edition:

Death toll reaches 80

LOVELAND – The death toll from the Big Thompson Canyon flash flood climbed to 80 Monday night as helicopters evacuated the last of the survivors from the devastated 25-mile canyon west of here.

As darkness approached Monday, fog which had blanketed the area all day lifted briefly, allowing pairs of U.S. Army helicopters to fly

along the canyon floor. Within an hour, about 75 persons who had been stranded since the Saturday night flood were plucked from the canyon and returned to Loveland.

Eventually, the Big Thompson flood would be blamed for the deaths of at least 145. According to the Bureau of Reclamation history, only one resident of the canyon possessed flood insurance.

Strange newsfellows

In the same edition that the *Rocky* first reported the Big Thompson flood, it carried another unrelated, but noteworthy story on page 20 under the headline:

FBI heard plan to 'grab' Hoffa, paper says

The legendary union chief had disappeared almost exactly one year before.

DETROIT (AP) – The FBI overheard reputed Mafia figures discussing a plan to "grab" ex-Teamsters boss James R. Hoffa as long ago as 1963, years before the union leader disappeared, the Detroit News said Sunday.

Paper inflation

For more than 100 years, anyone could buy the *Rocky* on the streets of Denver for a nickel. Now, for the second time in less than 20 years, the price of the paper had risen again: it was now 15 cents. □

Farewell to 'The King'

Elvis had left the building for good – we think – and the world was all shook up.

The man whom many credit with breathing life into rock 'n roll music was already a cultural deity by 1977, and when he died suddenly the *Rocky* gave his death page 1 prominence. The paper ran side-by-side photos of Presley, one from his 1968 television special, the other from a recent concert in Lincoln, Nebraska. Only former President Gerald Ford's support of President Jimmy Carter's pending Panama Canal agreement was bigger news.

MEMPHIS, Tenn. (AP) – Elvis Presley, the Mississippi boy whose rock 'n'roll guitar and gyrating hips changed American music styles, died Tuesday afternoon of heart failure. He was 42.

Dr. Jerry Francisco, medical examiner for Shelby County, said the cause of death was "cardiac arythmia," an irregular heartbeat. He said "that's just another name for a form of heart attack."

Francisco said the three-hour autopsy uncovered no other sign of any other disease, and there was no sign of any drug abuse.

... Presley, who had rarely emerged from his mansion grounds in recent years except for performances, had been hospitalized at Baptist (Hospital) in April ... His weight was said to have ballooned from the 175 pounds he weighed as a young man.

The paper ran several sidebars, local and national, inside.

Elvis, who earned millions of dollars from selling his records, making 31 motion pictures and especially Las Vegas shows, made his first appearance in Denver in 1956. He earned $4,000 for two shows that drew 16,000 fans to a sold-out Denver Coliseum. Presley performed in Denver only a handful of times over the next 20 years. When tickets went on sale for a 1973 concert, promoter Robert Garner said more than 30,000 tickets were ordered, although only 11,000 were available.

But more than any song, more than any movie, Presley is remembered in Denver for the legendary habit of giving away Cadillacs to special friends he made during trips to the city.

Remembering Elvis

The *Rocky* was developing a star-studded lineup of columnists in 1977, and a few of them wrote about Elvis' death. The newspaper's own TV columnist, Walter "Dusty" Saunders, recalled Presley's few television appearances. Syndicated columnist Bob Greene covered Elvis' drug addictions and incidents.

On the editorial page, a young Jack Anderson criticized President Ford for botching an oil purchase from Iran and the Soviet Union. In Sports, Jimmy "The Greek" Snyder was giving odds on anything – except Elvis' return. □

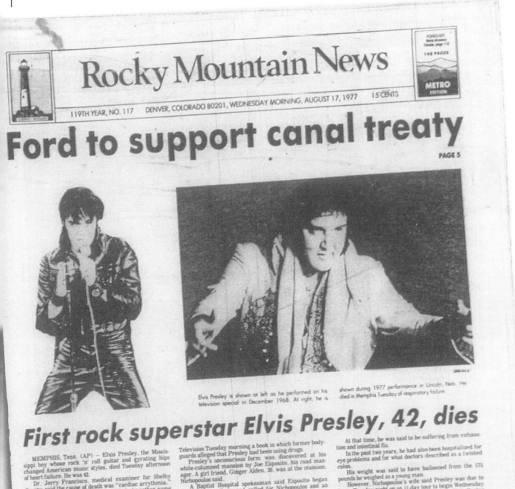

Rise of the 'brown cloud'

It was blamed on hundreds of belching chimneys in the city in 1910.

By 1935, officials pointed to scores of smoldering rubbish dumps.

It was called "smaze" in the late1950s.

A state health department report in 1964 said the problem was hundreds of tons of pollutants spewing from automobile exhaust pipes.

It was infamously known as the "brown cloud" by early 1977.

A few months later, on Nov. 5, 1977, the page 1 banner and story in the *Rocky* stated what many were thinking. And seeing. And smelling.

> The new director of the Environmental Protection Agency Friday termed metropolitan Denver's air pollution "a tragedy."
>
> … (Douglas) Costle told reporters that his flight into Denver for a weekend energy symposium had "a striking impact on my recognition" of Denver's air pollution problem.
>
> As Costle spoke, the city was shrouded in the notorious "brown cloud" – a harmful buildup of carbon monoxide and particulate matter from automobile emissions – common to metropolitan Denver during fall and winter months.
>
> Pollution levels were nearly high enough Friday morning for the Colorado Health Department to declare an alert, in which the elderly and persons with cardiovascular or respiratory ailments are advised to stay indoors.

It would take six years, but on Sept. 4, 1983, the front-page banner – and the air – looked a lot better.

Denver air quality improving

> Air quality in metropolitan Denver is finally improving – thanks to cars that contribute less to carbon monoxide and air pollution, a copyrighted staff story reported.
>
> "It appears to me that the trend is gradually downward, slowly but surely," said Michael Henry, former chairman of the state Air Quality Control Commission. "It may not be happening fast enough, but it's happening."
>
> Although levels of the two invisible, odorless pollutants still violate federal air quality limits, pollution fighters are confident they'll meet the 1987 cleanup deadline for ozone. Whether they make the same deadline for carbon monoxide is harder to tell.

Twelve more years passed before another page 1 headline made it official.

Denver's air healthiest it has been in decades

> Denver's air is relatively clean now, but growth could worsen it again.
>
> The metro area did not violate federal air-quality standards during 1994, the Colorado Department of Public Health and Environment announced Wednesday. That makes 1994 the cleanest air year in more than two decades.

Hazy, smazy days

The same day in 1957 that another Denver health official was lamenting the city's "smaze" problem, the *Rocky* was trying to pump up circulation by blowing some hot air about a story in the next day's Sunday *Parade* magazine.

> Lloyd Shearer, PARADE'S top Hollywood reporter, will tell you how leaders of the movie capital feel about Elvis' future now that his first picture is behind him.

Love Me Tender was the movie. Elvis would eventually try to put 31 motion pictures behind him. □

New Beginnings

Rocky Mountain News

Wellington Webb, with wife Wilma at his side, takes the mayor's oath of office, administered by Colorado Chief Justice Luis D. Rovira.
(Ken Papaleo /Rocky Mountain News)

Wellington Edward Webb became Denver's first black mayor
by literally walking the city. His habit and trademark throughout the campaign
was to don a pair of huge sneakers and knock on every door he came to.

Rocky Mountain News

June 19, 1991

Rocky Mountain News

119TH YEAR, NO. 255   DENVER, COLORADO 80201, MONDAY MORNING, JANUARY 2, 1978   15 CENTS

METRO EDITION

Super Bowl bound!

An Orange Crush coming up! Oakland's Fred Biletnikoff has just caught a pass from Ken Stabler, and Denver's Joe Rizzo is about to apply the crush. Rizzo did it with such vigor that Biletnikoff suffered a shoulder separation. The Raider receiver played no more. DETAILS OF DENVER'S VICTORY BEGIN ON PAGE 64.

NEWS PHOTO BY MEL SCHIELTZ

Broncos play Cowboys next after winning 20-17

By WOODROW PAIGE, JR.
News Staff

SUPER NEW YEAR!

Ring out the old — the Oakland Raiders — and ring in the new — the Denver Broncos.

Denver's Destiny Darlings are headed to the Super Bowl.

On New Year's Day, before 75,000 Broncomaniacs, the Broncos turned a chilly afternoon into the warmest day in Denver history by winning the National Football League's American Conference championship over the Raiders 20-17. Denver earned the right to advance to the NFL's Ultimate Game in New Orleans two weeks hence against the National Conference champions, the Dallas Cowboys.

In the meaningless regular-season final game between the two "Big D's", Dallas prevailed 14-6.

There was dancing in the streets Sunday after the Broncos provided Denver with its most exciting sports moment ever. Horns blared. The masses shouted. Goal posts were torn down and carted off. Sections of the field at Mile High Stadium were ripped up and taken away for souvenirs. People drank like there was no tomorrow and kissed strangers.

It was all the New Year's Eve parties rolled into one. The celebration goes on. Dance to the music of the Broncos.

But the triumph wasn't overwhelming against last year's Super Bowl winner. Only when running back Otis Armstrong & Denver stabbed at right end with just under two minutes remaining to pick up a first down did the Broncos and their followers finally let out an incredible sigh of relief.

The third time was indeed a charm for Denver, which took the first regular-season contest with the Raiders in Oakland then lost the return match in Denver.

The Broncos had not defeated Oakland in Denver since 1962. Repeat: 1962.

(Continued on page 32)

Super day for Colorado

Going to the Super Bowl, this very first time, turned out to be much more exciting for Colorado and its beloved Broncos than playing in it.

After 18 years – first as an American Football League stepchild, then a National Football League afterthought – the Broncos finally made Denver and Colorado feel like they were big-time.

The *Rocky* made it a tradition, unspoken and unplanned, to feature the Broncos on page 1 on most Mondays after games. Unless war or pestilence broke out. On Jan. 2, 1978, the football team really was a front-page story. The Broncos had beaten The Hated Raiders and were going to play America's team, the Dallas Cowboys, in Denver's first championship game.

The page 1 story began in cheerleader fashion:

SUPER NEW YEAR!
Ring out the old – the Oakland Raiders – and ring in the new – the Denver Broncos.
Denver's Destiny Darlings are headed to the Super Bowl.
On New Year's Day, before 75,000 Broncomaniacs, the Broncos turned a chilly afternoon into the warmest day in Denver history by winning the National Football League's American Conference championship over the Raiders 20-17.
... There was dancing in the streets Sunday after the Broncos provided Denver with its most exciting sports moment ever.

Even the cliché-filled sports writing was acceptable on this day. Broncomania truly had been born.

Inside, there was only one story in the local news section – a reaction story that ran with a photo of Mercy Medical Center nurses who had dyed two newborn babies' blankets orange and printed "Go Broncos" in blue on each. The Sports section provided five pages of coverage – puny today for even preseason games.

The next day there were zero stories in local news. Broncos fans learned that the team had been allotted 10,000

Jack Foster and the Zook building.
(Carl Iwasaki/LIFE Magazine/Rocky Mountain News)

tickets for the Super Bowl back in the Sports section.

By Wednesday, Jan. 4, the newspaper *got it.* Over a page 1 photo of a fan camped first in line overnight outside Super Bowl ticket windows, the banner headline read:

Bronco holiday declared

In a move that provoked a storm of public criticism, more than 65,000 state and city employees have been given a paid holiday on Friday – compliments of Gov. Dick Lamm – to celebrate the success of the Super Bowl-bound Denver Broncos.

A crowd estimated at 100,000 lined downtown streets to send off the team to New Orleans for the game. The orange-clad fans may not have even noticed the day's bummer banner story:

Market hits two-year low

The Broncos lost to Dallas 27-10. The paper gave the game nine pages of coverage, including page 1.

It certainly would have consoled Colorado to know that it would have five more trips to the Super Bowl in future years to get it right.

The passing of giants

The *Rocky* gave page 1 treatment to the deaths of two much-respected men in the week before the Super Bowl – Sen. Hubert Humphrey, a former vice president, and Jack Foster, the scrappy editor who rescued the newspaper in the 1940s and led it into its tabloid golden years.

One photo of Foster showed the fedora-topped editor sitting on the roof of the *Rocky's* old offices on West Colfax Avenue with the Zook Building over his shoulder. In 2007 the Zook was converted into million-dollar lofts, but in 1952 it had a three-story-tall whiskey bottle as an advertisement perched on its roof. Foster successfully campaigned to have the bottle removed because, he said, it cheapened the view of the mountains from his office. *Life* magazine took the photo. □

DCPA's mixed debut

The Denver Center for the Performing Arts did for music and theater what Apollo 11 did for moonwalking. It elevated the arts in Colorado's capitol to a place it had not been before.

The complex at 14th and Curtis streets, after six years of controversy and political brawling before its opening, immediately became the city's cultural sun.

Despite the unfortunate juxtaposition of page 1 headlines on Feb. 27, 1978, the day after the debut of one of the DCPA centerpieces, the *Rocky* hardly regarded it as a train wreck.

The first symphony concert in the unfinished Boettcher Concert Hall was a success Sunday with members of the audience remarking on the exquisite clarity of the sound.

The concert by the Denver Symphony Orchestra was dedicated to the "hard hats" who have spent more than 300,000 hours since October, 1975 constructing the $13 million circular hall, first in the country with the orchestra placed near the center and the audience close to the stage.

But following the hall's official opening one week later, the newspaper noted on March 5 that a few ears were feeling strained.

The question most asked in the audience at the Saturday night opening of the Boettcher Concert Hall was, "What do you think of the acoustics?"

The Denver Symphony Orchestra's new $13 million home seemed to receive a largely positive response from concertgoers. They seemed especially pleased during the orchestra's second piece, Tchaikovsky's Piano Concerto No.1 with Van Cliburn as the soloist.

However, there were a few complaints that voices – both from the speakers at the opening ceremonies and from the chorus during the initial selection, Williams' Serenade to Music – were difficult to hear.

Despite the overall success of the new DCPA, the strains of discontent grew louder.

Rocky Mountain News

67 persons hospitalized

Two more train wrecks spill toxic cargoes; 8 persons die

Chlorine gas, lye fumes released

Concert hall's opening

Members of the audience take some fresh air during intermission Sunday at the new Boettcher Concert Hall. It was the first symphony concert in the $13 million hall and was dedicated to the "hard hats" who built the facility. STORY ON PAGE 6.

Israelis won't change new settlement policy

Jimmy Connors wins tennis title

Amole's Corner

Gene Amole was the *Rocky's* longtime local columnist, resident expert of everything Denver and, unfortunately for the DCPA, a respected classical music aficionado. "Geno," as he was known in the newsroom, waited nearly two weeks after Boettcher's opening before he finally spoke up in "Amole's Corner" on March 9:

The new DCPA Boettcher Concert Hall does have some drawbacks, despite all the rave notices.

Solo singers can't be heard too well from those seats behind the orchestra. Choruses seem to come off better, though. Also difficult to hear was the harpsichord in Bach's Fourth Brandenburg Concerto.

… Worst of all, though, are the front seats. They are too high. Spectators under 5'8" will find that their feet won't touch the floor. Legs just dangle. Without some kind of foot support, the old rear end can get pretty numb, particularly during Mahler.

A mighty voice

The day of the Boettcher opening, the *Rocky* reported on page 5 the death of Gen. "Chappie" James.

Daniel "Chappie" James Jr., a controversial figure who became the first and only black four-star general in the U.S. armed forces, died at the Air Force Academy Hospital early Saturday morning.

James, 58, had commanded the North American Air Defense Command (NORAD), the joint U.S.-Canadian air defense system, and the U.S. Air Force Aerospace Defense Command, both headquartered in Colorado Springs. But as the story noted, James was much more than silver stars and ribbons.

As a young officer during World War II, James risked a possible court-martial to protest segregation in the armed forces.

He remained an articulate spokesman for black rights throughout his career. But he was a strong critic of black militants during the '60s. ☐

For 444 days, U.S. held hostage

The hand-drawn image on page 1 of the *Rocky* Jan 21, 1981, was of a gaily furled – presumably yellow – ribbon. Except the paper still didn't yet print daily color on the front page. But readers knew what the now familiar shape symbolized.

After 444 days, the hostages from the American Embassy in Tehran were coming home.

Next to the ribbon, the old-fashioned, overlay-box photo held even more good news – Marine Sgt. Billy Gallegos, of Pueblo, was among them. The United Press International story:

> RHEIN-MAIN AIR BASE, West Germany – Exhausted but unbowed, the 52 Americans who survived 444 days of Iranian captivity returned to American surroundings before sunrise Wednesday near the end of one of the most dramatic chapters in U.S. history.
>
> Twelve hours and 20 minutes after Islamic Revolutionary Guards jeered them out of Tehran with chants of "Down with America," and 4,055 miles after a final cruel twist of the knife kept them prisoners until Ronald Reagan became president of the United States, the two women and 50 men came back to something like home.
>
> … Wearing yellow ribbons in their hair, Elizabeth Ann Swift and Kathryn Koob, the two women among the hostages, were the first to step off the red and white jet, into the glare of television lights and the cheering applause of diplomats and reporters.

Yellow ribbons, of course, had become a symbol that America had not forgotten the hostages since they were taken by a mob of Iranian students on Nov. 4, 1979. That was a Sunday, and in Denver the story was the *Rocky's* front-page banner, although it had to compete with a photo of the Broncos' win over New Orleans.

The "twist of the knife" in the UPI story referred to the last-minute transfer of unfrozen Iranian funds from the U.S. to Iran, and the transfer of the presidency from Jimmy Carter to Reagan. An escrow account to temporarily hold the funds in England had not yet been set up, and Iran would not allow the plane to take off until the transaction was completed.

Reagan's inauguration as 40th president was reported the same day on the front page beneath the yellow-ribbon banner.

Hometown hero

Two *Rocky* reporters, David Freed and John Baron, were at the Pueblo home of Billy Gallegos' parents, Dick and Theresa, the morning of his release. As they reported:

> "They're out! They're out, baby," Dick Gallegos shouted jubilantly as he hung up the phone over which a State Department spokesman had just told him that Billy and the 51 other American hostages had been freed and were airborne from Tehran to Algiers.

The *Rocky* reporter sent to Wiesbaden to meet Billy Gallegos really wasn't a reporter. David L. Cornwell was a staff photographer, but he also filed stories from West Germany.

More yellow ribbons

Less than four years later, Thomas Sutherland was dragged from the limousine he was using as dean of agriculture at American University in Beirut, Lebanon. The Colorado State University professor was among more than 100 foreign hostages taken by the Islamic Jihad over a 10-year period. It's believed the terrorists were really hunting the university president who loaned Sutherland use of the limo. Iran and Syria were widely suspected of playing a major role in the kidnappings.

Sutherland was held hostage 2,354 days, second-longest after Terry Anderson, chief Middle East correspondent for the Associated Press. Sutherland eventually won a $353 million verdict in a lawsuit against Iran's frozen assets. □

Rocky Mountain News

208 PAGES

METRO EDITION

122ND YEAR, NO. 274   DENVER, COLORADO 80201, WEDNESDAY MORNING, JAN. 21, 1981   15 CENTS

Day 444 – freedom

PAGE 3

HAPPY DAY
The families and friends of 52 Americans find much to be happy about Tuesday as the hostages finally are free of their Iranian captors. And in Plains, Ga., it's a happy homecoming for former President Jimmy Carter, who will greet those Americans Wednesday in West Germany.

CELEBRATE!
Church bells ring, sirens wail, yellow ribbons are tied and a nation rejoices as the hostage crisis becomes history. The financial dealings that resulted in freedom for the hostage were incredibly complex and incredibly huge.

Several of the 52 freed Americans, including Marine Sgt. Billy Gallegos, of Pueblo, Colo., second from top, arrive about

Outbreak of twisters

It wasn't as if Denver hadn't seen a tornado before. It was just particularly unnerving when they dropped out of the sky onto Main Streets across the metro area one summer afternoon. It was the worst tornadic weather in memory, the *Rocky* reported in the next day's editions.

Numerous tornadoes touched down in the Denver area Wednesday afternoon, injuring about 45 people and causing extensive damage.

The lead reporter was the intrepid Al Nakkula, on the big story again, with numerous staffers contributing.

There were up to 50 sightings of funnel clouds in the metropolitan area, with fewer than a dozen that actually touched the ground.

... At least one storm-related death was reported. Mary McCarthy, 21, of Wharton, N.J., was killed when lightning sheared through a tree under which she and two companions sought refuge from a hailstorm about 1 p.m. while hiking near Red Rock Lake west of Ward.

Sue O'Brien, press secretary to Gov. Richard D. Lamm ... said Lamm had activated 100 military policemen in the Colorado National Guard to patrol stricken areas on foot and in jeeps to prevent looting. A dozen state patrolmen also were designated for traffic control duty.

National Weather Service forecasters said they couldn't recall a storm in Denver that matched Wednesday's series of tornadoes and funnel clouds.

"We can't see anything in the past that matches this. This is definitely the strongest in recent years. They could see this storm on radar in Salt Lake City," 500 miles west of Denver, said forecaster Tom Schwein. "Normally, about 125 miles is the range to see a thunderstorm on radar."

Tornadoes struck in Denver at West Fifth Avenue and Sheridan Boulevard, Thornton, Northglenn Shopping Center, Lakewood, near Sloans Lake, at Cherry Creek Reservoir and many other metro residential areas.

The immediate toll of damage: 16 single-family homes destroyed, 56 single-family homes with major damage, 28 apartments with major damage, 224 single-family homes with minor damage, 57 apartments with minor damage and 12 small businesses with minor damage.

Lamm requested that the U.S. Small Business Administration designate Adams, Denver, Jefferson and Weld counties as disaster areas.

Destructive decade

The '81 Denver tornadoes marked the beginning of a decade that seemed to spawn the weather monsters up and down the Front Range. Other episodes:

- May 29, 1981 – A tornado touched down three miles north of Stapleton International Airport, and lightning killed a woman in Aurora.
- July 6, 1984 – Five houses are damaged when a tornado hit an Aurora subdivision.
- July 19, 1985 – 10 homes in Douglas County damaged.
- June 8, 1986 – Three tornadoes injured six people and sheared off roofs in Aurora.
- Oct. 18, 1986 – Near New Raymer, a tornado damaged a farm and several outbuildings in eastern Weld County.
- May 13, 1987 – Tornadoes touched down twice in southeast Denver, damaging an apartment complex.
- June 18, 1987 – A tornado blew down about 200 trees in Roosevelt National Forest and damaged a Colorado State University retreat in Larimer County.
- April 21, 1988 – An Adams County girl is killed by lightning caused by thunderstorms and a small tornado.
- June 5, 1988 – Tornadoes with winds up to 157 mph touched down in Denver and Adams County, ripping roofs off houses.
- June 13, 1988 – Several homes in the community of Proctor suffered $100,000 in damage from a tornado.

Rocky Mountain News

METRO EDITION

123rd year, No. 43   Denver, Colorado 80204   **Thursday**   June 4, 1981   15 cents

Tornadoes rake Denver

45 are injured; damage heavy

By AL NAKKULA
News Staff

Oil shale project crumbles

Readers opening the *Rocky* on Monday morning, May 3, 1982, naturally assumed the bad news was at the top of the front page – England's war with Argentina over the Falkland Islands was escalating. Then they read the bottom of the page.

Exxon pulls plug on Colony shale project

Exxon Co. USA, one of the world's oil giants, announced Sunday that it will abandon the Colony shale oil project in Western Colorado, a move that cripples the state's shale industry.

Sandy Graham was the *Rocky's* Energy/Science Writer. The boom in energy exploration and development in the state had justified the paper designating an energy specialist.

Officials, including Colorado Gov. Richard D. Lamm, estimated that as many as 10,000 potential jobs would be lost as a result.

... Exxon said it hasn't decided what to do with the 8,800-acre property. The project employs 2,100 people, most of them in Colorado. The project will be shut down in "an orderly manner," the company said.

It became known as Black Sunday. Workers, most of whom lived in Parachute, Rifle and the company town of Battlement Mesa, were given no warning. When some tried to report to work at Colony on Monday, they were turned away.

Only months earlier, two federal oil shale leases, Cathedral Bluffs and Rio Blanco, laid off most of their workers. That left only Union Oil's Parachute Creek as the sole surviving oil shale project. Exxon eventually abandoned what was estimated as a $1 billion investment.

The Colony failure sent tremors across the state. City Market, the grocery chain, ceased work on a 55,000-square-foot "super store" that it had planned to open in Battlement Mesa in September. Contractors from Denver hoping to bid on school and office construction tabled their plans, and banks wondered what to do with their Battlement Mesa charters.

Colorado had dreamed of a cost-effective method of cooking the oil out of the rocks on its Western Slope since

1915. Most recently, with the overthrow of the Shah of Iran, it appeared the rising cost of crude oil made the timing right for major oil shale projects. But in 1981, a sudden world oil glut doomed the Colony plant.

Union Oil, or Unocal, continued to develop Parachute Creek into the late 1980s. Iraq's invasion of Kuwait in 1990 once again raised hopes for oil shale, but the allies' swift victory dashed them.

On March 27, 1991, oil shale was in the *Rocky* again with this headline:

Unocal closes oil shale plant in Parachute

The story seemed to be the death knell for oil shale development in Colorado.

But the latest Gulf War and, for a time, the highest prices for crude oil around the world in history, have investors eyeing oil shale yet again.

Pain at the pump

Black Sunday added to Colorado's growing unease with higher gasoline prices. The cost in 1982, as the *Rocky* reported, was much lower than today, but the tone of concern was just as high.

American motorists could see gas price hikes of 3 to 4 cents a gallon at the pump by as early as mid-May because of the first wholesale price increases to be imposed in more than a year.

... The average U.S. pump price had dropped by 20-cents a gallon in mid-April from an all-time high of $1.38 in March 1981.

More strange newsfellows

On the same day – on the same page – that the *Rocky* reported Unocal shuttering Parachute Creek, its Business section updated another bust:

The bankruptcy trustee liquidating Blinder, Robinson Inc., the huge Englewood-based penny stock brokerage, clocked nearly $1 million in legal fees in his first three months of work.

Meyer Blinder built the brokerage into a nationwide firm in the 1970s and '80s. But after a lengthy federal investigation he was sentenced to four years in prison. □

Snowstorm piles it on

Colorado has long brandished a personal pride in its winter challenges and its ability to weather them. The morning after Christmas, 1982, it had a lot to be proud of.

The state has had worse snowstorms – before and since. But no other one seems to have deposited memories as deep as snowdrifts, or caused those who shoveled through it to nearly whistle in awe when they echo the *Rocky's* Sunday headline:

BLIZZARD OF '82
City begins digging out

Denver began digging itself out Saturday from a record-breaking blizzard that stranded thousands of holiday travelers, brought traffic to a standstill and spoiled Christmas weekend festivities for 1.6 million metropolitan area residents.

The snowstorm – the city's worst in 69 years – left Denver and its suburbs buried under 2 to 3 feet of snow Christmas Day before moving into Nebraska early Saturday.

At least one death was attributed to the blizzard, that of an unidentified man who apparently walked away from his crippled 4-wheel-drive vehicle and froze to death in a field near Bennett, east of Denver.

The newspaper paid homage to the 1913 storm that dropped 47.5 inches of snow in five days, compared with 24 inches in 24 hours that slammed the area starting Friday. A half-page graphic charted the impressive snow depths around the metro area: Wondervu 42 inches, Wheat Ridge 35, Golden 34, Thornton 32, Conifer 31. Pueblo received little more than one inch.

Within a couple days, five deaths had been attributed to the storm.

For the first time in the history of both newspapers, the *Rocky* and *The Denver Post* called off publication of their Saturday papers. The *Rocky* estimated it was able to deliver only 55 percent of its Sunday papers because of the snow-choked streets.

The impact of the storm on Denver, though, was far from over. It took the city five days before it began to effectively clear city streets.

"The people who think I can make it snow also think I can take it away," Mayor Bill McNichols was quoted by the *Rocky* in the face of mounting criticism. "I can't do either."

Nevertheless, city residents never forgave McNichols for the wimpy response. A year later, they voted to give his job to Federico Peña.

A ton of reading

In 1982, the *Rocky* still employed "paper boys" – and girls – to deliver the paper. Carrying the Sunday "Blizzard" paper would have been a monumental task even without the snow – it was 460 pages including advertising inserts. The main news section was 200 pages.

Inside, the paper included a 14-page Business section, 56 pages of features and entertainment, a 48-page TV Dial and 12 pages of full-color comics. On the Monday after the blizzard, the new SportsPLUS section totaled 28 pages.

A new newspaper war

"*The Rocky,*" as the paper had been affectionately called for decades by fans and critics alike, was riding a resurgence. After years of trailing its rival in circulation, in early 1980 it passed *The Post* in weekday deliveries for the first time in memory, printing nearly 316,000 papers. By 1983, under the leadership of editor Ralph Looney and general manager William "Bill" Fletcher, it would wrench away the all-important Sunday lead as well with nearly 356,000 circulation.

But the latest newspaper war in the sizzling Denver market had only just begun. □

Rocky Mountain News
Weather
Warmer
Page 199
460 PAGES

SUNDAY — Sunday, December 26, 1982 — 50c

t year, No. 248   Denver, Colorado 80204

BLIZZARD OF '82

People helping people made the blizzard a little more bearable, as one unhappy motorist stuck in the snow on East 16th Avenue found out.

City begins digging out

Fighting epidemic, panic

Acquired immune deficiency syndrome, or AIDS, appeared on Colorado's radar when the first case was reported in the state in 1982. It didn't show up on the *Rocky's* front page until Oct. 20, 1985.

While the banner headline might seem alarming today, little was known about the disease 20 years ago, and the purpose of the two-day series was as much to educate as it was to alleviate the growing stigma. The headline over the story inside by Joseph Verrengia:

Maze of myths traps hapless victims

Combine the astonishing mortality of AIDS with the mysterious nature of its victims and you get what public health officials dread: a prescription for panic.

"The myths surrounding the disease are just abominable," says Dr. David Cohn, assistant director of the Denver Center for Disease Control and one of America's leading researchers of acquired immune deficiency syndrome.

"Clearly, we're in the middle of an epidemic, and the ramifications are unprecedented," Cohn says. "But lets keep things in perspective. You don't have to worry about the hot tub or the communion chalice."

More and more, the newspaper was assigning specialties to reporters. Pamela Avery was the paper's medical writer and as part of the series, she contributed a story about how AIDS had become the nation's No. 1 public health crisis. Reported Avery:

The disease is among the most deadly known to humanity. Of the 14,125 AIDS cases reported nationwide as of mid-October, more than half have resulted in death.

Following the trend in journalism of breaking down stories and subjects into shorter, more easily read chunks, the series presented an "AIDS Q&A" of basic questions and helpful answers.

Less than a year later, AIDS was on page 1 again in a troubling national story. The banner headline on June 20, 1986:

Blood passed test, but 2 get AIDS

In what researchers say is the first such incident in the nation, two Colorado men have been exposed to the AIDS virus from a blood donor who tested negative for the fatal disease.

(The two men) were innocent victims of an unusual set of circumstances. They were infected by transfusions last summer during surgery. Both received blood from the same donor, who had given blood so soon after he was infected that he hadn't developed AIDS virus antibodies – "fingerprints" of exposure that can be detected in blood tests.

National AIDS cases were now up to 21,000.

One year later, the *Rocky* reported that Denver was one of 30 major U.S. cities chosen to take part in the first survey to estimate the number of people carrying the AIDS virus. Denver ranked 19th highest in the nation in number of AIDS cases with 409.

Nationally, the number of cases had more than doubled to over 45,000. ☐

Rocky Mountain News

DENVER, COLORADO
© Tuesday, January 28, 1986

EXTRA

25¢

SHUTTLE EXPLODES

All 7 in Challenger crew die after liftoff

ASSOCIATED PRESS

The fireball that signaled disaster for shuttle mission 51-L occurred only 1 minute, 15 seconds after liftoff from Kennedy Space Center. NASA officials said there were no apparent problems at the time.

From hope to horror

The explosion of the space shuttle Challenger and death of its entire crew of seven stunned America and the world all the more because we all witnessed it on live television, or hurried to screens when we heard the news. There we found replay after replay, but no definitive reasons for the accident.

The shuttle blew apart at 9:39 a.m. Mountain time on Jan. 28, 1986, the very beginning of the news day for newspapers. With the *Rocky* and *The Denver Post* locked in the latest battle for circulation, the *Rocky* reacted as both messenger and opportunist.

Within three hours of the tragedy, it published an eight-page "Extra" edition, wrapped around the already-printed morning paper, that it could sell on the streets of Denver and count as daily circulation.

The "Extra" included details of the liftoff and explosion and the first theories about possible causes. Eight of the 15 stories in the section were written by *Rocky* staff members, including an eye-witness account by reporter Charlie Brennan, who was at Kennedy Space Center in Florida to cover local angles about the flight. Martin Marietta, the Denver aerospace company, built the huge orange fuel cells attached to the shuttle. And one crew member, Ellison Onizuka, was a graduate of the University of Colorado's aerospace engineering program.

The first wire service report:

> CAPE CANAVERAL, Fla. – The space shuttle Challenger blew up in a huge fireball 75 seconds after blastoff this morning and hurtled into the Atlantic Ocean. The crew of seven, including teacher Christa McAuliffe, was feared killed.
>
> … There was no announcement of the fate of the crew but it appeared there was no way they could survive. No American astronaut has ever been killed in a flight.
>
> The explosion occurred while two powerful booster rockets were attached to the shuttle. There was no way for the crew to escape the out-of-control spacecraft, which fell into the ocean eight miles off the coast.

The shuttle explosion was still the paper's main story the morning after the "Extra" edition, beneath a page 1 headline that quoted President Ronald Reagan:

**'We've never had
a tragedy like this'**

The teacher-astronaut

Christa McAuliffe was the first civilian to serve as an astronaut. The mission of the 37-year-old social studies teacher, who was chosen from more than 11,000 applicants, was to bring the space program into classrooms across the country.

One of the other stories Brennan was following during the liftout was attendance by a group of six Boulder

University of Colorado graduate Ellison Onizuka speaks at a press conference along with the rest of the Challenger crew. Christa McAuliffe is next in line.

County schoolchildren and their teacher. In a flash of flame and smoke, his story changed. Brennan wrote in his "Extra" story:

> It was the children's teachers who shed tears, perhaps feeling a special pain at seeing one of their own perish before their eyes in the clear blue Florida sky,
>
> "I just want to hold you, Phillip," a weeping Bill Dennler said to fourth-grade Phillip Boothby.

Dennler was a teacher, and Phillip a student at Boulder's Foothill Elementary School.

The 'Extra'

The special edition was the *Rocky's* first in 41 years, since "VJ Day" in 1945, when Japan surrendered to end World War II.

The day after the shuttle exploded, the paper announced it had published more than 60,000 copies that were available in news racks across the metro area by mid-afternoon. □

Bowing out of presidential race

It was another page out of the *Rocky's* circulation strategy book that made it official Gary Hart would not be president of the United States.

On May 8, 1987, when the former Colorado senator took himself out of competition for the Democratic presidential nomination, the newspaper reported it first in its "Stock Final" edition, an afternoon reprinting of its morning edition with fresh news and closing stocks – again, so it could count the papers in paid circulation.

Hart, 50, withdrew after *The Miami Herald* reported that he was having an affair with 29-year-old actress-model Donna Rice.

A defiant, unapologetic Gary Hart reluctantly took himself out of the presidential race yesterday with a final blast at the news media and a demand that the presidential primary system be changed.

The *Rocky's* political writer, Peter Blake, wrote the story.

Hart actually did withdraw on May 8. The "yesterday" reference was because Blake's story was also written to run in the next morning's edition, May 9, and the story wasn't edited for two different issues.

But for a brief moment at the beginning of the 11-minute speech, it looked as though he had changed his mind and was going to make a liar out of every newspaper and television station that had predicted his retreat.

"I intended, quite frankly, to come down here this morning and read a short, carefully worded statement saying that I was withdrawing from the race, and then quietly disappear from the stage," began Hart, who has spent the week looking at headlines suggesting he was engaged in an affair with Miami actress and model Donna Rice.

"And then, after, frankly, tossing and turning all night, as I have for the last three or four nights, I woke up about 4 or so this morning with a start. And I said to myself, 'Hell, no.'"

But withdraw, Hart did. He just didn't do it with any apology. As Blake's story went on:

Hart said the nation should "seriously question the system for selecting our national leaders, that reduces the press of this nation to hunters and presidential candidates to being hunted …

"I've made some mistakes," he said in the closest thing to an apology. "I've said so. I said I would because I'm human, and I did. Maybe big mistakes, but not bad mistakes."

Virtually the same story would run May 9, following the page 1 banner headline:

**Hart exits with blast
at media and system**

More strange newsfellows

Gary Hart wasn't the only national figure backing away from the bright lights in May of 1987. The day before *The Miami Herald* reported Hart's tryst, the *Rocky* carried Jim Bakker's first public appearance with wife Tammy since he gave up leadership of the PTL evangelical empire after a sexual scandal the previous March.

PALM SPRINGS, Calif. (AP) – Disgraced television evangelist Jim Bakker said yesterday that he and his wife won't fight to regain leadership of the $129 million PTL empire and that "without a miracle of God, we will never minister again."

"Tammy and I are alive. We may not be too well," Bakker said.

"Barely," Tammy Bakker tearfully interjected at the brief meeting with reporters outside their home here. □

Stapleton's worst crash

Continental Flight 1713 roared down runway 35L at Stapleton International Airport the afternoon of Nov. 15, 1987. At the same time, one of Colorado's fickle fall snowstorms bore down on the Denver metro area from the north. At least one result of the collision of weather and aircraft was the crash of the DC-9 in what became the worst accident in Stapleton's 65-year history. The *Rocky's* story:

> At least 26 people were killed when a Continental Airlines DC-9 carrying 82 passengers and crew crashed on takeoff during a snowstorm at Stapleton International Airport yesterday afternoon.
>
> … Rescue workers described the scene as "carnage" as they battled below-freezing temperatures and blowing snow to reach passengers trapped in the crumpled fuselage.
>
> Rescue work was complicated because the plane was upside down after it crashed, leaving many passengers hanging in their seats.

The paper's report the next day covered seven pages. The storm left 6 to 9 inches of snow in the metro area.

Eventually, 28 would die from crash injuries.

'It's a miracle'

As with so many other air disasters, victims and survivors of Flight 1713 seemed determined by pure chance.

"It's a miracle that so many people survived," Continental president Frank Lorenzo would later be quoted in the *Rocky*.

Two of the lucky ones were Debi Paschkov and her 6-year-old daughter, Melissa, who were seated near the left wing on the plane headed for Boise. The morning after the crash, the paper reported just how lucky they had been.

> "I remember the plane slipping, and I thought, 'Maybe they'll get it back to normal.' But people started screaming, and that's when the plane flipped," Debi Paschkov said.
>
> … Melissa was strapped in her window seat, hanging upside down and screaming, her mother said.
>
> Paschkov unbuckled her daughter's belt and her own, and then pushed Melissa through "a little tiny hole" between the seat and the floor.

The Alan Berg case

Three days after the crash of Flight 1713, the *Rocky* reported the final chapter in one of Denver's strangest murder cases.

2 guilty, 2 cleared in Berg case

A federal jury yesterday convicted two white supremacists and cleared two others of civil rights violations in the slaying of Denver radio host Alan Berg.

Bruce Pierce, accused of killing Berg outside his Denver town house with a MAC-10 machine gun, and David Lane, accused of driving the getaway car, were found guilty of violating Berg's civil rights by killing him because he was Jewish and employed as a talk-show host on KOA radio.

The case fully exposed Denver to a host of social factors that the city and world around it would be dealing with for decades to come – the phenomena of talk radio itself, the reality of white supremacist organizations, and the plague of hate crimes. □

Rocky Mountain News

129th year, No. 208   DENVER, COLORADO   **MONDAY**   ©NOVEMBER 16, 1987   25 cents

26 die in crash
Jet with 82 aboard flips at Stapleton

Rescuers free passengers from a Continental Airlines jet that overturned while taking off from Stapleton International Airport yesterday. Five crew members and 77 passengers were aboard the DC-9, which was bound for Boise, Idaho. The flight had originated in Oklahoma City. Blowing snow and below-freezing temperatures hampered rescue efforts, and some bodies and survivors remained trapped for several hours after the crash.

CRASH AT STAPLETON

The fall of The Wall

The *Rocky* as well as *The Denver Post* had grown circulation enough to rank among the top 20 largest newspapers in the nation. Still, the *Rocky* has always considered itself a "local" paper. At no time was that connection with its readers more evident or more important than when historic changes swept eastern Europe in the late 1980s and early 1990s.

The page 1 headline on Nov. 10, 1989, spoke of upheaval. The story on page 2 told of unbridled joy.

BERLIN (AP) – East Germany opened the Berlin Wall and its other borders yesterday, and its cheering citizens crossed freely to the West for the first time since 1961. Hundreds of people danced on the wall.

Also yesterday, Egon Krenz, East Germany's new leader, advocated a law that would ensure free and democratic elections in his communist nation, which has been disrupted by pro-reform demonstrations and weakened by mass flight to the West.

… Near Brandenburg Gate, East Germans raced through streams of police water cannon and were pulled up the wall by the young West Germans atop it. Some Germans used hammers to chip away at the barrier for keepsakes or in their own small way try to destroy the infamous symbol of East-West division.

The first day after the momentous change the *Rocky* scrambled to provide analysis of what the fall of the wall meant, and stories that connected its Colorado readers. It ran five pages of coverage.

Sidebars told the story of an Arapahoe High School teacher who immigrated with her parents from East Germany when she was 13. Local political science experts were sought out for their predictions about the chances for a reunified Germany.

The second day the paper devoted nearly the entire front page and five more pages inside to a "Special Report" on Germany's upheaval. The page 1 banner:

**All Berlin revels
in historic reunion**

There were more staff-written stories about an Aurora woman who risked crossing a mine field with her mother to flee East Germany in 1948. And the Regis College professor who as a tour guide was slapped in the face at the East German border and held and interrogated.

By the next edition, a Sunday, the full import of the political shift became clearer. The *Rocky* pushed a special local business package down on page 1 to make room for another banner from Germany:

**Germans join hands in joy
1 million pour across border to sing, cry, laugh**

BERLIN (AP) – It was a day like no other. More than 1 million people poured across borders from East to West yesterday and all Germans were the same for the first time in 40 years – embracing, laughing, singing and crying together.

Sound familiar?

The special business package that the paper shifted for the news from Germany showed the early cracks in one of America's own fundamental institutions. The headline on it that Sunday in 1989:

**A HOUSE OF CARDS
Denver's foreclosure fallout:
Only now is the real
impact being grasped.
Deep scars will linger for
years to come as
homeowners, neighborhoods
and businesses struggle
to cope.** □

City of invention
Innovations both famous, infamous born in Denver
Page 70

Rocky Mountain News

DENVER, COLORADO • 131st year, No. 202   **FRIDAY**   November 10, 1989 • 25¢

Egon Krenz
New East German leader

The Wall comes tumbling down

■ E. Germany opens border; citizens cheer new freedom/**2**   ■ Leaders in East, West hail quickening pace of reform/**54**

Beating triggers into plowshares

The end of plutonium processing and the dismantling of the Rocky Flats weapons plant northwest of Denver would close the chapter on one of Colorado's most controversial patches of land in history.

The *Rocky's* story on Nov. 30, 1989:

Plutonium processing at the Rocky Flats nuclear weapons plant has been temporarily shut down amid allegations of chronic safety problems, federal officials announced last night.

David Simonson, the plant manager for the Department of Energy, said in a statement that "a major curtailment of plutonium operations" began Nov. 13 and will continue through January.

But the 10-square-mile plant, which built triggers for hydrogen bombs, would never resume full operation. It was placed on the nation's list of "superfund" sites, and by the turn of the century the entrances which once were the targets of anti-war demonstrations were re-landscaped and ceased to exist.

Rocky Flats left a trail of ugly headlines behind it:

(April 30, 1978) **5,000 congregate for Rocky Flats protest**

(Feb. 15, 1975) **Rocky Flats disaster plan unproven**

(Dec. 12, 1970) **Rocky Flats denies radiation danger**

(May 13, 1969) **Radioactive Blaze Fells 1 Fireman**

The fire occurred on a Sunday and took firefighters six hours to control but wasn't reported in the *Rocky* for two days. Even then, the story ran under a one-column headline on page 5 without a byline:

A fireman at the Dow Chemical Co. Rocky Flats plant is being treated for exposure to radioactivity following Sunday's fire at the weapons-making facility.

… Contamination was confined to the area immediately surrounding the fire, the spokesman said. Monitoring teams found no health hazards at air sampling stations located outside the plant.

… Officials said the building and equipment is valued at $18 million and that nearly 40 per cent of the first floor of the building is destroyed.

Cleanup costs for the fire exceeded $48 million – $3 million more than it cost to build the facility in 1951, according to *Colorado: A History of the Centennial State*. Eventually, once the plant was closed, the final cleanup would cost billions of dollars. Former workers at the plant and nearby landowners who sued the operators for damages are still settling claims and seeking reparations today.

Locker room change

By 1989, when Rocky Flats operations were curtailed, the *Rocky* had introduced one of the few women sports columnists in the country at the time, Teri Thompson ☐

Hubbub over Hubble

On April 25, 1990, the day after the Hubble telescope was launched into space, the *Rocky* called the ultra-sophisticated engineering marvel the world's "window to the stars." Joseph Verrengia, now the paper's science writer, reported from Florida:

> CAPE CANAVERAL – The $2 billion Hubble Space Telescope finally is ready to take its front-row seat in the heavens this morning following a thunderous launch yesterday aboard the space shuttle Discovery.

The *Rocky* made itself and Verrengia experts on the aerospace industry. After all, the company that built Hubble's spectrographic equipment and the shuttle rockets that lifted it into space, Martin Marietta, was based in the red-rock canyons southwest of Denver.

> … Within seven minutes, the shuttle approached its deployment altitude of 380 miles – the highest orbit ever reached in 35 shuttle missions.
>
> From that dizzying perch, Hubble is expected to revolutionize our knowledge of the universe.

Hubble's mission, in essence, was to photograph the universe. Space telescopes had been proposed as early as the 1940s. What made Hubble infinitely superior to earlier designs was that its high orbit virtually eliminated background light, and combined with its imaging capability made it possible to capture extremely sharp images.

Initially, there was just one hitch. Scientists discovered that the telescope's primary mirror had been ground incorrectly. Early images were fuzzy, as if out of focus. However, there was one other difference between Hubble and other space telescopes – it is the only one so far designed to be serviced in space by astronauts. Two years later, Hubble's imaging flaw was corrected.

Finally, the first improved images were transmitted and they immediately justified Hubble's lofty price tag. Already, it has helped resolve several long-standing astronomy issues. Hubble has helped refine estimates of the age of the universe. It returned truly science fiction-looking images, such as the gassy "pillars of creation," where stars are formed in nebula. And in 1994 it captured the collision of a comet with the planet Jupiter.

The bigger picture

Interest in Hubble's capabilities, as well as revitalization of the shuttle program, opened eyes to Colorado's growing stature in the aerospace industry.

The *Rocky* tracked the original Glenn L. Martin Company, which prospered by building intercontinental ballistic missiles used to face down the Soviet Union during the Cold War, according to *Colorado: A History of the Centennial State*. Martin built the first Titan missile. A merger transformed it into Martin Marietta, which constructed Mars landers such as the Viking I, responsible for transmitting the first images from the surface of Mars in 1976, and the Magellan, which traveled to Venus. Another merger created Lockheed Martin.

In addition, the University of Colorado's aerospace program claimed a rich history and several NASA astronauts.

Even stranger newsfellows

In the same edition that the *Rocky* reported the Hubble launch, it marked the death of two old stars that had flamed out.

Michael Milken, the billionaire financier who pioneered the use of high-yield debt securities known as junk bonds, pled guilty to breaking federal securities and tax laws and agreed to pay a record $600 million in penalties.

And the Ogden Theater, a Capitol Hill landmark since 1917 and Denver's oldest operating theater, was to close in a matter of months. The cult following that had shown up for midnight screenings of the *Rocky Horror Picture Show* on Saturday nights at the Ogden for the past 13 years would have to dress up somewhere else. □

New weapons of war and words

Iraqi President Saddam Hussein called Bush a "hypocritical criminal" and vowed to crush "the satanic intentions of the White House."

Operation Desert Shield grew into Desert Storm, utilizing a multi-national force that drove Iraqi forces from Kuwait in 43 days.

The newspaper tried to match the moment with smothering coverage. The first edition of the war carried 17 pages of stories. The same afternoon, the *Rocky* published its first "Extra" edition – 32 pages entirely on the war – since the Challenger shuttle exploded in 1986. The second day it introduced readers to "wrap-around sections" – 12 pages of war coverage wrapped around the regular daily paper, which included 13 more pages of war-related stories from throughout Colorado.

"Bush 1" called a ceasefire on Feb. 27, 1992, with Iraq's elite Republican Guard army in full retreat. For the following Sunday's edition, the *Rocky* printed a special 16-page commemorative section "dedicated to the Colorado servicemen and women who served in the gulf."

The Gulf War vocabulary

The Gulf War introduced an entire strata of new names and faces to the world. Scuds and Warthogs. Norman Schwarzkopf and Tariq Aziz. Imbedded journalists and weapons of mass destruction. Peter Arnett and Wolf Blitzer. The Baath Party and AWACS planes. CNN and MREs (Meals Ready to Eat).

The Gulf War also changed in a fundamental way the communications of the world. The Internet and Cable News Network (CNN) delivered news and images almost instantaneously, and it would lead to a technological revolution in journalism within the next 10 years.

Birth of a new *Rocky*

When the *Rocky's* new "electronic newspaper," called A LA CARTE EDITION, splashed the headline "WAR" at 5:29 p.m. on Jan. 16 – 12 hours before the newspaper reporting it thumped on Denver doorsteps – it gave readers a taste of what the new journalism was all about.

It was the first "newspaper" in the U.S. to report the start of the war. The newspaper had introduced A LA CARTE, which could be accessed by computer running Prodigy software, only two months before. The paper committed one editor, Denny Dressman, to lead a staff of four in "posting" stories produced in the newsroom to the new service.

The war was the *Rocky's* first electronic scoop. □

The huge, stark headline was reminiscent of the *Rocky Mountain News* of 1917, announcing America had entered World War I. But on Jan. 17, 1991, everything else was different.

Different enemy. Different motivation. Different weapons. Different technology. Different journalism.

It was evident from the earliest Scripps Howard News Service report on page 1:

> President Bush launched a war in the Persian Gulf last night with devastating air raids against Iraq and its occupation army in Kuwait. There was almost no immediate retaliation.
>
> At 5 p.m. MST, exactly on schedule, wave after wave of American F-15E jets, backed by British Tornados and squadrons of Saudi and Kuwaiti air forces, began hitting Iraqi Scud missile bases, chemical plants, command and control centers, air bases and other military targets.
>
> "The liberation of Kuwait has begun," Bush declared. "The world could wait no longer …"

Colorado makes the big leagues

The page 1 banner was simple. Direct. Correct. And, first.

It was the sports story every journalist in Denver wanted for the past 35 years.

The copyrighted story by Norm Clarke, the baseball writer without a baseball team, led the *Rocky's* Sports section inside the June 5, 1991, edition.

Denver and Miami are the National League expansion committee's recommendations for the two new Major League Baseball franchises, the Rocky Mountain News confirmed yesterday through several high-level sources.

… The committee will continue talking with other owners this week as it attempts to garner support for the recommendation before the National and American League club owners vote June 12.

Denver is "the surest thing there is," said a source close to the commissioner's office.

Clarke, a gregarious, eye-patch wearing, man-about-any-town, was hired by the *Rocky* in October, 1984 – nearly seven years before he broke the story. It would be two more years after the story before the Colorado Rockies took the field. Clarke's hiring was a news bulletin to the city of Denver about the paper's commitment to getting the team and the story.

How excited was Denver about the possibility of finally getting a Major League Baseball team? On the same day Clarke broke the news, a short story ran deep inside the Sports section. The headline:

Ehrhart denies report
'Grizzlies' team name

Everyone in town knew the expansion recommendation was coming and speculation was rampant over the slightest detail that might indicate Denver was finally one of the chosen ones. Steve Ehrhart was president of the Colorado Baseball Partnership, the ill-starred original group of owners pitching for a franchise. "Grizzlies" was one of dozens of early favorite suggestions for the team name.

"That's news to me," Ehrhart said. " … Right now, we're just focusing on trying to get the team."

One month after Clarke's big scoop, the National League made it official and the *Rocky* ran another page 1 baseball banner story by Clarke:

Rockies safe at home

This is how Major League Baseball finally came to Denver. The phone rang in a Hyatt Regency suite yesterday. Bill White, president of the National League, answered. He smiled, turned to the members of the Colorado Baseball Partnership and said, "Congratulations. It was unanimous."

On the same day, the paper printed the official team name – Rockies – and logo, a baseball rocketing out of a purple mountain background.

Right man, right job

Clarke proved the perfect choice to win the baseball race for the *Rocky*. He was a straight-forward, hard-news reporter who thrived on competition.

About the time the call of "Play ball!" was heard at Denver's first hometown major league game in 1993, Clarke wrote in his book, *High Hard Ones,* about the newspaper battle for baseball:

"Looking back, I have no doubt that I would have left Denver had we not been first with the story. I'd probably be back in California now, trying to live down the darkest chapter of my life."

Clarke went on to become the *Rocky's* "Talk Of The Town" columnist where he fought for every news morsel on Denver's appetizing political, social, entertainment and sports smorgasbord. □

Rocky Mountain News

June 5, 1991   **DENVER, COLORADO**   133rd year, No. 44   25¢

It's Denver, Miami

Baseball expansion franchise for Denver is 'surest thing there is,' top source says, but NL's decision-making process continues and changes could be made. **Page 65**

Minorities shifting to suburbs

Bloody Sunday

The United Bank robbery rivaled the Denver Mint heist in 1922 for its audacity, ferocity and confounding execution. There was one major difference, though, in the two crimes.

The day after Father's Day, 1991, the *Rocky* laid out the robbery with a page 1 graphic and veteran reporter John Ensslin's story inside:

> Four United Bank of Denver guards were shot to death yesterday in the bloodiest bank holdup in modern Colorado history.
>
> A well-dressed, silver-haired gunman slipped past an elaborate electronic maze and escaped with an undisclosed amount of cash.
>
> "This is one of the most grotesque and horrendous crimes I've ever seen," a somber District Attorney Norm Early said as he emerged from the bank. "I've never been to a crime scene like this."
>
> None of the guards were armed and some were shot execution-style, police said. The bank recently changed its firearms policy for guards.

The new policy banned the carrying of guns.

There were no suspects. Police believed the robber fled the scene before they arrived. Nevertheless, a search began of every room in the 52-story United One Bank Center and the inter-connected 22-story United Bank building.

A sidebar story inside, also written by Ensslin, posed the problem police faced at the end of the day.

Cops hunting smart robber who's also a cunning killer

The man who masterminded the United Bank of Denver heist and the slaying of four guards is a calculating, cold-blooded killer, investigators said last night.

But the elaborate plot that enabled the robber to decode a high-tech security system and walk undetected into an underground cash-counting area on a quiet Sunday morning is unlike any other holdups that FBI agents have encountered in the area.

Unlike the Denver Mint heist, in which one guard was killed but no one was ever charged, three weeks after the United Bank robbery, authorities arrested a suspect. However, James W. King, 54, a retired Denver Police sergeant who had worked as a United Bank guard until four months before the holdup, was acquitted by a jury one year later.

Reporter-investigator

Seven days after the United Bank robbery, James King greeted a stranger at his modest bungalow in the Pleasant View neighborhood near Golden.

The visitor was John Ensslin. The *Rocky* reporter recounted the meeting in a first-person story he wrote the day after King's arrest. The headline over it:

Reporter beat cops to King's door

One week after the bloody heist at United Bank, former bank guard and retired Denver cop James W. King wondered aloud why no one other than a Rocky Mountain News reporter had questioned him about it.

"Don't worry," I told him. "They'll get around to you."

They did.

Ensslin, who remained on the staff of the newspaper until its end, went on to write:

> King agreed the heist appeared to have been planned by someone with detailed knowledge of the security system.
>
> But who did it? Nobody he could imagine, he replied. ☐

Rocky Mountain News

June 17, 1991 DENVER, COLORADO **MONDAY** 133rd year, No. 56 25¢

4 slain in bank heist

Gunman slips into underground cash-counting room in downtown United Bank, kills unarmed guards, grabs undisclosed amount of cash before escaping. **Pages 6, 7**

An unidentified woman and her escort leave the United Bank building, where four guards were killed, soon after Denver police gave permission for employees to leave.

What happened

Who guides | Gandhi party

Walking tall

Wellington Edward Webb became Denver's first black mayor by literally walking the city. It became the habit and trademark of the 6-foot, 5-inch tall candidate throughout his campaign to don a pair of huge sneakers and knock on every door he came to. And Denver let him in, as the *Rocky* reported June 19, 1991.

Wellington Webb walked the city but sprinted past Norm Early in the stretch yesterday to become Denver's first black mayor in one of the most stunning come-from-behind victories in the city's history.

Once a longshot to even make the runoff, Webb parlayed a popular image and a managerial message into an astonishing 58% of the vote to Early's 42%. He won by nearly 18,000 votes.

The election was marred by the worst voter turnout in years, with only half of Denver's 234,250 registered voters casting ballots. About 10,000 fewer voters turned out this time compared to the May 21 general election.

Early suffered a trend by being the third district attorney to lose the mayoral race, after Bert Keating and Dale Tooley. Even though he was expected to be a huge favorite if he ran, he had to be begged, and his campaign was criticized for being negative and joyless.

That palooka Blake

The same day election results were reported, the paper's veteran political columnist, Peter Blake, admitted he might also have read the race wrong.

"One last thing," Blake wrote, tongue wadded in cheek.

Seven months ago, on the day Mayor Federico Peña dropped out, a local political observer – I forget which one – predicted that if Early entered the race soon, "he would quickly lap the huge field and win going away."

… Let's check and see which palooka wrote those words and now, heh, heh, has to eat them.

… Oops, well, never mind.

A different palooka

Also on election day, the *Rocky* reported that another one of the mavericks Denver has watched preside over financial boondoggles in its history, had his hand slapped by the government. Neil Bush, the other son of President George Bush, was found guilty of violating conflict-of-interest regulations in what the paper had labeled as The Silverado Saga.

Bush, 36, was director of Silverado Bank when it collapsed in 1988. He was one of 13 defendants who settled a $200 million lawsuit by the Federal Deposit Insurance Company. They shook hands on a $49.5 million settlement.

As the paper's story goes …

A large part of Bush's legal fees – estimated at $250,000 – are being paid by a defense fund set up by former Rep. Thomas Ashley, a longtime friend of President Bush.

"Neil has got a negative net worth," Ashley told the Associated Press."

Asked for Neil Bush's comment after the settlement, his attorney, James Nesland, told the paper, "His comment is, he's glad it's over, but he's not glad it happened." □

Rocky Mountain News

June 19, 1991 DENVER, COLORADO WEDNESDAY 133rd year, No. 58 25¢

Webb in a walk

Auditor beats Early 58% to 42%, completing a come-from-behind, shoe-leather drive to become Denver's first black mayor. **6-page report, with precinct map, starts on page 6**

Wellington Webb hugs Norm Early, back to camera, after sweeping to victory over Early yesterday in the Denver mayoral election. Webb's wife, Wilma, is at left.

INSIDE

Break Time	149	Movies	80
Business	29	Obituaries	147
Classified	84	People	154
Comics	150	Science	34
Dear Abby	57	Sports	70
Editorials	52	Stocks	44
Entertainment	69	TV listings	68
Lifestyles	55	Weather	155

For circulation information, call 892-6397
For classified information, call 892-7111
For all other information, call 892-5000

Multitude of questions haunts massacre probe

■ Police follow slayer's electronic pass-card trail through United Bank; source says card belonged to one of 4 security guards shot to death by robber.

■ Slain guard Scott McCarthy aspired to be cop.

■ Slaying victim Mankoff former bank executive.

Jerry McElhanney and daughter Jennifer McCarthy, widow of guard.

Page 8

Startling view of Red Square from the Rockies

In the 150-year history of the *Rocky*, there may not have been a more striking, more significant world development than the breakup of the Soviet Union.

Soviet president Mikhail Gorbachev ushered the upheaval in the late 1980s with his policies of *glasnost*, a revolutionary openness in the USSR. But that was only the beginning. With U.S. President George Bush as a staunch supporter and eventual friend, Gorbachev pushed even harder for *perestroika*, the restructuring of the entire Soviet political machine. Gorbachev's surprising sidekick in the reform became Boris Yeltsin, the hard-drinking, stage-stomping new president of the Russian republic.

Half a world away, they created a memorable *Rocky* front page headline on Aug. 24, 1991. The headline, in the paper's revived conversational tone, combined with the photo of Gorbachev casually shrugging, confirmed the Cold War indeed was a thing of the past. The Associated Press story ran on page 2:

> **MOSCOW** – Mikhail Gorbachev and Boris Yeltsin teamed up to strike at the pillars of the Soviet establishment Friday, stripping power from the Communist Party and taking control of the army and KGB.
>
> The party was banned from the KGB nationwide and from the national army and police in the Russian republic. Its offices in Moscow were sealed, its hard-line chapter in the Russian republic shut down. Even its telephones were cut off.

The story was accompanied inside by photos of Russian citizens tearing down monuments in Red Square to the architects of Communism.

Only three days before, events in Moscow set off a series of newspaper headlines hardly imagined in the West, and certainly not the Rocky Mountain West. On page 1 of the *Rocky*:

(Aug. 21) Coup turns deadly

Soviet hard-liners had removed Gorbachev from office and hundreds of thousands of countrymen had answered Yeltsin's call for them to resist the Communists.

(Aug. 22) Back in power

Leading some experts to wonder if Gorbachev hadn't orchestrated the coup against himself, the Soviet leader regained power and revived his people's fervor for reform.

(Aug. 23) Kremlin cleanup

Gorbachev purged the government of those who tried to oust him, and Yeltsin was hailed for leading the way to democracy.

Two weeks later, Gorbachev succeeded in undoing 70 years of the Soviet system. The *Rocky's* headline:

Lawmakers dismantle USSR

International experts

Call it unreal luck. Perfect timing. Or smart journalism. *Rocky* editor Jay Ambrose had put the newspaper in an enviable position to cover major international stories like the fall of the Berlin Wall, the disbanding of the Soviet Union and the first Iraq war by hiring an international editor. It was a luxury the relatively small staff never had in recent years.

The first was Clifford D. May. His successor was Holger Jensen, a former war correspondent who held the position during Gorbachev's rise. Jensen had a clean writing style and the sources and savvy to give readers an insider's perspective.

His analysis of the Soviet coup ran on page 1 – ahead of the AP news story – during the Soviet coup:

> ... However, those who ousted Gorbachev would have to be very thick not to have realized by now that they gravely miscalculated the extent of popular outrage at home, the swiftness of the economic fallout from abroad and the loyalty of the armed forces. □

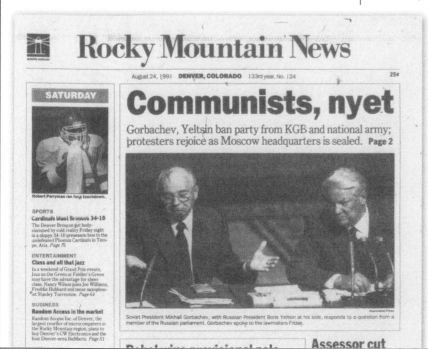

Rocky Mountain News

August 24, 1991 **DENVER, COLORADO** 133rd year, No. 124 25¢

SATURDAY

Communists, nyet

Gorbachev, Yeltsin ban party from KGB and national army; protesters rejoice as Moscow headquarters is sealed. **Page 2**

Robert Perryman ran for a touchdown.

SPORTS
Cardinals blast Broncos 34-10
The Denver Broncos got body-slammed by cold reality Friday night in a sloppy 34-10 preseason loss to the undefeated Phoenix Cardinals in Tempe, Ariz. *Page 75*

ENTERTAINMENT
Class and all that jazz
In a weekend of Grand Prix events, Jazz on the Green at Fiddler's Green may have the advantage for sheer class. Nancy Wilson joins Joe Williams, Freddie Hubbard and tenor saxophonist Stanley Turrentine. *Page 64*

BUSINESS
Random Access in the market
Random Access Inc. of Denver, the largest reseller of microcomputers in the Rocky Mountain region, plans to buy Denver's CW Electronics and the four Denver-area BizMarts. *Page 51*

Soviet President Mikhail Gorbachev, with Russian President Boris Yeltsin at his side, responds to a question from a member of the Russian parliament. Gorbachev spoke to the lawmakers Friday.

Assessor cut

Pinch me: Opening Day in Denver

It was a scene every baseball fan in Denver – no, every sports fans – imagined, but didn't believe would ever come true:

The players of Denver's home team lining the field on Opening Day of the first major league baseball game in the city. Caps off, heads bowed for the national anthem. Mile High Stadium jammed with the largest Opening Day crowd in baseball history. Blue-bird clear skies.

This was the front and back cover of the *Rocky's* wraparound Souvenir Edition April 10, 1993, the day after the Colorado Rockies played their first home game. The story was written by Tracy Ringolsby, the paper's second baseball writer:

THE DREAM COMES TRUE
Rockies 11, Expos 4

When the major league baseball team they had coveted for three decades finally arrived at Mile High Stadium on Friday afternoon, Rocky Mountain baseball fans were given a chance to savor it.

And they did.

… And by the time the Rockies finished off their 11-4 winning debut against Montreal, the majority of the 80,227 paying customers … were standing on their feet, lauding their new heroes.

"This was a dream come true for the people of Denver," catcher Joe Girardi said. "The players … we know we're going to win. There's no chance of losing 162 in a row. But I'm glad we were able to help these people fulfill their dreams with a game like this."

Most memorable moment

Ask any Rockies fan what their favorite moment in team history is, even after the club reached its first World Series in 2007, and 95 percent of them will recall Eric Young's shocking home run in the Rockies' first major league at-bat in Denver.

With the victory, amid all the pageantry and celebration of the home opener, Young's home run wasn't mentioned until the 14th paragraph of the game story. But it remains one of the most thrilling plays in Denver sports history. Young had only 11 homers in 454 previous professional games. He finished the day 4-for-4.

In a sidebar story, Young was asked if he was surprised?

"As far as the home run, yes. As far as getting hits, no. I think I can hit."

Bittersweet frames

Two photos inside the Souvenir Edition serve as reminders today of the fleeting nature of baseball and the game of life.

On page 2, a robust-looking Bob Howsam basked in a good seat at the game. Howsam, who ran the Denver Bears minor-league team for decades and brought the Denver Broncos to life, was the first to seriously campaign for major league baseball in the Mile High City. He died in February, 2008, at age 89.

On page 8, Rockies founding partners Charlie Montfort and Jerry McMorris, sitting one behind the other, grasped hands in an "I-can't-believe-it's-happening" moment. Monfort and brother Dick would later buy out McMorris' financial interest in the franchise. □

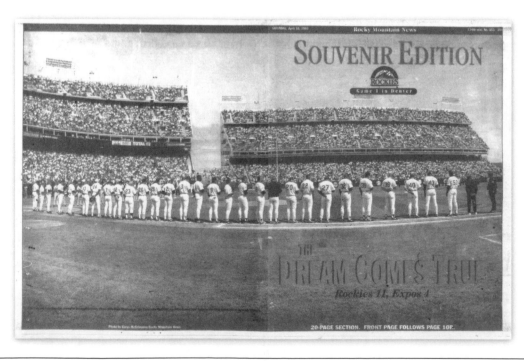

Sermons from the mountains

It was called World Youth Day.

For the *Rocky,* it was a solid week of Pope sightings, monster crowds, emotional renewals of Catholic faith and more than one hundred pages of coverage of the largest gathering in Colorado's history.

The Roman Catholic celebration of the world's youth had been in planning since 1992 when Pope John Paul II announced he had chosen Denver for the intermittently scheduled conference. Approximately 186,000 registered for the event. Over four days, masses and events presided over by the Pope attracted crowds totaling nearly 1 million people.

The *Rocky's* week-long coverage began with sending a reporter and photographer to Jamaica to meet the Pope on his way to Denver.

The first official event in the city was a mass at Civic Center Park attended by 100,000 worshippers – but not the Pope. He made his first appearance the next day, Aug. 12, 1993, when he welcomed 90,000 young people packed into old Mile High Stadium. But throughout the week, he shared top billing on page 1 with President Bill Clinton. The paper's banner story the next day:

Pontiff thrills youths after chat with Clinton

Jack McElroy, an assistant managing editor, took the role of weaving together the lead story each day from dozens of sources and staff reports from the field.

> **The skies brought two heads of state to Denver Thursday, then bathed them in rain. Far from dampening spirits, though, the shower that greeted Pope John Paul II and President Clinton seemed to suit their purpose: a salute to rejuvenation and unity through the world's youth.**
>
> **"America, I express gratitude to you for receiving me ... with rain," said the pope after landing at Stapleton International Airport.**

The newspaper treated the meeting of the two leaders like an international summit, which unofficially, it was. It assigned its former international editor, now associate editor, Clifford May, to put that part of the spectacle in perspective. Wrote May:

> **Pope John Paul II arrived in Denver Thursday and immediately tackled an issue that has put him in sharp conflict with many Americans: abortion.**
>
> **"If you want equal justice for all, and true freedom and lasting peace, then, America, defend life," the pontiff said as Bill Clinton, an abortion-rights president stood beside him.**

The next night, the Pope spoke to 250,000 pilgrims at Cherry Creek State Park. Then on Sunday he said mass as 375,000 filled the state park and summer temperatures soared to 98 degrees. Fourteen thousand ailing worshippers had to be treated for dehydration and heat exhaustion and threatened to overwhelm medical teams.

A busy President

President Clinton made his own headlines while in Colorado.

Just before leaving Washington, he unveiled a controversial anti-crime package that the *Rocky* crammed onto the bottom of page 1. On his way to Denver, he stopped in St. Louis to sign a flood relief bill for the Midwest. Then on the same day that the Pope exulted in the mountain scenery of Camp St. Malo on the edge of Rocky Mountain National Park, Clinton signed the much-debated bill adding more than 600,000 acres of Colorado mountainland to the nation's wilderness preserve.

Worst juxtaposition of the week

In the same edition it bannered the opening mass of World Youth Day on page 1, in the small "sky box" at the top of the page a copy editor wrote a "refer" headline to the entertainment section:

Money is god in Hollywood. Page 11C □

Rocky Mountain News

50¢ in Designated Areas

July 8, 1994   **FRIDAY**   ★ 136th year, No. 77   35¢

'Hell caught us'

Mountain gives up 12 charred bodies as questions swirl

Thomas Kelsey/Rocky Mountain News

The body of a firefighter who died Wednesday on a steep slope of Storm King Mountain is removed from a helicopter at the Glenwood Springs airport Thursday.

Lost were 'the best of the best'

— Bruce Babbitt, secretary of the interior

- **Richard Tyler**, Palisade
- **Robert Browning**, Grand Junction
- **Don Mackey**, Hamilton, Mont.
- **Roger Roth**, McCall, Idaho
- **James Thrash**, McCall, Idaho
- **Jon Kelso**, Prineville, Ore.
- **Terri Hagen**, Prineville, Ore.

- **Bonnie Holtby**, Prineville, Ore.
- **Tami Bickett**, Powell Butte, Ore.
- **Kathi Beck**, Eugene, Ore.
- **Scott Blecha**, Clatskanie, Ore.
- **Levi Brinkley**, Burns, Ore.
- **Rob Johnson**, Redmond, Ore.
- **Doug Dunbar**, Redmond, Ore.

Two firefighters react to the tragedy Thursday. The badly burned remains of 12 firefighters were recovered west of Glenwood Springs. Two others were missing and presumed dead.

Dennis Schroeder/Rocky Mountain News

14 PAGES OF COVERAGE BEGIN ON 4A

Storm King killer

The tragedy occurred July 6, 1994. The unforgettable front page that serves as a memorial to 14 wild land firefighters who died on Storm King Mountain published July 8.

The *Rocky* and other media reported the first day that the Canyon Creek Fire had blown up and chased and killed 11 firefighters up the steep canyon west of Glenwood Springs, and that three others were missing. By the next day 12 bodies had been recovered, making it the deadliest wildfire in Colorado history. The two remaining missing were found slightly removed from the main group on July 8. Nine of the fallen were members of the elite Prineville Hot Shots from Oregon.

What made the *Rocky's* July 8 edition so memorable were its gripping front page, the emotional stories from survivors, and the reporting that asked questions which eventually – months later – contributed to harsh lessons learned about how the fire was mismanaged.

On July 8, the paper printed the names of all 14 firefighters on page 1 beneath a subhead quoting Bruce Babbitt, secretary of the interior:

Greg Lopez

Lost were 'the best of the best'

GLENWOOD SPRINGS – The charred bodies of 12 firefighters were removed Thursday from Colorado's deadliest wildfire amid smoldering questions about what went wrong.

The questions include:

- Why wasn't the killer blaze put out days ago?
- Why were firefighters dispatched to such a steep mountainside despite forecasts of high winds?
- Why wasn't a safety officer sent with firefighters to help them escape danger?

The bodies were found within a 200-yard radius on an ashen mountainside, dotted with the tiny aluminum-foil tents some had crawled under in a desperate attempt to survive.

… "Hell caught up with us," said Brad Haugh, a Gypsum (Colo.) firefighter who outran the Canyon Creek Fire.

Ann Carnahan, a talented and versatile staff writer, wrote the lead story. Five other reporters on the scene contributed to Carnahan's account and wrote other stories that filled 14 pages.

The fire wasn't fully contained until July 11 after what had begun as a 50-acre fire started by lightning consumed nearly 2,200 acres of worthless scrub oak and pinyon-juniper and cost 14 lives and more than $4.5 million.

'People' storyteller

Another piece of the *Rocky's* coverage was its regular 'People' column written by a young man, Greg Lopez, who had a knack for telling extraordinary stories about everyday people.

Lopez also interviewed Haugh, who was with some of the firefighters who tried to scramble over the ridge and escape the fire. Haugh was one of the lucky ones. He helped another volunteer off the mountain, Erik Hepke from Seattle, who burned his hands. Lopez asked Haugh if he dreamed the night after he escaped:

"You know what I dreamed of?" (Haugh) said. "I thought it would be a nightmare – me caught in the fire again – but it was just a regular fire. It was a regular fire, and I was just clearing a line with Erik, just doing our job.

"I have no idea why, but I had a nice dream." □

DENVER

Rocky Mountain News

February 28, 1995   **TUESDAY**   ★★ 35¢

At last

Linda McConnel/Rocky Mountain News
Steve Swain guides DIA's first cargo flight Monday.

Glenn Asakawa/Rocky Mountain News

The sun sets on DIA's last idle day Sunday. "Denver has staked out its competitive environment for the next century," said federal aviation administrator David Hinson Monday.

INSIDE

DIA

- **Move beats storm.** Page 3A
- **Bags will vanish.** Page 3A
- **Bondholder files suit claiming city lied.** Page 4A
- **Handy guide to using your new airport.** Page 5A
- **DIA's first cargo flight lands on Monday.** Page 38A

Denver soars into the future

Snow unlikely to dampen historic opening of $4 billion airport

By Kevin Flynn
and Christopher Broderick

Rocky Mountain News Staff Writers

The waiting is over.

Denver International Airport opens this morning with ceremony, the thunder of jet engines — and a sense of relief.

After 16 months of delays caused chiefly by a futuristic but faulty baggage system, the first major new U.S. airport in 21 years is ready to go to work.

The first passenger plane — United Airlines Flight 1062 to Kansas City, Mo. — is scheduled to depart at 6 a.m. The first arrival — United Flight 1474 from Colorado Springs — will land at the $4 billion airport five minutes later.

Federico Peña and Wellington Webb, the two Denver mayors responsible for the new airport, will greet the first passengers.

The biggest obstacle might be weather: Snow and freezing drizzle could ice up runways.

See **MOVE** on 2A

COMPLETE INDEX ON PAGE 2A

~ 138 ~

New airport carries some baggage

The page 1 banner on Feb. 28, 1995, read as it was intended – as if the entire city of Denver and state of Colorado exhaled in a sigh of accomplishment.

After all the construction delays, all the worries about the baggage system, all the cost overruns, the Rocky Mountains had a spanking new airport. The secondary headlines:

**Denver soars into the future
Snow unlikely to dampen historic opening
of $4 billion airport**

The newspaper started the story on page 1, which it rarely did in its recent tabloid days of a single dominant photo surrounded by what staff jokingly referred to as "refer madness" – stacks of headlines promoting stories inside.

The waiting is over.

Denver International Airport opens this morning with ceremony, the thunder of jet engines – and a sense of relief.

After 16 months of delays caused chiefly by a futuristic but faulty baggage system, the first major new U.S. airport in 21 years is ready to go to work.

DIA's originally scheduled opening date was Oct. 31, 1993.

The day before the actual debut, the paper displayed four missed opening deadlines and the final date in a graphic timeline, each date represented by one of DIA's trademark white "tents" that were part of the main terminal's distinctive design.

The *Rocky* had already published a special section leading up to the airport opening, including detailed graphics of the terminal layout and how the baggage system was supposed to work.

The day of the opening it ran 18 pages of coverage. That didn't include the full-page ad taken by USWEST, the largest telecommunications company in the region, which copied the strategy of history's big advertisers that tied their ads to the news.

Damaged In Action

The problem with DIA's new $225 million automated, code-reading baggage system was it didn't work. A story inside the *Rocky* on opening day quoted the head of the company that manufactured the system estimating that about 1,000 bags a day would be lost until the bugs were worked out.

If the system didn't lose your luggage, it ate it alive, mangling bags. And the labyrinth of trolleys, tracks and wheels vibrated so badly that it shook shops on upper floors of the terminal.

To limit the chaos, only United Airlines used the system when DIA opened. Eventually, Denver threw out the whole thing.

United Airlines' original baggage handling system was the joke of the city when DIA opened in 1995. Pete Leabo, owner of this computer, wasn't laughing, however, after it was damaged and then plundered in delivery at the airport. *(Glenn Asakawa/Rocky Mountain News)*

Editor's note

For some time, Jay Ambrose, the *Rocky*'s editor, had been writing a 30- or 40-word note to readers that appeared each day on page 2A along with an expanded index of sections and stories inside the paper. Ambrose's note on the morning DIA came alive:

Forget the investigations. Forget the delays. Forget, even, the malfunctioning baggage system. Denver International Airport opens today, and that's a major historical event for this city and state.

Buy a paper, get a deal

Beneath Ambrose's daily message, the Daily Deal appeared.

With both the *Rocky* and *The Post* still locked in a costly, bruising cage match for circulation and advertising supremacy, the Marketing Dept. had begun printing daily coupons that readers could redeem for everything from free hash browns at McDonalds to movie tickets.

The Daily Deal the day DIA opened – a free cup of coffee. □

The Oklahoma City bombing

Terrorism had officially and publicly wreaked death within the shores of the United States. The *Rocky's* page 1 banner on April 20, 1995, and the image of the blasted-out Alfred P. Murrah Federal Building in Oklahoma City left no doubt.

> **OKLAHOMA CITY** – A huge car bomb tore apart a federal building in Oklahoma City Wednesday, killing at least 31 people, 12 of them children, Reuters news agency reported.
>
> Authorities said more than 300 people were missing after the worst act of terrorism on U.S. soil. The death toll was likely to rise to 80 or more as rescue and body recovering efforts wore into the night.
>
> The blast blew away an entire side of the building, gutting several floors and sending glass shards flying through city streets.

Within days, the country learned the toll was much worse: 168 killed, 19 of them children in the federal building's day-care center, and more than 500 injured.

The newspaper devoted six pages to first-day coverage. One full page looked at the vulnerability of Denver's own federal facilities. The lead headline and staff-written story on page 6A:

Security tightened at federal buildings

> The U.S. Marshall implemented contingency plans for a terrorist attack on Denver's courthouse Wednesday while security was beefed up at federal buildings in the area.
>
> In the wake of the Oklahoma City bombing, Denver authorities also evacuated a day-care center in the U.S. Custom House downtown, posted guards at three federal day-care centers and placed Denver International Airport on alert for heightened security.

The morning after the bombing, as rescue teams and families and friends sorted the living from the dead, the nation began looking for those to blame and answers to the question: Why?

The *Rocky's* second-day front page again led with a simple yet dramatic banner:

Wanted:

the word followed by drawings of two suspects for whom the FBI had issued arrest warrants. Both were identified only as "John Doe."

Timothy McVeigh, a 27-year-old former Army soldier, was arrested little more than one hour after the bombing, but on a firearms charge when an Oklahoma state trooper stopped him for not having a license plate on his Mercury Marquis. Two days later he was arrested in the bombing and eventually charged and tried for the act.

At that point, Denver and its citizens had no idea how intertwined their lives would become with that of the short-haired, off-looking man over the next two years.

The baby and the fireman

Tragedies have a way of producing unforgettable photographs in journalism. They are branded in the public's memory and become the iconic image associated with the event. In Oklahoma City, it happened within minutes of the bombing.

The *Rocky* published the photo of Chris Field emerging from the rubble cradling a bruised and bleeding child, whose limbs hung limp from the firefighter's arms. Golden hair curled from the soot and dirt on the baby girl's head. The photo happened to be taken by an amateur photographer, a bank clerk.

The day after, the paper carried an Associated Press story at the top of one of its inside pages:

Year-old girl pictured in photograph dies

> **OKLAHOMA CITY** – The baby who was carried from the ruins of the federal building in a photograph displayed worldwide has died.
>
> ... The child was identified Thursday as a girl who had turned a year old the day before the bombing.
>
> Baylee Almon's mother, Aren Almon, 22, met with a TV reporter Thursday to talk about her grief and then had a tearful meeting with the police officer and firefighter who had tried to rescue her daughter. □

Not as simple as black and white

The front-page photo of a young African-American girl headed home from school was arresting.

The *Rocky's* banner headline and story on Sept. 13, 1995, were history-making.

U.S. District Judge Richard Matsch on Tuesday released Denver from more than two decades of busing to desegregate schools.

In a historic 66-page decision that took a year to write, Matsch said Denver has scrupulously followed every court order to end segregation. Although those efforts haven't resulted in racial equality in student achievement, the district has met the requirements of federal law, Matsch held.

"The United States Constitution does not burden public education with remedying all of the disadvantages experienced by racial or ethnic groups in this nation's history," he wrote.

But the man who sued the Denver School District in 1969 in order to desegregate Park Hill schools, and whose victory changed the way the U.S. measured desegregation, did not agree with Matsch's view. On page 9 of the newspaper, Wilfred Keyes recalled growing up in Kansas City, Missouri, gazing at a school that he couldn't attend because he was black. Guy Kelly reported:

Wilfred Keyes stands at the center of a case that rocked Denver's foundations and changed its social, political and economic landscape.

But looking back, nothing's really changed, Keyes said Tuesday after a federal judge lifted the busing order.

"I don't see it being any better," Keyes said. "I really don't.

" ... I'm not saying the education is not going to be equal, but we're right back to neighborhood schools, something I stood up against more than 23 years ago, and I'm not happy about that at all," Keyes said.

In 1973, when the U.S. Supreme Court upheld Keyes' position, it was also the *Rocky's* lead story on page 1. One additional story ran inside.

In 1995, the page 1 decision was accompanied by five more stories inside plus extensive examination of ethnic education trends in Denver.

The eyes of a child

The paper's "People" columnist, Greg Lopez, had a way of helping readers see complex issues through crystal-clear eyes. The day after Matsch's decision, those eyes belonged to a first- and second-grader busing from Park Hill. The way Lopez saw it:

Bus No. 2167 left University Park Elementary School on the way to more educational opportunities, and Taisha Brown started to count the street signs.

The kids who live close enough to come here waved goodbye, and the kids who live far enough away to come here waved back.

... Every day, Taisha counts the street signs on the way home, at least until she gets to 59.

"My mom, she's never been this far," Taisha said. "I want her to come to my school sometime. So I'm trying to show her it's not too far, but I lose count."

... The way second-grader Lawrence Mason put it, "Maybe I won't get bus-sick and throw up anymore."

And that is pretty much what busing comes down to for first- and second-graders. □

Avalanche of emotions

Denver "enjoyed" its first championship in any major professional sport so much, the *Rocky* decided it was worthy of two EXTRA! editions.

The first EXTRA! showed a jubilant Patrick Roy beneath the screaming headline

ROY-HOOOO!

and was distributed minutes after the Colorado Avalanche's Game 4 victory for the Stanley Cup.

The 2nd EXTRA! was planned, but it also became necessary in order to report how Denver fans had gone loony since the first EXTRA! was printed.

The morning of June 11, 1996, readers woke up to the complete story with team captain Joe Sakic hoisting Lord Stanley's coveted cup on page 1H to prove it. The headline inside on page 2H:

'It's ours! The Cup is ours!'

The Stanley Cup is Colorado's.

After years of big-game frustration – and 44 minutes of pulse-popping overtimes – Colorado's sports fans can finally boast about a big-time championship.

"It's ours! It's ours! The Cup is ours," Darrell Good yelled as pandemonium erupted in LoDo Monday night after Uwe Krupp scored in the third overtime.

Denver still loved the Broncos football team, but it had lost all four Super Bowls it which it played. The Nuggets basketball team had never reached the NBA Finals.

The 2nd EXTRA! included details and photos from the match in Miami. But most of the 2nd EXTRA! covered how fans exploded in Denver overnight. Photos showed a young woman being passed along above a sea of fans in Lower Downtown, and two men leaping through a bonfire at 15th and Larimer streets. The headline on the page:

Revelers a little rowdy

Lower downtown Denver became the flash point for the raucous postgame celebration.

... Up to 50,000 revelers swarmed Larimer, Blake and Market streets leaving streets littered with trash and motorists helpless to do more than lean on their horns.

After all, Denver was new at this.

What EXTRA! ?

The "ROY-HOOOO!" EXTRA!, not by coincidence, didn't include the score or any game details.

The front-page photo, not by coincidence, showed the goaltender in his red road sweater. The caption stated up-front the photo was from Game 3. But it could have been Game 4.

And none of the four pages, not by coincidence, carried the edition date.

That's because the EXTRA! was printed before the game – justified as a "tribute" to Colorado's season. There wasn't a bigger Avalanche fan in Colorado than *Rocky* Editor Bob Burdick. This one time, the edition flew under his usual policy of not printing ahead of "hard" news.

Hockey Mountain News

When the Avalanche made the playoffs, the newspaper committed to printing several "wraparound" sections around the regular daily edition that included local, national and international news. Hoping to sell more papers in the heady playoff environment, it was Burdick who suggested the twist on the *Rocky's* page 1 flag, turning "Rocky" into "Hockey" with the aid of two hockey sticks and a puck.

Who was that guy?

Covered by the hockey "wrap" the morning Denver woke up to its championship, an historic photo on the regular front page of the paper could have been overlooked. The fact it was white-haired, Russian president Boris Yeltsin rocking out on stage with two young attractive ladies only days before his country's election, guaranteed that it wasn't. □

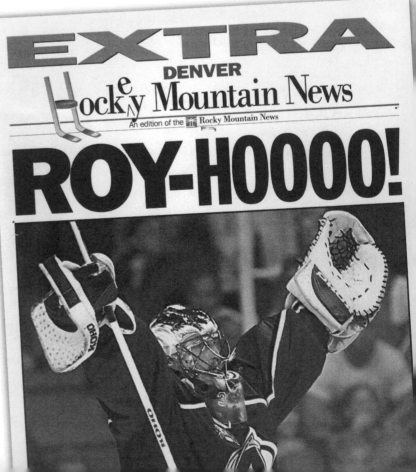

Unsolved, but absolved

In its first report the morning after Christmas, 1996, the *Rocky* didn't print a picture of the photogenic blonde girl. It spelled her name with a small "b" – Jonbenet. And the headline was on page 1, but small, near the bottom:

Boulder executive's daughter, 6, found dead in her home.

By the next day, Dec. 28, the murder of JonBenet Ramsey had become a national story that would command page 1 for years, spin off books and movies, and to this day remain an unsolved crime. One photo of the girl, among several that would become posters for her case, smiled from the front page. Charlie Brennan, one of the paper's most dogged reporters, wrote the second-day story.

The headline and story on page 5A:

Police puzzle over girl's slaying

BOULDER – JonBenet Ramsey was last seen alive at bedtime Christmas night, the owner of a brand-new bicycle and a personality that would light up a room.

Sometime after that, a killer strangled the 6-year-old who had been crowned Little Miss Colorado this year, hiding her body in the basement of her well-to-do famly's home.

John Ramsey discovered the body Thursday afternoon, nearly eight hours after Patsy Ramsey found a ransom note demanding $118,000 in exchange for her kidnapped daughter.

JonBenet's death remained a mystery Friday.

Two years later, the case remained unsolved, while theories could be found at every supermarket checkout stand.

The headline on Brennan's story on Dec. 28, 1998:

The restive murder case of JonBenet

One says there will be a conviction. The other says no way.

... Gerry Spence, the Wyoming lawyer known for his fiery defense of civil liberties, thinks one or both of the little girl's parents will stand trial. And he's betting on a guilty verdict for one or both.

Stephen Jones, who defended Oklahoma City bomber Timothy McVeigh, thinks John and Patsy Ramsey might well end up on trial. But he doesn't expect they'll be convicted.

Boulder police were assailed for their handling of the crime scene and initial investigation. Future Boulder Police chief Mark Beckner was placed in charge of the case. But when a grand jury closed in 1999, District Attorney Alex Hunter reported there were still no indictments.

In 2006, the case took a bizarre turn when John Mark Karr claimed he was present when JonBenet died. But after Karr was arrested in Thailand, DA Mary Lacy dropped the case against him when DNA tests failed to match evidence.

Epilogue

The *Rocky's* front-page headlines on July 10, 2008:

DA: Ramseys didn't do it
Lacy offers apology, says new evidence, tests clear family.

Twelve years after JonBenet Ramsey's murder, science took a leap that provided new hope of finding her killer and led authorities to exonerate her family.

On Wednesday, Boulder District Attorney Mary Lacy announced that a new method of collecting and analyzing DNA generated powerful forensic evidence that an unidentified man murdered 6-year-old JonBenet in her home on Christmas night 1996.

Lacy also gave JonBenet's father, John Ramsey, a written apology expressing deep regret for contributing in any way to the public perception that someone in the Ramsey family had committed the crime.

Patsy Ramsey died in 2006 after a long battle with ovarian cancer. ☐

Challenge

Denver District Judge Richard Matsch
(Essdras Suarez/Rocky Mountain News)

*"A Colorado jury today convicted
Timothy McVeigh of waging the deadliest act
of domestic terrorism in American history."*

Rocky Mountain News

June 2, 1997

McVillain

Oklahoma City was shattered by the bombing of the Alfred P. Murrah Building. Denver shared in the aftershocks.

Almost eight months after the bombing, the 10th U.S. Circuit Court appointed Denver District Judge Richard Matsch to preside over the trials of Timothy McVeigh and Terry Nichols, both charged with murder and conspiracy in the case.

Despite leaked newspaper stories and defense claims that the resulting publicity made a fair trial impossible, the rigid judge set the trial start date for March 31, 1997. Jury summonses were sent to 1,000 Coloradans. Extreme security measures were put in place around the downtown courthouse just blocks from Denver's 16th Street Mall. The trial started March 31.

In mid-afternoon on June 2, the *Rocky* hit the streets of Denver first with a four-page EXTRA! edition bearing one of the largest headlines in the paper's history. The story on the cover:

A Colorado jury today convicted Timothy McVeigh of waging the deadliest act of domestic terrorism in American history.

The 29-year-old former soldier was convicted in the Oklahoma City bombing that killed 168 people, including 19 children.

U.S. District Judge Richard Matsch read the verdict at 1:34 p.m. in Denver's Federal Courthouse. The jury deliberated approximately 23 hours over four days before convicting McVeigh on all 11 counts.

The verdict was immediately hailed by bombing victims in the courthouse plaza outside.

And it was greeted with cheers and tears in the still-grieving state of Oklahoma.

The remaining matter: sentencing, which Matsch and Colorado would also preside over.

Eleven days later on June 13, the newspaper published another EXTRA! edition with an equally immense banner headline:

**DEATH
SENTENCE**

The headline inside over the story on page 2:

ONE LIFE FOR 168 LIVES

A Colorado jury today sentenced Oklahoma City bomber Timothy McVeigh to die.

The panel of five women and seven men voted unanimously to condemn the 29-year-old former soldier to death instead of life in prison.

EXTRA! What about it?

The newspaper war between the *Rocky* and *The Post* was at its zenith at the time of the McVeigh trial, and every paper sold counted toward all-important circulation reports. The *Rocky* staff genuinely relished covering big stories and rising to deadline and production challenges because it was a chance to compete head-to-head, EXTRA!-to-EXTRA!, with its rival. As the assistant managing editor who oftentimes was responsible for watching the clock down to the minute in such races, I can honestly swear the *Rocky* seldom finished second.

Editorial and Production departments historically fought each other. But at the *Rocky* at the time, they were intense partners. As the verdict drew near, Paul Gledhill, vice president of production, devised an EXTRA! strategy in which all the page plates from each morning's complete edition were left on the presses. When the verdict came in, Editorial dashed to "remake" only four pages – the single outside sheet of the paper, cover and back, minimizing the time to start the presses and sell papers on the street.

In the case of the "GUILTY" EXTRA!, Editorial prebuilt two of the four pages with the important background of the bombing in Oklahoma City. It included the name of every victim. Some newspapers have been known to preprint two EXTRA! editions – each one reporting a different verdict or outcome. But *Rocky* Editor Bob Burdick had a strict policy of not getting ahead of "hard" news.

The *Rocky* staff waited anxiously for the verdicts, then raced to tell all of Denver. □

The Princess and the Saint

The shock of the death of England's Princess Diana in a car crash was soothed one week later, for *Rocky* readers, by coverage of her royal and loving funeral.

The Sunday banner headline Sept. 7, 1997, floated over a photo of her royal cortege in front of which stood five integral men in her life – former husband Prince Charles, sons Prince Harry and William, brother Earl Charles Spencer, and Prince Phillip, the queen's husband. The *Rocky's* wire service compilation:

LONDON – The British people by the millions poured out their hearts Saturday in a final farewell to Princess Diana.

They cried at the courage of Prince William, 15, and Prince Harry, 12, as the brothers walked behind their mother's funeral cortege.

They sang along with hymns of old and Elton John's new version of his pop hymn, *Candle In The Wind,* in which he bids "Goodbye, England's rose."

But mostly they stood and watched and reflected on the tragedy that snuffed the life of the Princess of Wales six days earlier.

It was, by most accounts, the largest crowd in London since VE Day, the 1945 celebration of the Allied victory over Germany.

Hundreds of thousands of people pressed around Westminster Abbey, site of the funeral.

Like every other newspaper in the world, the *Rocky* had carried countless stories every day since Diana's death in the early morning of Aug. 31 in Paris. The Sunday edition in which her death was reported, the paper included only one 5-inch local sidebar about her skiing vacations to Vail and Aspen.

With each day that passed, with enormous media coverage and growing speculation about her relationship with Dodi Al Fayed, the Egyptian playboy who was also killed in the crash, the paper printed more stories about Colorado's reaction to her death.

The day of Di's funeral the *Rocky* devoted seven pages of coverage, including three color photo pages, one a gallery of movie actors, rock stars and First Lady Hillary Clinton in attendance.

'Saint' gets page 2

The Sept. 7 edition of the *Rocky* also mourned the death of another woman, known as well as Diana all over the world for her care of India's sick and poor – the esteemed Roman Catholic nun, Mother Teresa. The single second-day story appeared on page 2:

**World joins to honor
'Saint of the Slums'**

CALCUTTA, India – The world paid homage to Mother Teresa on Saturday as India cast tradition aside and decided to hold a state funeral for the tiny saint of Calcutta's slums.

Find it if you can

Beneath the Mother Teresa story, in its now familiar home, the *Rocky* printed its weekly Sunday "treasure map." In its zeal to sectionalize the bulging edition, and because of the production limitations of printing the smaller tabloid, section after section had to be "nested" in each other's fold. The graphic map was intended to show readers how easy it was to find the 19 different sections. □

SUNDAY
Rocky Mountain News
September 7, 1997 • LATE SPORTS DENVER www.denver-rmn.com ★ 50¢ ($1.00 at Designation Areas)

'Goodbye, England's rose'

Millions say farewell as Britain's beloved Princess Diana is laid to rest. **3A**

Prince Charles, Prince Harry, Earl Charles Spencer, Prince William and Prince Philip stand as the coffin bearing Princess Diana's body is carried into London's Westminster Abbey for her funeral Saturday. The princes represent three generations of Britain's royal family. Crowds lined the city streets in an emotional send-off.

NINE PAGES OF COVERAGE BEGIN ON PAGE 3A

SPORTS
CU roars past stubborn CSU 31-21
No. 8 Buffs overcome slow start, beat Rams 7th straight time. **1C**
▶ BRONCOS GUARD AGAINST OVERCONFIDENCE IN SEATTLE. **1N**

**Jail guards caught
sleeping on the job.** 5A

If you think Colorado's crowded now, just wait a few years. **4A**

The Killer and the Country Boy

On Oct. 14, 1997, the *Rocky* presented a front page of extreme contrasts. It marked the death of one man Colorado wanted to forget, and it celebrated the life of another whom it dearly wished to remember.

The banner on page 1 and story inside carried the tones of finality and justice.

> CANON CITY – Eleven years after he raped and murdered Ginny May, Gary Lee Davis was executed Monday night, the first criminal put to death in Colorado in 30 years.
>
> An alcoholic with an appetite for abusing women sexually, Davis, 53, was pronounced dead at 8:33 p.m. after prison officials injected lethal drugs into his arm in the Colorado State Penitentiary's death chamber.
>
> Davis had no last words – to his family or his victim and her family.

The history-making element of Davis' execution was the reinstatement of the death penalty in Colorado, and the resumption of the national debate over the moral justification for it. Colorado's return to executing criminals came during a surge in capital punishment in the U.S. Seventy-four convicts were executed in 1997 in this country.

The newspaper's coverage of Davis' execution was in depth, seven pages in addition to the front page. It included brief profiles of the 12 witnesses, including Ginny May's father and brother. It also ran a minute-by-minute chronology of the last hour and 25 minutes of Davis' life.

Rod MacLennan, May's father, was quoted in his profile:

> "Tonight Colorado fired a shot heard around the state that gave fair warning to all its people that if you deliberately take the life of one of us, you will pay the price.
>
> "And the price is death.
>
> "... Our family will not waste any more time thinking about Gary Lee Davis any more."

Colorado's country boy

At the opposite end of page 1, the *Rocky* reported the accidental death of beloved singer and songwriter John Denver. He was 53 – the same age as Davis.

> John Denver, the boyish singer who captured the optimism of Colorado with his hit *Rocky Mountain High,* died Sunday when his experimental plane plunged into the Pacific Ocean near Monterrey Bay.
>
> ... The singer had made his home in Aspen for 30 years and had taken "Denver" for his stage name from Colorado's capital city.

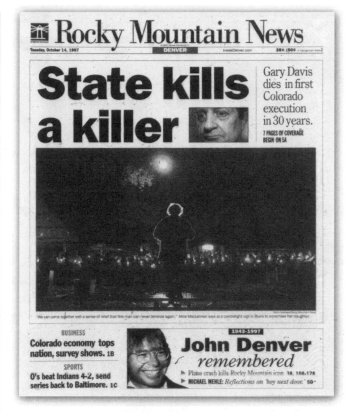

> Gov. Roy Romer called Denver's death a personal and statewide loss. "I knew him as a friend and a pilot," Romer said.
>
> "He was not only a longtime resident of Colorado but our best ambassador in describing what Colorado is, and its vibrant beauty."

The story ran on page 3 alongside a classic photo of Denver dressed in jeans and cowboy boots, belting out *Thank God I'm a Country Boy* from the top of the Baltimore Orioles' baseball dugout at a game only one month before.

In an inside sidebar, staff writer Joseph B. Verrengia put Denver's worldwide appeal in perspective:

> No one – not even John Elway or gonzo journalist Hunter S. Thompson – is so closely associated with Colorado in the world's imagination as John Denver.

Denver trivia

The trivia question over Denver's real name is as much a piece of Colorado lore as the singer is. He was born Henry John Deutschendorf Jr. in Roswell, New Mexico. His father was an Air Force pilot and his family moved frequently. His mother and brother lived in Aurora at the time of his death. □

Rocky Mountain News

© 1998 Denver Publishing Co.

Monday, January 26, 1998 | **DENVER** | InsideDenver.com ★ ★★ **35¢ (50¢** in Designated Areas)

7th Heaven

Elway finally brings home Super Bowl title

48-PAGE SUPER NEWS SECTION INSIDE

Cyrus McCrimmon/Rocky Mountain News

Teammates carry Denver Broncos quarterback John Elway after the team's 31-24 victory over the Green Bay Packers in Super Bowl XXXII in San Diego on Sunday.

2 gunshot deaths, looting, rioting after victory. 5A

Worth a Mile High Salute

The Denver Broncos had finally won a Super Bowl.

The *Rocky* told its readers so on Jan. 26, 1998, not once. Not twice. But in three editions. Colorado had a long love affair with its professional football team. Residents shuddered whenever they were reminded the Broncos had lost the same number of championship games as the – ugh! – Buffalo Bills.

Finally, the wait was over, and Denver was going to relish it.

The paper's first EXTRA! on the street told the story with a simple full-page headline:

No.1

Squeezed amidst the big type was the score: Denver 31, Green Bay 24.

The 2nd EXTRA! front page was more sentimental. After all, future Hall of Fame quarterback John Elway had led the team for 15 seasons:

THIS ONE'S FOR JOHN!

They were the words of Broncos owner Pat Bowlen at the Lombardi Trophy presentation.

The main edition, with #7 riding a tide of teammates on page 1, was a fat orange and blue production of 140 pages. It included a 48-page "Super News" section inside with the cover headline and story:

AB-SALUTE-LY!

SAN DIEGO – To those whose faith never wavered.

To those who dreamed their team could win a Super Bowl title.

And to those who hoped and prayed that John Elway would capture the one prize that has eluded him during his glorious 15-year NFL career.

The Denver Broncos salute you.

John Elway in Super Bowl XXXII. *(Rocky Mountain News)*

The Mile High Salute became the team's calling card over the season after running back and Super Bowl Most Valuable Player Terrell Davis began saluting fans after touchdowns. Teammates, teachers, pizza delivery boys, construction workers across the city and state began imitating him.

A bad trend

Unfortunately, as with the city's celebration of the Avalanche's Stanley Cup two years before, back home Denver created some embarrassing headlines, as John Ensslin reported on page 5A:

Jubilant city erupts in chaos

They hung from wires above the streets. They hugged and danced with strangers. Then, they set the night on fire.

Police threw so much tear gas at revelers overturning cars and ransacking downtown stores that they had to borrow more gas from Lakewood.

Paramedics set up a triage center at Coors Field, and Denver Health Medical Center overflowed with injured.

Meanwhile, back at the White House

The same Monday morning, on page 2A, another national story was unraveling as it neared its conclusion:

Pals defend Clinton honor; Lewinsky 'dying' to tell story

WASHINGTON – President Clinton's allies defended him Sunday against charges of sexual misconduct as Monica Lewinsky's lawyers said again that she was "dying" to tell her story in exchange for immunity from prosecution. □

Paired for history

The *Rocky's* front page on Dec. 20, 1998, was undeniably history-making. As in, Andrew-Johnson-history-making.

But for Colorado and the nation, it was also a prelude for another front page to come. The first part of the two-act drama, as reported by the Associated Press:

WASHINGTON – On a day of history and upheaval, President Clinton was impeached by the Republican-controlled House Saturday for perjury and obstruction of justice.

The 42nd chief executive became only the second since the nation's founding to be ordered to stand trial in the Senate. In the trial, expected next month, a two-thirds majority is required to remove Clinton from office.

The White House vowed a vigorous defense and turned aside fresh calls for Clinton's resignation – even as House Speaker-elect Bob Livingston abruptly announced he would leave Congress over his own marital indiscretions.

The House passed two of four articles facing Clinton. Article 1 alleged the president committed perjury before Independent Counsel Kenneth Starr's grand jury when asked about his relationship with former White House intern Monica Lewinsky.

The House also passed Article 3, citing Clinton for efforts to influence grand jury testimony by Lewinsky and Betty Currie, his secretary.

The vote came 11 months after an emotional, indignant Clinton appeared on television and told the nation: "I did not have sexual relations with that woman, Ms. Lewinsky."

The *Rocky* published the second front page in the drama 24 days later. Above the bold verdict on page 1, the paper quoted Clinton from the prepared statement he delivered after:

"I want to say again to the American people how profoundly sorry I am."

Acquitted

WASHINGTON – President Clinton on Friday survived only the second impeachment of a president in American history as a weary, mostly partisan Senate acquitted him on charges of perjury and obstruction of justice.

Men of the Year

On the same page Dec. 20, 1998, that the paper published the story of Clinton's House impeachment, the paper ran a small boxed item reporting that *Time* magazine had announced its ritual choice for Man of the Year. The magazine wrote:

"The (impeachment) news reinforced our decision, which we had been wrestling with until the final hours, to choose as our Men of the Year Bill Clinton and his pursuer Kenneth Starr, whose shared obstinacy but radically different personalities and values caused them to become entwined in a sullied embrace and paired for history."

Let history be served

For at least a decade the *Rocky* had tried every trick to obtain syndicated rights in the Rocky Mountain region to *The New York Times* wire service, which *The Denver Post* possessed. Finally, it bargained partial rights, and the day after Clinton was acquitted it printed a *Times* analysis. In it, the newspaper quoted Arthur M. Schlesinger Jr., the eminent historian, on what the entire impeachment episode would mean to history.

"The failed impeachment of Andrew Johnson left a wounded, weakened presidency – one that lasted for many years," Schlesinger said, "and I think the failed impeachment of Bill Clinton will do the same thing." ☐

Denver Rocky Mountain News

Judged Colorado's best newspaper   for the third straight year

December 20, 1998 • LATE SPORTS   **SUNDAY**   ★ 50¢ ($1.00 in designated areas)

Impeached

Clinton faces trial in Senate after historic House vote

First lady Hillary Rodham Clinton watches her husband promise supporters outside the White House he will serve as president "until the last hour of the last day of my term."

The toast of Colorado

It's difficult to imagine, here in the land of predominately orange-painted tract houses and Bronco-tattooed babies, anything overshadowing the local pro football team.

Leave it to John Elway.

In editions Feb. 1, 1999, the *Rocky* gave full treatment to Denver's second straight Super Bowl victory. The 52-page special section reporting the team's win over the Atlanta Falcons even topped the first Super Bowl celebration section by four pages.

But which of the following two questions do you think more Coloradans can answer today:

- The score of Super Bowl XXXIII? or

- Elway's final words to 75,000 Denver fans in his final game in Mile High Stadium after the Broncos won the AFC Championship?

The *Rocky's* front page and story inside on Jan. 18 are probably more memorable, as Lynn DeBruin wrote:

> There were no tears of joy or sadness, only an ear-to-ear grin and three words: "I love you."
> The fans at Mile High Stadium certainly showed John Elway they love him, too.
> They serenaded their hero with deafening chants of El-way, El-way as he climbed to the podium to hold the AFC Championship trophy, then shouted in unison a more urgent message.
> "One More Year, One More Year."

The Broncos' 16-year quarterback didn't make it official until some time after the Super Bowl win that he would, indeed, retire. He remains today the most recognized and revered athlete in Colorado history.

Super Bowl win No. 2

The headline and photo of Elway chugging for a touchdown said it all on the cover of the *Rocky's* Super Bowl section:

SWEET REPEAT

MIAMI – This one was for John.
Again.
Only this time, it was even better.
… Elway was named the Most Valuable Player of Super Bowl XXXIII after a 336-yard passing performance that made you wonder why he wouldn't want to come back for, you guessed it, one more season.

Back in Denver

The packs of lunatics on the streets were smaller. The police arrests were fewer. Otherwise, the *Rocky's* photos and stories of the celebration on facing pages 4-5A looked and read like 1998 all over again.

> Clouds of tear gas and police in riot gear rolled through downtown Sunday, breaking up post-Super Bowl crowds that smashed windows and overturned cars in a repeat of last year's violence.
> Within an hour of the game's end, well-prepared police on horseback and on foot formed lines across LoDo streets and marched toward hundreds of fans who poured into the area to celebrate the Broncos' second straight Super Bowl victory. □

Denver Rocky Mountain News

Most awards in Colorado for the fourth straight year

WEDNESDAY

April 21, 1999 • InsideDenver.com

25¢ (May vary outside metro Denver)

Heartbreak

2 student gunmen terrorize Columbine High in deadliest school shooting in U.S. history. **2A**

George Kochaniec Jr./News Staff Photographer

Columbine students are overwhelmed by emotion during Tuesday's rampage. As many as 25 people, including the gunmen, were killed, and 21 were wounded.

Columbine

There did not seem words capable of telling such a story. Yet throughout history, newspapers have found the words and photographs to report war, destruction, terror.

But these were children. Young adults.

On April 21, 1999, the *Denver Rocky Mountain News* performed possibly its most difficult job ever. The front page was wrenching. The headline and story on page 2A were chilling.

TRAGEDY AT COLUMBINE
Death goes to school
with cold, evil laughter

The two came to school Tuesday in fatigues, pipe bombs strapped to their chests and shotguns and high-powered pistols under long black coats.

About 11:30 a.m., they went to work, wearing masks, shredding their classmates with bullets and bombs, laughing as they went, turning Columbine High School, home of the Rebels, into the scene of the deadliest school shooting in American history.

The lead writer was Mike Anton, a veteran *Rocky* staffer, who reported and compiled the story with accounts from dozens of fellow reporters and photographers.

As many as 25 died maybe even more, police said. Twenty-one were wounded, half of them critically. They were shot in the chest and back, head and legs. One girl had nine shrapnel wounds.

"We're talking a war zone," said Steven Greene, whose son, a senior, escaped unharmed.

One teacher was among the dead.

The carnage ended when the gunmen – Dylan Klebold and Eric Harris, both juniors at Columbine, shot themselves while they were in the school library. A SWAT team found the bodies shortly before 4 p.m.

But the agony was just beginning.

That night President Clinton addressed the nation on television, expressing his sadness. The next day the newspaper devoted its first 23 pages, surrounding only five ads, to coverage.

Authorities didn't know for sure, at first, how many could be dead. Pipe bombs had exploded around the school. Bodies inside were left where they fell for fear some might be booby-trapped. It wasn't until the next day that the toll was made official: 12 students and one teacher were killed, 23 wounded. The two murderers killed themselves.

Columbine High School remained closed for the rest of the school term.

'From the publisher'

On the cover of a 24-page special wraparound section, April 22, the *Rocky* printed a letter from its publisher, Larry Strutton. It was one of the few times since even the days of founder William Byers in 1859 that the publisher spoke out in the newspaper. Strutton's message ran beneath a small headline on page 1:

Columbine students mourn their classmates. *(Rodolfo Gonzalez/Rocky Mountain News)*

A letter to our community

I write as the publisher of this newspaper, but also as a longtime member of this community and the father of two children educated in public schools, one who became a teacher.

In this time of terrible grief, so many of us are looking for ways to help the victims of the tragedy at Columbine High School.

… It's up to the community to decide what needs to be done.

… If students, teachers and parents feel there is no way they can return to the classrooms of Columbine, the *Denver Rocky Mountain News* will lead the charge to raise the funds to build a new school and urge legislators to help.

In the meantime, Strutton announced, the newspaper would lead a drive to raise funds for a memorial and it would contribute $25,000.

Columbine students returned to their high school for the fall semester. ☐

Denver Rocky Mountain News

RockyMountainNews.com

25¢ (May vary outside metro Denver)

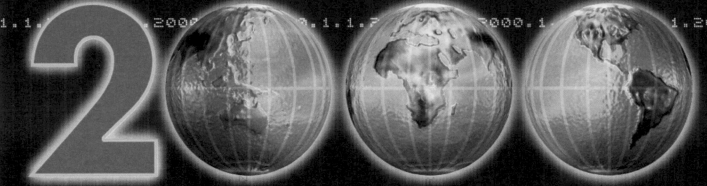

2000

World finds Y2 is OK. 2A

Rodolfo Gonzalez/News Staff Photographer and Associated Press

AROUND THE PLANET

Above left, Jim and Peggy Charleston of Gunnison share a midnight kiss at Denver's Brown Palace Hotel. Lower left, the Sydney Harbour Bridge and Opera House are illuminated by fireworks as Australia welcomes the new year. Center, the Eiffel Tower in Paris rises majestically nearly 1,000 feet into the night sky amid a halo of fireworks. Right, the ball drops at New York's Times Square, signaling the United States' smooth entry into the year 2000.

Yeltsin resigns, hands power to Putin. 5A | Hijackers release hostages. 5A

Three centuries of newspapering

One hundred years after the *Rocky Mountain News* postponed recognition of the dawn of the next century on Jan. 1, 1900, there was no delaying the arrival of the 21st century. Something called Y2K wouldn't allow it.

On New Year's Day, 1900, the newspaper published what it boasted was "the best paper ever printed in Colorado." An ambitious 54-page special section heralded the new year. But it didn't recognize the date as the start of the new century. The reasoning then – and even by some a century later – was that technically the century was from 1801 through 1900, because theoretically there was no "zero year." The *Rocky* reasoned then that the last day of the century wasn't until Dec. 31, 1900.

In the final days of 1999, there still was some debate in the newsroom – even around the world – about the mathematics of century-changing, when it ended, when it began. But there was a whistling-through-the-graveyard urgency that it was now.

The concern was that after decades of advancing technology, no one was really sure what would happen when all the world's clocks and timers and computers and odometers rolled over to read "000." The *Rocky* was pretty sure its own computers, needed to write stories and run its presses, would work. But no one was taking any chances. Thousands of hours of planning were devoted to setting up backup plans as well as marking the new millenium.

So the banner headline of a decidedly non-traditional front page on Jan. 1 carried a very real tone of relief.

The world was OK. And the paper ran photos of jubilant celebration from around the world to prove it. Its lead story chased the arrival of the new century around the globe.

The magic moment sped westward, from a windswept atoll in the South Pacific to the skyscraper canyons of Manhattan to the rock-ribbed foothills of the Front Range.

Y2K advanced relentlessly Friday, hurtling across 24 time zones and joining the world's nations in an unprecedented global block party.

… In Denver, the party was on in the bars and restaurants of LoDo and at the Pepsi Center, where Neil Diamond performed in front of 15,000. Much of downtown, though, was a no-parking zone with a heavy police presence in an attempt to prevent a repeat of rioting that struck after the Broncos' Super Bowl victories the past two years.

A century of journalism

The *Rocky* was no less ambitious than its editors one hundred years before. It published what amounted to three

newspapers in a single day – the New Year's Day Y2K paper, a special 24-page time capsule edition entitled "Dusk to Dawn" wrapping the next day's paper, and continuous electronic publication of its Internet site, rockymountainnews.com.

The Y2K edition captured the tension of the time. A reporter filed a story from outside the Year 2000 Strategic Stability Center in Colorado Springs where American and Russian military personnel together monitored each other's nuclear arsenals. Another reporter wrote about members of a local militia, the Colorado State Defense Force Reserve, stocking hotel rooms near Denver with food and weapons – just in case.

Given all the technology, all the advancements in journalism, it made the journalism of the *Rocky* one hundred years before still strikingly impressive.

Y2K wedding

Journalism had changed dramatically in 100 years. And it hadn't changed at all.

In keeping with the great tradition of newspaper stunts, at midnight on Dec. 31, 1999, the paper's Internet editor, Jack McElroy, staged a wedding in the paper's lobby and streamed live video of it on the Web site. □

Pride and pain

One hundred and 41 years, nearly to the day, after the first *Rocky Mountain News* was printed, a cheer went up once again a few blocks from the paper's birthplace along Cherry Creek. The newspaper had won its first Pulitzer Prize, the most prestigious award in journalism.

It wasn't the lead headline on page 1, and the paper shared the day with its rival, *The Denver Post,* as the story April 11, 2000, explained.

> Denver's two daily newspapers won journalism's highest honor Monday, each garnering a Pulitzer Prize for coverage of the tragedy at Columbine High School.
>
> The *Denver Rocky Mountain News* won for spot news photography.
>
> *The Denver Post* won for breaking news reporting.
>
> It was a bittersweet victory for both papers.
>
> Reporters, photographers and editors hugged each other and offered congratulations, but the moment was tinged with sadness.
>
> "I am proud that this newsroom and this newspaper have been recognized, but I sure wish we never had to get it this way," said Rocky Editor John Temple."

The murder of 12 students and one teacher at the suburban high school, and the suicides of the two fellow students and executioners, were fresh in everyone's minds. The staff was still reporting on official findings and controversies surrounding the incident. The story went on:

> "This is supposed to be a happy day," Temple said. "It's this newspaper's first Pulitzer Prize. It's my first Pulitzer Prize as an editor. But these prizes pale when you think of what we covered. You just think of the magnitude of this tragedy and those people whose lives were lost on that day."

The prizes changed the *Rocky* in one other way: It added the two faces of the Pulitzer Prize medal to the page 1 flag, although they were removed before the end of the year.

More Pulitzers

The *Rocky* won three more Pulitzer Prizes over the next six years.

The tabloid format is perfect for dominant display of photographs. Over the years, director Janet Reeves developed a talented staff of editors and photographers. This team won a second Pulitzer for breaking news photography in 2003 for its coverage of an endless summer of Colorado wildfires, particularly the Hayman Fire, the most destructive ever in the state.

And in 2006, reporter Jim Sheeler and photographer Todd Heisler both collected Pulitzers for feature writing and feature photography for the powerful series, "Final Salute." Sheeler and Heisler spent a year following Maj. Steve Beck, a Marine casualty notification officer responsible for telling families that their loved ones had been killed during the Iraq War.

A busy news day

The page 1 banner on April 11, 2000, was a significant story. Gov. Bill Owens signed the law requiring the first public school report cards based on Colorado Student Assessment Program (CSAP) tests, to be issued following the next school year as part of education reform.

Elsewhere in the paper, Elian Gonzalez, the 6-year-old boy rescued at sea trying to reach America, was close to being returned to his Cuban home; Colorado's Supreme Court ordered a Vail man to face felony charges in the collision death of another skier, a landmark case; Hantavirus, a lethal disease transmitted by exposure to infected rodents, had claimed its first victim of the year; and, the paper ran the first excerpts from the new book *JonBenet: Inside the Ramsey Murder Investigation.* □

The beginning of the end

In the century-long Denver newspaper war, it was the cruelest, yet bravest front-page headline the newspaper had ever printed.

The "truce" between the *Rocky* and *The Denver Post* brushed away exhausting, expensive efforts by both papers for decades to put the other away, once and for all. Yet – at least on paper, as they say – the agreement saved one or both from the nation's growing heap of failed newspapers, at least for a while, and offered owners the prospect of making a buck.

The *Rocky* explained on May 12, 2000:

The Denver Rocky Mountain News and *The Denver Post* declared a truce Thursday in the nation's last major newspaper war, ending a bitter battle that spanned a century and took a financial toll on both papers.

The dailies agreed to merge their business operations while maintaining separate newsrooms, an arrangement known as a joint operating agreement or JOA. The 50-year agreement requires approval from the U.S. Justice Department, which will receive the application today.

"The war has exacted a cost which threatens this community's rich newspaper heritage," said Kenneth Lowe, president and chief operating officer of the E.W. Scripps Co., which owns the *News*. "It has been an incredible battle."

Despite record circulation gains, the *News* has lost $123 million in the past decade and faces probable financial failure, Lowe said. *The Post* has been consistently profitable, making $200 million in the past 10 years, but the fierce competition has cut into those profits, said William Dean Singleton, chairman and CEO of the MediaNews Group, which owns *The Post*.

Recent audits showed the *Rocky* ahead in circulation by more than 30,000 daily. Yet one of its latest subscription campaigns offered the paper six days a week for one penny a day.

How does it work?

To this day, some Coloradans think the *Rocky* and *Post* were owned by the same company under the JOA. They were not.

The two parent companies, Scripps and MediaNews Group, formed and shared equal ownership in a third company named the Denver Newspaper Agency. The DNA consolidated the business operations of the two papers – advertising, marketing, circulation, production, finance, technology, etc. – which resulted in operational savings.

The gravest fear in the community when JOAs are formed is that it will lose the competitive voices of two independent newspapers. But in Denver, the two editorial staffs operated separately, and still reported to their respective owners.

As one example, after the two papers moved into new offices at Broadway and Colfax Avenue, they worked and even parked on separate, secure floors. Staff members were not permitted on each other's floors.

Competition was as keen as ever.

It's like football

The public understands competition. But some have never really grasped the intensity of the rivalry between the *Rocky* and *Post*.

During Bill McCartney's first season at the University of Colorado in 1982, the new football coach railed one day at the *Rocky's* beat writer over a story he had scooped *The Post* on but which McCartney didn't like. The football coach said he didn't understand the scrutiny his program was under.

"I look at *The Post*," the writer explained, "like you look at Nebraska."

McCartney looked like he'd experienced an epiphany. "Ohhhh," he said, smiling. "Now I get it." □

Denver Rocky Mountain News

Winner of the 2000 Pulitzer Prize for news photography

May 12, 2000 • RockyMountainNews.com **FRIDAY** 35¢ (May vary outside metro Denver)

News-Post truce

Newspapers end 108-year battle, agree to merge business operations. 4A

A duplex in Los Alamos, N.M., is engulfed in flames early Thursday. Firefighters watched helplessly as the blaze ravaged the town for a second day. More than 20,000 people have evacuated the region.

RUNAWAY INFERNO

Hundreds of homes lost in Los Alamos firestorm. 2A

BOB KRAVITZ: *Turnabout's fair play: Avs will earn spot in NHL finals.* 1N Rocky Mountain News 8-PAGE SECTION FOLLOWS 14C ► Avalanche braces for knock-down, drag-out playoff rematch with Stars. 2N

The 35-day election

The progression of headlines in the *Rocky Mountain News* in the 2000 presidential election gave Colorado a lesson in civics, and pages of history.

Between election result editions, Nov. 8, the newspaper changed the front-page banner. When the first edition had to go to press around 11 p.m. it was:

CLIFFHANGER
Gore, Bush swap lead through wild night.

It was too close to call, so the paper had to hedge. George W. Bush held 246 electoral votes to Al Gore's 241. The constitutional majority necessary to win was 270. But four states were still undecided.

By the time the *Rocky* had to close its final edition at 12:30 a.m., editors called it:

BUSH ON TOP
**Texas governor edges out
Gore with win in Florida.**

Bush now had 271 electoral votes to Gore's 249. But the vote in the pivotal state of Florida had been extremely close. At one point television networks gave the state to Gore. But when more votes were counted and Bush surged ahead, they reversed and declared him the winner in Florida.

Gore challenged the results. Florida had to recount some counties, an exercise so painstaking that election officials were forced to examine individual ballot punches, leading to the infamous late-night comedy punchline asking "what's a hanging chad?"

The *Rocky's* front page banner on Nov. 27:

It's 'official' but not over
**19 days later, Florida declares Bush victory;
Gore vows legal fight.**

Florida certified its vote and Bush's triumph. Still, Gore, the sitting vice president, insisted the vote was incomplete, and the U.S. Supreme Court agreed to hear his case. Eight days later, on Dec. 5, the *Rocky's* front page reported that not much had changed:

2 strikes on Gore
**27 days after election, Florida judge,
U.S. Supreme Court reject recounts,
dimming VP's hopes for White House.**

Four more days and the Florida Supreme Court, by a 4-3 vote, jolted the nation by restoring enough Gore votes to leave him only 154 behind Bush, and declaring an immediate recount of thousands of state ballots. The *Rocky's* headline:

Stunner
**Florida high court gives Gore
new life in presidential race.**

The next day, Dec. 10, provided yet another pendulum-swing banner:

Not so fast
**U.S. Supreme Court halts
recount, deals blow to Gore.**

Finally, three days later, the headline in the Dec. 13 newspaper appeared to end the national drama:

5-4 for Bush
**Historic decision clears
path to presidency**

WASHINGTON – The Supreme Court effectively handed the presidential election to Gov. George W. Bush Tuesday night.

Exactly five weeks after one of the most unsettled elections in history the Texas governor appeared to have swept away any lingering legal obstacles, achieving the right to call himself "president-elect."

The court overturned the Florida Supreme Court, ruling by a 5-4 vote that there could be no further counting of Florida's disputed presidential votes.

While the campaigns of Bush and Vice President Al Gore were still processing and digesting the Supreme Court's tangled and elaborate ruling as midnight approached in Washington, officials in both camps said it was now virtually impossible for Gore to become president.

It had taken 35 days to elect a president in the United States. ☐

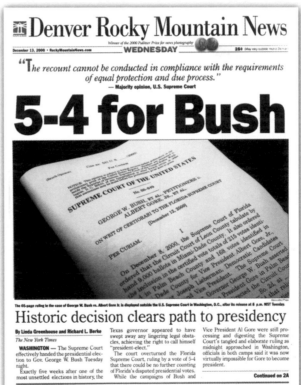

Broadsheet madness

Longtime readers might have thought they'd received a special introductory, souvenir thank-you, bonus prize instead of their regular *Rocky* on Saturday, April 7, 2001.

Why, Mabel, look – it's a jigsaw puzzle dressed up as a newspaper.

As part of the joint operating agreement signed with *The Denver Post* 11 months before, it was agreed that in the near future only the *Rocky* would continue to publish on Saturdays and only *The Post* would print on Sundays as a joint cost-saving measure. But because of the logistics of printing and delivering 800,000-plus newspapers to both *News* and *Post* customers on back-to-back days, it was now necessary to print both weekend editions in the same format, the same size.

For the first morning since 1942, the *Rocky* was a broadsheet again, on Saturdays only.

The editors wanted to retain the look and feel of the daily tabloid, yet they were limited by the physical capabilities of huge printing presses. The result was ... interesting.

The Saturday *Rocky* was the same size as *The Post*, but page 1 was printed sideways so that it still looked like a magazine-shaped tabloid.

When readers turned the front page, they found themselves in the Sports section. And the broadsheet pages inside were, of course, at right angles with the cover. That was intentional, so readers would know this was still the *Rocky*. But it was as if you boarded an airplane to Omaha and got off and found yourself in Istanbul.

The paper also added the word *Weekend* in front of *Rocky Mountain News* to distinguish it as a larger non-weekday edition.

Editor John Temple tried to put the best face on the contrivance in his column.

> **Today the *Rocky Mountain News* introduces a new newspaper, a Weekend edition bigger and better than any Saturday paper Denver's dailies have ever produced.**
>
> **Today, for the first time in more than 100 years, subscribers of the *Rocky Mountain News* and *The Denver Post* are receiving the same newspaper.**
>
> **I welcome you all – those of you who are not familiar with the *News* and those of you who are our old friends – to a new newspaper, a newspaper we've designed especially for Colorado weekends.**

Deep down, the *Rocky* staff hated what they felt was a jury-rigged product.

Though the Saturday paper remained a broadsheet, the *Rocky* greatly improved the organization of sections and quickly quit printing the cover sideways. It's a collector's edition, if you saved the first one.

New: Insight

To bolster the new Weekend edition, the newspaper introduced the Insight section, full of in-depth journalism and commentary. The first front-page banner story ran there. It was a special report on the unfairness of Colorado's probate system and how it mangled the lives of fragile, usually elderly citizens.

Turn to page Somewhere-A

Doing everything they could to help readers navigate through the new Saturday format, editors wrote "refer" blurbs on the many section covers, directing readers and promoting top stories inside. The blurb on the cover of Insight sent readers to an analysis of the changing newspaper industry on page 29A. Only problem was, the section ended on page 28A. Readers' instincts, no doubt, helped them find the piece on 26A. ☐

Rocky Mountain News

September 12, 2001 • 24/7 @ RockyMountainNews.com

WEDNESDAY

50¢ May vary outside metro Denver

'Our nation saw evil'

Kristen Brochmann/The New York Times

An inferno engulfs the World Trade Center after two hijacked jets slammed into the towers Tuesday. President Bush vowed to hunt down the terrorists. 2A

America shaken

There was no describing the horror, deceit and sadness of 9/11. The *Rocky* attempted to do so with straightforward, comprehensive journalism.

The words on page 1 came from President George W. Bush's live televised speech to the nation.

Inside, spread across page 2 and 3, the story unfolded beneath the headline:

U.S. in shock after deadly day

NEW YORK – In the most devastating terrorist onslaught waged against the United States, knife-wielding hijackers crashed two jetliners into the World Trade Center on Tuesday, toppling its twin 110-story towers.

The calamity was witnessed on televisions across the world as another plane slammed into the Pentagon, and a fourth crashed outside Pittsburgh.

... Establishing the death toll could take weeks. The four airliners alone had 266 people aboard, and there were no known survivors. Officials put the number of dead and wounded at the Pentagon at about 100 or more, with some news reports suggesting it could rise to 800.

In addition, a union official said he feared 300 firefighters who first reached the scene had died in rescue efforts at the trade center – where 50,000 people worked – and dozens of police officers were missing.

The paper used 48 pages of its 68-page main section to cover the attack. Forty-one were full pages. With Business and Sports sections both carrying stories on the impact, 60 of the paper's total 88 editorial pages carried the story. Most were labeled with the "header" agreed upon by editors to tie the pages together:

AMERICA UNDER ATTACK

All eight staff columnists and cartoonists, plus six editorials, focused on what the nation had already begun referring to as "9/11." The lead editorial ran in a heavy black box:

The act of war against the United States on Tuesday succeeded in inflicting slaughter and shock on a superpower. But it did much more than that, of course.

It also changed everything. It altered the way Americans think of their personal safety, national security and relationship with the rest of the world.

Sports and Business

Since World War II, as the reality of world events visited our lives, newspapers learned that none of its pages were insulated from tragedy. At the *Rocky*, gone were the days when the Sports section could ignore a life-altering event outside its realm.

On Sept. 12, 2001, the lead Sports story wasn't about a game. Bernie Lincicome's column led the section beneath the headline:

There's no fun in games today

The next story on the Sports cover reported the Broncos and NFL were reviewing whether to play games the weekend after the national tragedy. On page 2C, the paper's sports cartoonist, Drew Litton, drew the image of a distraught baseball player walking off the field with the word "GROUNDED" hovering above the diamond.

Major League Baseball suspended games that day. No one had any qualms about interrupting Barry Bonds' home run record quest. Three days earlier, Bonds had swatted No. 63 in Denver on his way to a record 73.

The Business section was equally reflective. The lead headline:

Economists say recession likely

U.S. stock markets would remain shut down at least through Sept. 12. The last time the New York Stock Exchange closed for more than a day was in 1933.

One year later

In all, more than 3,000 people died as a result of the 9/11 attack. One year later, in a 24-page memorial section, the *Rocky* printed the name of every one of them. The stark, nearly empty section cover bore a simple headline beneath a small photo of the smoking, but still standing twin towers:

We remember

America strikes back

Less than a month after the 9/11 attacks, the United States delivered its response. The *Rocky* summed it up in one word on page 1 on Oct. 8, while departing from its usual format and starting the text of the Associated Press story, accompanied by an intricate battle map.

> WASHINGTON – American and British forces unleashed punishing airstrikes Sunday against military targets and Osama bin Laden's training camps in Afghanistan.
>
> The strikes were aimed at terrorists blamed for the Sept. 11 attacks that murdered thousands on the East Coast.
>
> ... "I gave them a warning," the president told one adviser.
>
> The opening of a sustained campaign dubbed Enduring Freedom, the assault was accompanied by airdrops of thousands of vitamin-enriched food rations for needy civilians – and by a ground-based attack by Afghan opposition forces against the ruling Taliban.

The page theme **"AMERICA UNDER ATTACK"** had been replaced by **"AMERICA STRIKES BACK."**

The headlines of a new war began a daily march across the paper's front page:

(Oct. 9) **Bush warns Americans 'This will be a long war'**

The same day, George W. Bush created the Office of Homeland Security with former Pennsylvania Gov. Tom Ridge in charge, and America dealt with a new threat – anthrax deaths in Florida.

(Oct. 11) **Day 4 brings rain of bombs**

The U.S. stepped up, if possible, the bombardment of Afghanistan. The White House unveiled a "most wanted list" of 22 suspected terrorists with bin Laden at the top.

(Oct. 12) **'America is strong'**

Marking the one-month anniversary of 9/11, President Bush went on national TV again, offering the Taliban regime in Afghanistan a "second chance" to surrender bin Laden and leaders of the al-Qaeda terrorist network.

International insight

From the start of the war, the *Rocky* used its international editor, Holger Jensen, to good advantage. His strength was interpreting for readers the stream of foreign names and motives and beliefs that came hurtling at them, and providing the perspective of a journalist who had been to these places. Samples from his columns in October, 2001:

■ This war in Afghanistan will not be pretty. ... It is not a war for territory but a war against terrorists, and it can only be won if we convince the Afghans that we are on their side against a common enemy.

■ Has Osama bin Laden succeeded in pitting Islam against the West? No, at least not yet. But he has cleverly elevated the Palestinian cause in his holy war against the infidel, making it that much more difficult for the Palestinians and their Arab supporters to distance themselves from bin Laden's brand of international terrorism.

■ His (bin Laden's) call for a holy war has not captivated much of the Islamic world ... (Anti-American demonstrations) have not attracted the silent majority there and appear to be waning as Muslim clerics and political leaders finally speak out in support of the United States. □

Rocky Mountain News

MONDAY

October 8, 2001 · 24/7 @ RockyMountainNews.com
★★★ 50¢ May vary outside metro Denver

"I gave them fair warning." — President Bush

Retaliation

U.S., British launch massive air attack on Afghanistan

By David Espo
Associated Press

WASHINGTON — American and British forces unleashed punishing airstrikes Sunday against military targets and Osama bin Laden's training camps in Afghanistan.

The strikes were aimed at terrorists blamed for the Sept. 11 attacks that mur-dered thousands on the

Operation Enduring Freedom

Weapons used

Forests blackened and a legend lost

Rocky Mountain News
WEDNESDAY

"More extreme than Yellowstone." — Joe Hartman, fire commander

Scorched earth: 150,000 acres

Firefighters on edge as blazes devour forests, threaten homes. 4A

■ Hayman Fire too dangerous to put crews on front lines, commander says. 5A

The *Rocky* headline –

Scorched earth: 150,000 acres

told a story that proved to be only the beginning of Colorado's worst wildfire season.

For the next three weeks a series of monster wildfires raged across the state, including what was to become the largest fire in history – the Hayman Fire. It began June 8, when a U.S. Forest Service worker, Terry Lynn Barton, first reported it as an abandoned campfire near Lake Ge orge in Park County. When it was finally contained, the Hayman Fire alone had burned more than 137,000 acres in four counties – Park, Teller, Douglas and Jefferson. One hundred fifteen residences and more than 445 other buildings were lost. And most tragic, four firefighters on their way to fight the Hayman died when their van rolled in an accident.

Barton confessed to accidentally starting the Hayman Fire. She was later convicted and served her sentence in prison.

2002 major wildfires

- ■ Snaking (near Bailey)
- ■ Black Mountain (Pike National Forest)
- ■ Schoonover (southwest of Deckers)
- ■ Trinidad Complex (east and west of Trinidad)
- ■ Iron Mountain (southwest of Canon City)
- ■ Hayman (near Lake George)
- ■ Coal Seam (west of Glenwood Springs)
- ■ Missionary Ridge (north of Durango)
- ■ Million (south of South Fork)
- ■ Valley (northwest of Durango)
- ■ Big Elk Meadow (near Estes Park)

Voice of Denver

A month before the summer inferno, the *Rocky* lost its most popular writer – maybe ever – and Denver lost one of its civic treasures when columnist Gene Amole died, only days shy of his 79th birthday. More than six months earlier, Amole announced in his column that he was dying. His body was giving out on him. But he said he intended to write a diary of his last days that he hoped would help others.

He died on May 12, 2002. The next day the paper printed the column he wrote to be read upon his death. The column began with Amole's customary clipped opening.

Goodbye, Denver

Grumbled.

In life, we ask where have I been, and where am I going? In death, I don't know where I am going or if I shall even exist. I have been to a lot of wonderful places, though, and I am grateful for the journey.

Gene Amole

Amole didn't start his job as the *Rocky's* columnist until he was 54. After serving with the Army in World War II, he came home to start jazz radio station KDEN and one year later KVOD, which became one of the most successful classical music stations in the country. But he said he always dreamed of writing for the *Rocky*.

From his very first column on Dec. 18, 1977:

I shall want to deal with the human condition in some of these columns. Perhaps we can laugh at ourselves on this page. Sometimes I suppose we'll cry. There's nothing wrong with that. It's OK to cry. Take it from me. I have been known to cry at supermarket grand openings and eighth-grade continuation ceremonies.

The *Rocky* published four books of Amole's columns over the years – *Morning, Amole Again, Amole One More Time* and, posthumously, *The Last Chapter.* □

The fall of Baghdad

The front-page headline beside the literal toppling of Saddam Hussein in Baghdad in the *Rocky* on April 10, 2003, gave readers reason for hope.

> **BAGHDAD, Iraq – Their hour of freedom at hand, jubilant Iraqis celebrated the collapse of Saddam Hussein's murderous regime on Wednesday.**
>
> **Crowds beheaded a toppled statue of their long-time ruler in downtown Baghdad and embraced American troops as liberators.**
>
> **"I'm 49, but I never lived a single day. Only now will I start living," said Yussuf Abed Kazim, a mosque preacher.**
>
> **… The scenes of liberation in Baghdad and celebrations in other cities unfolded as the Pentagon announced that 101 American troops had died in the first three weeks of Operation Iraqi Freedom.**

It had taken American and British troops only 21 days to slash across the desert country in their drive to bring down and capture the dictator, end his regime and prove the White House's claim that Iraq held weapons of mass destruction, or WMDs.

But now that they had reached Baghdad, neither Saddam nor the WMDs were anywhere to be found.

In another AP story:

> **Defense Secretary Donald Rumsfeld laid out several possibilities: "(Saddam's) not active. Therefore, he's either dead, or he's incapacitated, or he's healthy and cowering in some tunnel someplace."**

Rumsfeld, who was later asked to resign by President George W. Bush, was right about one thing. In a few months, Saddam was flushed out of an underground burrow. The front-page headline:

> **'Got him'**

The tyrant stood trial and was eventually executed.

No evidence that Iraq possessed weapons of mass destruction at the start of the war has ever been discovered.

Imbedded

Coalition forces granted unprecedented presence of journalists in the battlefield in Iraq and Afghanistan. "Imbedded with the troops" became the most sought after media calling card and a badge of courage around the world.

Five staff members from the *Rocky* were imbedded at different times during the war. Photographer Todd Heisler was with the Seabees of the 1st Marine Expeditionary Force at the start. In December, 2003, he and columnist Bill Johnson joined the 3rd Brigade Combat Team, then the 3rd Armored Cavalry Regiment, both out of Fort Carson. The two journalists "re-upped" with the 3rd Armored for about a month in 2005 before an armored vehicle they were traveling in was blasted by an IED – improvised explosive device. They were brought home safely soon after. Reporter Charlie Brennan was with the Army V Corps in Kuwait on the day of the invasion. Washington correspondent M.E. Sprengelmeyer was attached to the 101st Airborne Division. Photographer Ahmad Terry was assigned to the 4th Infantry Division, also deployed out of Fort Carson.

Blizzard of '03

Denver and the rest of Colorado couldn't have felt any farther away from the blazing sands of Iraq on the day Baghdad fell. Three days after the largest snowstorm in 90 years struck, residents were still digging out from snow piled from 2 to 8 feet deep.

The American troops' arrival in Baghdad pushed continuing storm coverage in the newspaper back to page 37A.

> **The first day of spring delivered a shirt-sleeve warm-up Thursday – bright sunshine melting a historic snowfall as the work of reclaiming driveways and rerouting travelers continued.**
>
> **While cars – the non-four-wheel-drive kind – reclaimed the streets, much of the metro area remained shut down for a third straight day, with schools and government offices closed.**
>
> **Denver International Airport, a tent city for 4,000 people since Tuesday, reopened for business, giving some stranded travelers hope they soon might be on the way out of town.** ☐

San Luis Valley saga

The re-election of George W. Bush wasn't any easier for the *Rocky* to call the next day, Nov. 3, 2004, than the President's election was in 2000. The first-edition page 1 banner carefully hedged:

Nail-biter
Bush, Kerry in dead heat on historic Election Night.

By the close of the final edition, the outcome remained undecided, but it looked like it was Ohio's turn to keep the nation awake overnight.

"Ohio loomed as this year's Florida," the Associated Press story inside reported.

But history had already been made on the front page with the raised Stetson and thumbs-up smile of Senator-elect Ken Salazar.

Ken Salazar's narrow victory over Pete Coors sends him to a U.S. Senate that has had only three Hispanics in its history, the last nearly 30 years ago.

That fact alone rockets Salazar to national prominence, said Denver pollster Floyd Ciruli.

"He'll be a player on the national stage immediately," Ciruli said.

In his victory speech, Salazar recalled his family's heritage. He grew up on a San Luis Valley ranch without electricity or a telephone.

But he was only half the story. A smaller headline at the bottom of page 1 also wasn't written until minutes before the edition closed:

Congress: John Salazar beats Walcher in 3rd.

Ken, twice elected Colorado's attorney general, and John, a potato farmer who was elected to the state legislature in his first campaign for office, became the second set of Democratic brothers in the 2004 election to take seats in the Senate and House. They joined Carl and Sander Levin of Michigan.

Someone was sleeping

At least one Salazar watching election results at the clan's ranch five miles east of Manassa, Colorado, home of boxing legend Jack Dempsey, couldn't stay awake any longer. Emma Salazar, 82-year-old mother of the two politicians, would have to dream of her sons' victories one more night.

"My heart doesn't let me stay up late. I usually go to bed at nine," Emma Salazar said, monitoring early returns from her recliner with a portable telephone in one hand and a TV remote control in the other. "Maybe they can wake me to tell me what happens."

Rocky reporter Joe Garner wrote about watching some of the returns with her. Ken Salazar called home after she went to bed, but still didn't know yet if he had won.

'America has spoken'

That was the front-page banner the second day after the 2004 election, burned into a photo of a smiling George W. Bush, who received 270 electoral votes to 252 for Democrat John Kerry. *The New York Times* report:

George Walker Bush declared victory in the race for president on Wednesday, driving a national election that bolstered Republican strength in Congress and led the White House to proclaim that Bush had captured a mandate for a second term.

"America has spoken," Bush said.

It was the postscript to a second night of quibbling and consternation over Ohio's close vote, before Kerry conceded. □

Blown away by Katrina

Five days after 145-mile per hour winds shredded southern Louisiana, Mississippi and Alabama, and waters swamped 80 percent of New Orleans, the *Rocky* added a "story header" to its coverage of the hurricane on Sept. 3, 2005. The purpose of such labels is to set a theme for multi-page, continued coverage. The header:

IN WAKE OF KATRINA

Indeed, the aftermath of the hurricane became the story and, tragically, it was just beginning. The Associated Press story on the Saturday broadsheet cover:

> **The cavalry finally arrived.**
> **With a cigar-chomping general in front, a convoy of at least three-dozen troop vehicles and supply trucks rolled through floodwaters Friday into a desperate and devastated New Orleans, where some survivors of Hurricane Katrina had died waiting for food, water and medicine.**
> **"Thank you, Jesus," Leschia Radford shrieked amid a throng of tens of thousands outside the city's convention center.**
> **Some people threw their arms heavenward, and others nearly fainted with joy as the soldiers arrived in the punishing midday heat in a scene that looked like a relief mission to a Third World country.**

New Orleans Mayor Ray Nagin's original estimate of "thousands" dead rivaled the San Francisco earthquake a century before as the worst natural disaster in U.S. history.

Rocky Mountain News
& THE DENVER POST
SATURDAY, SEPTEMBER 3, 2005 ★ 50 cents in Denver

IN WAKE OF KATRINA

Help at last

■ **Relief:** Soldiers, water, food roll into New Orleans. ■ **Bush:** Declares response 'not acceptable,' tours region. ■ **Scene:** Firsthand from streets – a walk through hell.

President Bush tries to comfort Bronwynn Bassier, 23, and her sister, Kim Bassier, 21, left, during a walking tour Friday in Biloxi, Miss.

The cavalry finally arrived.

With a cigar-chomping general in front, a convoy of at least three-dozen troop vehicles and supply trucks rolled through floodwaters Friday into a desperate and devastated New Orleans, where some survivors of Hurricane Katrina had died waiting for food, water and medicine.

"Thank you, Jesus!" Leschia Radford shrieked amid a throng of tens of thousands outside the city's convention center.

Some people threw their arms heavenward, and others nearly fainted with joy as the soldiers arrived in the punishing midday heat in a scene that looked like a relief mission to a Third World country.

But there was also anger and jeers from many in the crowd who questioned why they had to wait four days before they could get anything to eat or drink.

"They should have been here days ago," said 48-year-old Michael Levy, whose words were echoed by those around him yelling, "Hell, yeah!"

"We've been sleeping on the ... ground like rats," Levy added. "I say burn this whole ... city down."

The mayor and others had complained that the federal government had bungled the relief effort and let people die for lack of food, water or medicine.

Within minutes of the soldiers' arrival, they set up food and water lines. The crowd was mostly orderly, grateful for the first major relief to reach the arena.

Accompanying the convoy were dozens of buses, waiting to transport the bedraggled crowd to Texas.

President Bush toured hard-hit areas of Louisiana, Mississippi and Alabama and admitted of the relief effort, "The results are not acceptable."

Congress passed a $10.5 billion disaster-aid package, which Bush signed later Friday.

One group of Katrina's victims lurched from one tragedy to another: A bus carrying evacuees from the Superdome overturned on a Louisiana highway,

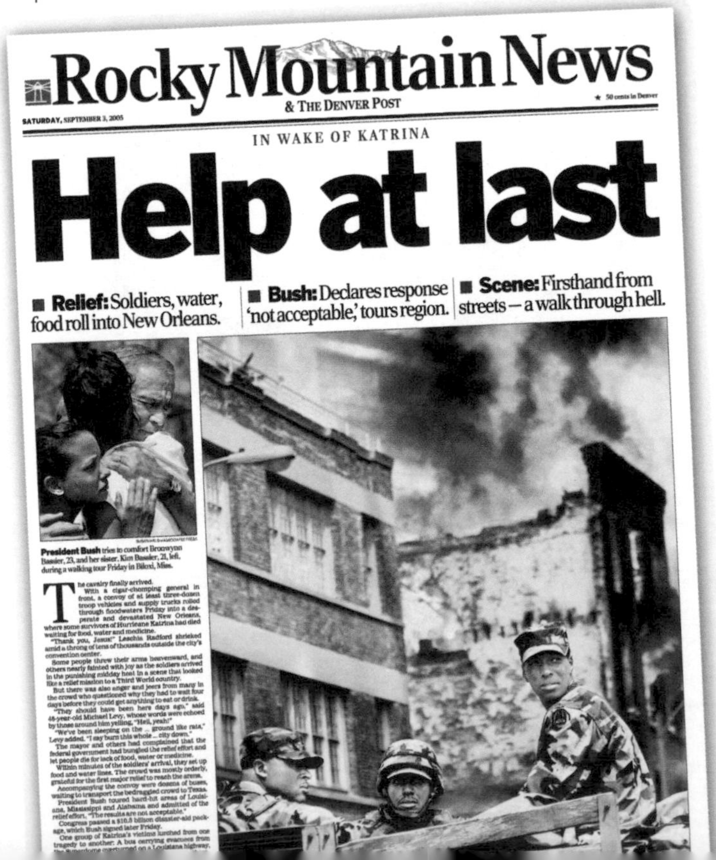

Countless numbers were trapped and drowned when two levees were breached, unleashing Lake Pontchartrain into the city. Most of New Orleans' poor and elderly didn't evacuate and many moved into the convention center and eventually the Superdome. More than two million Gulf Coast residents were without power or utilities.

Two days after the hurricane, the mayor was again quoted in the *Rocky's* main story:

> **"We're not even dealing with dead bodies," Nagin said. "They're just pushing them on the side."**

The Red Cross set up shelters. But government promises of more National Guardsmen to help stop looting and $10 billion in aid had yet to reach the city. As the newspaper reported on Sept. 2:

> **New Orleans' top emergency management official called that effort a "national disgrace" and questioned when reinforcements actually would reach the increasingly lawless city.**

The same day, President George W. Bush toured the devastated region and delivered ill-fated praise to his head of the Federal Emergency Management Agency, Mike Brown. The *Rocky* and papers across the country quoted him:

> **"Brownie, you're doing a heck of a job."**

Still, New Orleans suffered. The paper's header could have been shortened to **WAKE OF KATRINA.**

On Sept. 10 there was a new headline over an AP story:

Boss booted off job

> **WASHINGTON – The administration dumped FEMA Director Mike Brown as commander of Hurricane Katrina relief operations Friday as President Bush tried to rekindle memories of the 2001 terror attacks, hailing the "extraordinary bravery" of rescue personnel.**

Back in Denver

Squeezed among the front-page Katrina banners that lingered for weeks, *Rocky* readers found at least two headlines bearing more cheerful local news.

(Sept. 3) Grand entrance

The Ellie Caulkins Opera House, rebuilt like "a ship in a bottle" within the 97-year-old Auditorium Theatre, was ready to reopen after undergoing a $92 million overhaul.

(Sept. 8) United's new start

Denver's troubled hub airline was emerging from bankruptcy with a plan to replace stock and resolve $26 million in debts. □

Baseball reigns over a football town

The *Rocky* front page of Oct. 16, 2007, is memorable for at least four reasons:

- After 15 seasons in sports' most exclusive realm, Major League Baseball, the Colorado Rockies were going to their first World Series.

- The Rockies had to win 21 of their last 22 games to get there.

- Cover boy Todd Helton, the rock of the franchise and one of the best players in baseball never to have reached a World Series, was going to get his chance.

- And, soon, after spending the entire month of Rocktober on page 1, it would be over. The team would lose the Series in four straight games to the Boston Red Sox.

But baseball had never seen such a stretch run. The story inside, written by Tracy Ringolsby, recently voted into the media wing of baseball's Hall of Fame:

Dream World
Believe it: Rockies are NL champions

Todd Helton's going to the World Series. And he didn't have to leave town to do it.

He might no longer be the face of the franchise, but he is the foundation that the team has been built around – a championship team.

The Rockies added another chapter to the most dramatic late-season surge in baseball history Monday night with a 6-4 victory against the Arizona Diamondbacks at Coors Field to finish a four-game sweep of the National League Championship Series.

Usually by September, the *Rocky* had banished the Rockies to the back pages of the Sports section, never to be seen on page 1. They had reached the playoffs only once before, in 1995.

In 2007, though, the Rockies bumped even the adored Broncos from the cover. The paper began riding Rockies Fever in mid-September. On Oct. 3, when the team secured a playoff berth, the paper published a 28-page special section. It launched a daily Rocky Rocktober special section. A "Whiz Kids" special section wrapped the paper at the start of the NLCS on Oct. 11. Helton also stole the cover of a "NL CHAMPIONSHIP EXTRA" on Oct. 16. Then, starting Oct. 24, Game 1 of the World Series, the *Rocky* wrapped the main paper with a daily WORLD SERIES COLLECTOR'S EDITION until the ride ended Oct. 29.

Been there

Denver's sports fans finally got a championship and didn't dismantle downtown to celebrate. In fact, they even brought brooms to the game Oct. 15 to sweep up after the Diamondbacks. Jubilant fans blocked the intersection of 20th and Blake streets in front of Coors Field for 30 minutes after the last out, but they avoided the mayhem and destruction that followed previous big victories by the Broncos and Avalanche.

What else was going on?

On the day of Helton's page 1 appearance, inside the *Rocky* led local news with a story that Children's Hospital was throwing away old furniture for safety reasons, despite one church's efforts to salvage pieces. And – a story that had familiar sepia tones – air quality activists were demanding oil and gas polluters do more to reduce CO_2 emissions. □

DENVER • TUESDAY, OCTOBER 16, 2007 • 50 CENTS ★★

Rocky Mountain News

Yes!

Rox sweep into World Series with 6-4 win over Arizona.

Todd Helton squeezes the final out and celebrates the Rockies win Monday that ended 14 years of frustration and put the team in the World Series for the first time.

KEN PAPALEO/ROCKY MOUNTAIN NEWS

American history in Colorado

Win or lose the 2008 election, Sen. Barack Obama made history on the front page of the *Rocky,* June 4, by becoming the first African-American to secure a major-party nomination for president of the United States.

The headline and Associated Press story inside on page 20:

'America, this is our moment'

ST. PAUL, Minn. – Before a crowd of cheering thousands, Sen. Barack Obama of Illinois laid claim to the Democratic presidential nomination Tuesday night, taking a historic step toward his once-improbable goal of becoming the nation's first black president.

Hillary Rodham Clinton maneuvered for the vice presidential spot on his fall ticket without conceding her own defeat.

"America, this is our moment," the 46-year-old senator and one-time community organizer said in his first appearance as the Democratic nominee-in-waiting. "This is our time. Our time to turn the page on the policies of the past."

Obama's victory set up a five-month campaign with Republican Sen. John McCain of Arizona, a race between a first-term Senate opponent of the Iraq War and a 71-year-old former Vietnam prisoner of war and staunch supporter of the current military mission.

It was the end of a historic state primary campaign in which Clinton narrowly missed becoming the first woman nominated for president. By winning one of the final two primaries, Montana, Obama achieved the majority of state delegates necessary to win the nomination. In the months to come, Obama chose not to consider Clinton for vice president, dashing some Dems' hopes of a "Dream Ticket," and instead chose the experienced Sen. Joe Biden.

The presumptive nomination of Obama also marked a noteworthy milestone for the *Rocky.* Because of the historic significance of the primaries, the Democratic National Convention to be held in Denver in August, and the election to come, the newspaper had invested in the most comprehensive, multi-media, coast-to-coast election coverage in its history. Taking advantage of the Internet age, even before the primaries the paper launched an innovative Web site, red/blue America, inviting readers and Internet bloggers – a new electronic groundswell – to add their voices to the national political debate ahead. The paper moved Scripps political correspondent M.E. Sprengelmeyer from Washington to Des Moines before the Iowa caucuses, and columnist Mike Littwin criss-crossed the country to bring the candidates into Colorado homes.

But there was still more history to come.

Another Denver anniversary

One hundred years after Denver hosted the party of William Jennings Bryan, it staged its second Democratic National Convention.

The city went to enormous lengths planning and preparing for the event. In the post-9/11 world, security was a dominating concern. Protesters vowed to be seen and heard, and security was complicated even further when Obama chose to move the final night's nomination acceptance from the Pepsi Center headquarters to 75,000-seat Invesco Field, home of the Denver Broncos.

The *Rocky* printed huge convention special sections around the main paper every day. It packed its Web site with updates, video coverage, a daily animated convention cartoon, and a new cool tool called Twitter that reporters used to directly feed the Web with text messages.

The crowning edition was Aug. 29, the morning after Obama accepted the Democratic nomination on the 45th anniversary of Dr. Martin Luther King's "I have a dream" speech.

Obama, wife Michelle and their two daughters filled the front page. The banner headline, and the story inside by Kevin Vaughan:

'Time to change'

Thursday night, on a date symbolic of both the worst and the best of recent life for African-Americans, a black man stood in a football stadium in Denver and made history, accepting the Democratic Party's nomination for president.

More history

The next day, the *Rocky* delivered another dose of drama on page 1:

McCain regains spotlight with surprise veep pick
Choice of first-term Alaska Gov. Sarah Palin considered a shocker

Wealth-quake

It wasn't the beginning of the gravest economic disaster in America in 80 years. And it certainly wasn't the end of it.

But on Oct. 4, 2008, the *Rocky's* banner headline and story marked a seminal moment in the nation's history – an unprecedented government bailout that no one was even sure would pull the country out of its worst financial fix since the Great Depression.

The banner headline and Associated Press story inside the Saturday broadsheet newspaper:

$700 billion to the rescue

WASHINGTON – They held their noses and voted "yes."

Now lawmakers in both parties – along with President Bush – are waiting to see whether their historic $700 billion bailout for the financial industry can stabilize the tottering economy and prevent a broader meltdown.

... Friday's vote capped an extraordinary two weeks of tumult in Congress and on Wall Street ... The bailout, which gives the government broad authority to buy up mortgage-related investments and other distressed assets from tottering financial institutions, is designed to ease a credit crunch that began on Wall Street but is engulfing business around the nation.

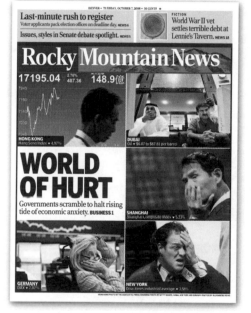

For several years, housing foreclosures had soared across the U.S. with Colorado holding one of the highest rates of failure. Housing values began to plummet. Pillars of the financial foundation – institutions like American International Group (AIG), Washington Mutual and federal housing behemoths Freddie Mac and Fannie Mae – had to be propped up.

By September, amid reports that national unemployment was marching upward, the stock market went into a tailspin. Front-page headlines became a taunting ticker:

(Sept 18) Hole in the Wall

Dow Jones industrials fell 450 points, and the market experienced its lowest close in three years.

(Sept. 30) What now? Dow plunges 777 points

The Bush bailout was first rejected by the House, resulting in the market's biggest single-day loss ever.

**(Oct. 1) BUILDING MOMENTUM FOR BAILOUT
Dow rises 485 points**

Prodding members with the argument that Congress had to do something to staunch the financial hemorrhaging, the House poised for another bailout vote. The bailout passed. But Wall Street wasn't watching.

(Oct. 7) WORLD OF HURT

Only three days after Bush signed the law enacting the bailout, stock markets suddenly suffered a global lack of confidence. The Dow dropped 370 points and fell below 10,000 for the first time in four years.

(Oct. 10) Peak to bleak

On the one-year anniversary of its all-time high of 14,164, the Dow crashed another 679 points to close at 8,579.

(Oct. 14) U-turn on Wall St.

After eight days of precipitous losses, the Dow opened the week with an astounding gain – 936 points – nearly doubling the largest single-day increase in its history.

Two weeks after Bush signed the bailout into law, only a small portion of it had been earmarked for a specific relief program. The American economy was only lurching forward. Waiting for direction. Waiting for a new president. Waiting for a fresh outlook.

The R word

The country was treating its economic downturn like tooth decay; it knew it was suffering, but officially it didn't want to admit it had a gaping cavity.

On Dec. 2, the *Rocky* decided not to tell everyone on page 1 what they already knew – the country was in a recession. The story ran on page 2 of the Business section:

WASHINGTON – The U.S. economy has been in a recession since December 2007, the National Bureau of Economic Research said Monday.

By one benchmark, a recession occurs whenever the gross domestic product – the total output of goods and services – declines for two consecutive quarters. If further confirmation of the nation's economic status was necessary, it came with the news that the country had lost nearly 2 million jobs in 2008.

Colorado financial experts said they believed the state could still avoid the deep recession in which many other states were already mired. □

Rocky Mountain News

OBAMA

Colorado key in electing first black president

Udall win boosts Dems' margin in U.S. Senate

A dream fulfilled

The cover of the *Rocky Mountain News* on Nov. 5, 2008, made it immediately clear that Barack Obama did not cheat history.

It took more than 230 years after America's founders wrote that "all men are created equal."

It took nearly 150 years after Colorado's first newspaper promised in 1859 that it was "hoping well to act our part."

Obama had fulfilled the dreams of many. Lincoln. King. Most importantly, his own dream of what was possible.

The *Rocky*, along with the rest of the world, reported what had forever seemed to be the impossible. The Associated Press story on page 2, beneath the headline

In historic vote, 'Change has come'

WASHINGTON – Barack Obama swept to victory as the nation's first black president Tuesday night in an electoral college landslide that overcame racial barriers as old as America itself.

"Change has come," he told a huge throng of jubilant supporters in Chicago's Grant Park.

"If there is anyone out there who still doubts that America is a place where all things are possible," Obama said, in the opening remarks of his victory speech, "who still wonders if the dream of our founders is alive in our time, who still questions the power of our democracy, tonight is your answer."

The son of a black father from Kenya and a white mother from Kansas, the Democratic senator from Illinois sealed his historic triumph by defeating Republican Sen. John McCain in a string of wins in hard-fought battleground states – Ohio, Florida, Virginia, Iowa and more, including Colorado and New Mexico.

Colorado, which voted Democratic for only the second time in 44 years, played a major role on a national stage.

Obama and vice president-elect Joe Biden visited Colorado 12 times. McCain and running mate Sarah Palin, recognizing the threat of losing the West, made 17 appearances in Colorado.

Mark Udall's successful run to replace retiring Republican Wayne Allard gave Colorado two Democrats in the U.S. Senate. Not since 1936 had the state voted for a Democratic presidential candidate and allowed that party to claim both

Sen. John McCain, Republican candidate for president, shares lunch with one of his most recognizable Colorado supporters, John Elway. *(Chris Schneider/Rocky Mountain News)*

senate seats, control the U.S. House of Representatives delegation, and hold the governor's mansion and the majority in both houses of the state legislature.

Wellington Webb, the first black mayor of Denver, may have stated the historical significance of the election best when quoted in the *Rocky:*

"In Colorado, we turned a red state blue."

Endorsement upheaval

The *Rocky* did not endorse Obama.

Nor did it endorse McCain.

Newspapers have a long tradition of endorsing candidates. For more than a hundred years, readers often chose their newspaper based on its politics.

But two weeks before the election, which would inspire one of the largest voter turnouts in U.S. history, the *Rocky* shook up two worlds – politics and its own industry. John Temple, the paper's editor, president and publisher, made the unprecedented announcement that the paper would no longer endorse political candidates, except in special circumstances.

Temple, one of the most aggressive editors in the country when it comes to use of the Internet, made the point that the electronic medium as well as television now offered the populace nearly instant and certainly constant access to candidates and their views. Instead, he said the *Rocky's* editorial pages would concentrate more than ever on probing issues and candidates' conduct rather than pushing its opinion. Temple wrote in his weekly column:

In the end, we'll leave it to you to come to your own conclusion, trusting that's what you want and believing this newspaper's editorial page can be most valuable to you if it helps you reach an informed decision, with an emphasis on informed. After all, ultimately that's our job. It's not to pick presidents, senators or representatives.

Editorial's last word

The morning after the election, the *Rocky's* editorial page nevertheless did provide the most succinct observation of Obama's rise to 44th President of the United States. The first line of its lead editorial:

Not even Abe Lincoln saw this coming.

DENVER • FRIDAY, FEBRUARY 27, 2009 • 50 CENTS

ROCKY MOUNTAIN NEWS.

THE MINES AND MINERS OF KANSAS AND NEBRASKA.

VOL. 1.   CHERRY CREEK, K. T., SATURDAY, APRIL 23 1859.   NO. 1.

1859 ⧗ FINAL EDITION ⧗ 2009

Goodbye, Colorado

IT IS WITH GREAT SADNESS THAT WE SAY GOODBYE TO YOU TODAY. Our time chronicling the life of Denver and Colorado, the nation and the world, is over. Thousands of men and women have worked at this newspaper since William Byers produced its first edition on the banks of Cherry Creek on April 23, 1859. We speak, we believe, for all of them, when we say that it has been an honor to serve you. To have reached this day, the final edition of the *Rocky Mountain News*, just 55 days shy of its 150th birthday, is painful. We will scatter. And all that will be left are the stories we have told, captured on microfilm or in digital archives, devices unimaginable in those first days. But what was present in the paper then and has remained to this day is a belief in this community and the people who make it what it has become and what it will be. We part in sorrow because we know so much lies ahead that will be worth telling, and we will not be there to do so. We have celebrated life in Colorado, praising its ways, but we have warned, too, against steps we thought were mistaken. We have always been a part of this special place, striving to reflect it accurately and with compassion. We hope Coloradans will remember this newspaper fondly from generation to generation, a reminder of Denver's history — the ambitions, foibles and virtues of its settlers and those who followed. We are confident that you will build on their dreams and find new ways to tell your story. Farewell — and thank you for so many memorable years together.

Rocky Mountain News

The End

The last front page of Colorado's oldest newspaper published 55 days short of what would have been its 150th anniversary.

The cover was a simple, elegant re-creation of the first edition printed by founder William N. Byers and overprinted with the last message from the 22nd editor in the paper's rich history, John Temple.

Byers had greeted his new readers with these words:

"Fondly looking forward to a long and pleasant acquaintance with our readers, hoping well to act our part, we send forth to the world the first number of the Rocky Mountain News."

Temple bid farewell with these:

"It is with great sadness that we say goodbye to you today …"

How it all went down

As long as it took to approach such a remarkable milestone as a 150th anniversary, the swiftness with which the venerable paper was shuttered was bewildering. It took only 85 days.

When Rich Boehne, president and CEO of owner E.W. Scripps Co., arrived unannounced in Denver on Dec. 4, 2008, he did not come in the role as Jack Foster had in 1942 to save the paper.

"We're not here today to close the paper," Boehne told the *Rocky* staff in the middle of the newsroom, the setting for so many casual and comradely gatherings in the past. "We're here today to say the status quo is not going to work."

Boehne estimated that the paper would lose $15 million in 2008. It turned out to be $16 million.

Scripps set an unspecified mid-January deadline for a potential buyer to come forward or the newspaper could be closed.

Even more shocking in the depressing days ahead, Temple wrote in the paper that since the formation of the joint operating agreement with *The Denver Post* in 2000, the business had lost more than $100 million in classified advertising revenue, once the lifeblood of the industry.

John Temple

Amid immense concern throughout the city that Denver could become a one-newspaper town, the *Rocky's* business staff broke a story that *The Post's* owner faced serious credit challenges from its banks, and that it had withheld payments to the JOA in order to cover payroll. Some began wondering if Denver might soon be a no-newspaper town.

For the next two months, even as Scripps' sale deadline passed, hardly a day went by that the *Rocky's* "Letters" page didn't include a reader's expression of hope that the newspaper would survive. Some even offered to pay more for their subscriptions.

The *Rocky* waited for Boehne's return.

In the final edition, reporter Katie Kerwin McCrimmon wrote about one of the many rumors. One of the city's media-obsessed Web sites reported that one of local radio's media-obsessed talk show hosts, Peter Boyles, claimed to have two sources confirming Scripps honchos were back in town. Wrote Kerwin McCrimmon:

"Two sources?" quipped one (Rocky) reporter. "Peter Boyles' idea of two sources is him talking to himself in a mirror."

That same day, Boehne stood in the newsroom once again. Kevin Vaughan, a Pulitzer Prize finalist reporter, was assigned to write the lead story.

"Tomorrow will be the final edition of the *Rocky Mountain News*," Boehne began simply. **"It's certainly not good news for any of you, and it's certainly not good news for Denver."**

Tradition destined to die

The symbol at the bottom of this page was used for decades by newspaper reporters to alert editors at the end of their stories, so they knew all pages had been submitted. Its origin was during the Civil War when reporters typed XXX at the end of stories – Roman numerals for 30. In newspapering, it has always meant The End.

It is appropriate to use here, after 150 years of the *Rocky*. ☐

Pages 2, 4-8
Pages 10-14
Pages 16-21
Pages 24-38
Pages 40, 43-55
Pages 57-70
Pages 72-80
Pages 82-92
Pages 94, 96-98
Pages 101-110
Courtesy, Colorado Historical Society

Pages 9, 22, 42
Courtesy, Western History Collection,
Denver Public Library

Pages 81, 100, 114, 122, 136
Pages 149-152
Pages 154-170
Page 172
Courtesy, *Rocky Mountain News*

Pages 111-112
Pages 116-121
Pages 124-135
Pages 138, 140-143
Pages 145-147
© 2009 *Rocky Mountain News*.
Reprinted with permission.
Image scanned from UMI® microfilm
produced by ProQuest CSA LLC.
All Rights Reserved.

Reader's Guide

Discussion Questions

- What events or front pages chosen for *Heroes, Villains, Dames & Disasters* do you think should not be included among the most significant in the newspaper's history? What would you add or substitute?

- How does the *Rocky's* reporting of events match your own knowledge or experience?

- Do you feel there is a balance of years and eras between past and present? Too many stories of frontier Colorado? Assassinations? Recent events? 21st Century events?

- Oftentimes, readers remark that all newspapers devote too much coverage to doom and gloom, death and destruction. Do you think that's true of this collection?

- What's your opinion of the vignettes, the slices of life, that were chosen to end most of the chapters? Do they complement the main historic event, or do they detract? Trivial, or timely? Frivolous, or added flavor?

- What is your favorite period of history over the past 150 years?

- What treasured stories, or memories, of Colorado history have been passed down to you through your family, or that you personally experienced?

- What did you learn that was new, or surprising, or changed your thinking about an event included in *Heroes, Villains, Dames & Disasters*?

- Why – or why not – should the death of a world leader be considered an important moment in history, or a history-altering event?

- How well do the selected events reflect the diversity of Colorado and American culture, race, religion, politics and common interests?

- What do you think of the *Rocky's* early reporting of events surrounding Native Americans?

- What do you think of the overnight review of the Beatles' 1964 concert at Red Rocks?

- What do you think of the number of sports events included as important dates in Colorado history? Were you surprised to find sports on the front page as far back as 1910?

- What date do you consider the start of the 21st Century – the Y2K date of Jan. 1, 2000, or 2001? Should 1900-1901 be any different?

- Do you think the *Rocky* treated Nikola Tesla's claim of a "message from another world" in 1901 as a legitimate news story, or a New Year's Day joke?

- Do you consider frontier reports like the Union troops' action at Glorieta Pass, or the death of Buffalo Bill, to be over-blown writing? Can you think of any current-day examples?

- What trends in the type of coverage, or in news judgment, over decades did you detect?

Author's Note

I am proud to play a role in collecting the *Rocky's* history in a book. In my daydreams, I always hoped that readers might like my stories and want to share in the experience. *Heroes, Villains, Dames & Disasters* proved that many readers have their own real-life accounts that are linked to events on Page 1. Some are as dramatic and entertaining as any that appeared in the newspaper.

I would be honored to share my stories and yours with your group, by phone or in person. If you are part of a book club, history or journalism class, senior center or other organization interested in discussing *Heroes, Villains, Dames & Disasters*, please feel free to contact me at **www.michaelmadiganauthor.com**.

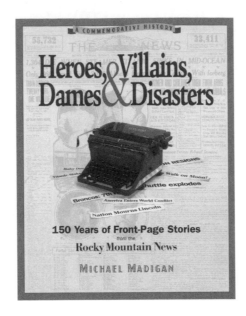

How to order additional copies of
Heroes, Villains, Dames & Disasters

CREDIT CARD
order at **www.michaelmadiganauthor.com**

CHECK / MONEY ORDER
Mail to:
MadIdeas LLC
15449 W. 77th Drive
Arvada, CO 80007

Please provide complete name, address,
telephone and email contact information with mail orders.

Retail price $29.95
Tax (Colorado resident rate) 2.45
Shipping (one book) 5.00

Total $37.40

PHONE
303-431-0499
for orders of 10 or more books
or if you represent a library or educational institution.